African Arguments

Written by experts with an un[...]
African Arguments is a series o[...]
the key issues currently facing Africa. Topical and thought-provoking, accessible but in-depth, they provide essential reading for anyone interested in getting to the heart of both why contemporary Africa is the way it is and how it is changing.

African Arguments Online

African Arguments Online is a website managed by the Royal African Society, which hosts debates on the *African Arguments* series and other topical issues that affect Africa: http://africanarguments.org

Published by Zed Books and the IAI with the support of the following organisations:

The principal aim of the **International African Institute** is to promote scholarly understanding of Africa, notably its changing societies, cultures and languages. Founded in 1926 and based in London, it supports a range of seminars and publications including the journal *Africa*.
www.internationalafricaninstitute.org

Now more than a hundred years old, the **Royal African Society** today is Britain's leading organisation promoting Africa's cause. Through its journal, *African Affairs*, and by organising meetings, discussions and other activities, the society strengthens links between Africa and Britain and encourages understanding of Africa and its relations with the rest of the world.
www.royalafricansociety.org

The **World Peace Foundation**, founded in 1910, is located at the Fletcher School, Tufts University. The Foundation's mission is to promote innovative research and teaching, believing that these are critical to the challenges of making peace around the world, and should go hand in hand with advocacy and practical engagement with the toughest issues. Its central theme is 'reinventing peace' for the twenty-first century.
www.worldpeacefoundation.org

About the authors

Mick Moore is a Professorial Fellow at the Institute of Development Studies, and CEO of the International Centre for Tax and Development.

Wilson Prichard is an Associate Professor at the Munk School of Global Affairs and the Department of Political Science at the University of Toronto, Research Fellow at the Institute of Development Studies and Research Director at the International Centre for Tax and Development.

Odd-Helge Fjeldstad is Research Professor at Chr. Michelsen Institute, Bergen, Norway, Extraordinary Professor at the African Tax Institute, University of Pretoria, and Senior Fellow at the International Centre for Tax and Development.

TAXING AFRICA

COERCION, REFORM AND DEVELOPMENT

BY MICK MOORE, WILSON PRICHARD
AND ODD-HELGE FJELDSTAD

In association with
International African Institute
Royal African Society
World Peace Foundation

ZED

Taxing Africa: Coercion, Reform and Development was first published in 2018 by Zed Books Ltd, The Foundry, 17 Oval Way, London SE11 5RR, UK.

www.zedbooks.net

Typeset in Haarlemmer by seagulls.net
Index by John Barker
Cover design by Jonathan Pelham
Cover photo © Robin Hammond/Panos

A catalogue record for this book is available from the British Library

ISBN 978-1-78360-454-8 hb
ISBN 978-1-78360-453-1 pb
ISBN 978-1-78360-455-5 pdf
ISBN 978-1-78360-456-2 epub
ISBN 978-1-78360-457-9 mobi

Printed and bound by CPI Group (UK) Ltd, Croydon, CR0 4YY

CONTENTS

ACKNOWLEDGEMENTS

Among our many creditors, we would like especially to acknowledge:

Stephanie Kitchen of the International Africa Institute for suggesting that we write this book; Ken Barlow of Zed Books for tolerating failed promises about delivery dates; Rhiannon McCluskey for a great deal of help with facts, figures and feedback; Louise Eldridge for editing; and a large number of people who have helped to create, animate and sustain the highly stimulating environment within which this book was nurtured: the International Centre for Tax and Development (ICTD) – Doris Akol, Merima Ali, Zilper Audi, Rished Bade, Mary Baine, Per Oyvind Bastoe, Rachel Beach, Ingvild Bergskaug, Richard Bird, Jean-François Brun, Thomas Cantens, Alan Carter, Gerard Chambas, Alex Cobham, Ben Dickinson, Rebecca Dottey, Mike Durst, Peter Evans, Max Everest-Phillips, Alex Ezenagu, Paul Fish, Riel Franzsen, Anne-Marie Geourjon, Tom Goodfellow, Vishal Gujadhur, Martin Hearson, Kari Heggstad, Samuel Jibao, Anuradha Joshi, Allen Kagina, Jalia Kangave, Agnes Kanyangeyo, Mick Keen, Adrienne Le Bas, Wazi Ligomeka, Olav Lundstol, Mary Maganga, Lincoln Marais, Giulia Mascagni, Rhiannon McCluskey, Kyle McNabb, Andualem Mengistu, Fariya Mohiuddin, Alvin Moisioma, Nara Monkam, Oliver Morrissey, Denis Mukama, Catherine Mutava, Susan Nakato, Milly Nalukwago, Adolf Ndunguri, Christopher Nell, David Nguyen-Thanh, Annet Oguttu, Olly Owen, Laura Paler, Sol Picciotto, Gael Raballand, Adam Randon, Simon Rees, Henry

Saka, Ingrid Sjursen, Tanja Ustvedt, Yolanda Vamusse, Vanessa van den Boogard, Ronald Waiswa, Camilla Walsh, Attiya Waris, Logan Wort, Wollela Yesegat, Nyah Zebong and Patrick Zzimbe.

Chapter 1

WHY DOES TAX MATTER?

Introduction

If asked to identify the most important issues facing Africa in the twenty-first century, few people would mention tax. For most of us, taxation lies somewhere on a spectrum between irritating and boring. At best, it is an unappealing necessity – rather like sewerage or vaccinations. 'Tax' is the domain of charisma-free account-ants, lawyers and number crunchers. It seems an unlikely place to encounter big societal questions about democracy, development, equity or good government. Yet it is exactly these kinds of issues that pervade the conversations about taxation that we, the authors, have with policymakers, business people, tax collectors, civil society activists, journalists and aid donors in Africa. Many of them think tax is central to African development. Let us begin by introducing you to one of these tax aficionados.

A ground-level view of taxation in Africa

Dr Samuel Jibao is now one of our close research colleagues. Samuel's original contact with the authors was in 2010, when he and Wilson Prichard worked together on an analysis of the (many) challenges facing the Sierra Leone tax system. At their first meeting, Samuel introduced himself as a native of Kailahun District, in the east of the country, and an economist by training. He worked initially as a lecturer at the national university before joining the newly created

National Revenue Authority (NRA) in 2003. There, he rose to become Acting Director of Research in 2010. In 2011, he left the NRA to create an independent research institute, the Centre for Economic Research and Capacity Building, which specialises in taxation.

Samuel's rise within the NRA reflected a keen intelligence and a deeply held commitment to honesty and public service. But what also distinguished him was that he regularly travelled around the country and got to know tax officials and taxpayers at every level. He sought to understand the tax system from the ground up, focusing not only on formal laws and institutions, but also on the lived experiences of taxpayers and tax collectors. It was this need to understand how the system actually functioned that he emphasised during his first meeting with Wilson – over several bottles of Heineken and a plate of palaver stew, in a small Freetown restaurant up the street from the headquarters of the NRA. Interrupted regularly by colleagues, jokes, personal stories and much else, Samuel explained why it was important to speak with taxpayers themselves.

The first thing you discover, he said, is that when you talk about 'taxes' in Sierra Leone, the word will mean very different things depending on who you are talking to. In the big cities, and among the national elite, 'taxation' generally means personal income taxes, corporate taxes, value-added taxes and customs duties. These taxes bring in most national revenue, and – probably for that reason – dominate international discussion of taxation. However, to people outside the big cities and small elite circles, 'taxation' means something very different: smaller taxes, levies and fees paid to local governments; 'informal' payments to tax collectors and state officials; and a wide range of payments to groups other than the government, including traditional chiefs. These kinds of payments – what in Chapter 7 we label *small taxes* – are easily overlooked by outsiders but are an integral part of the story of taxation in Africa.

In 2010, we, the authors, established the International Centre for Tax and Development (ICTD). Four years later, Samuel's Centre for Economic Research and Capacity Building worked with ICTD to conduct a large survey to find out exactly what citizens of Sierra Leone outside large cities pay in taxes and tax-like levies. Samuel had been exactly right. Few people outside the cities pay income tax or corporate taxes. About half of the tax and tax-like payments they make are to local governments. The remainder are 'informal taxes' collected by people and organisations who are not in any sense 'official' or part of the state: chiefs, community development organisations, religious organisations, informal defence groups and so on. More surprisingly, people on average had significantly more confidence that these non-state 'informal taxes' would be transformed into public services than that the formal taxes they paid to the local and national government would be (Jibao et al. 2017).

Back in the restaurant in Freetown, Samuel had gone on to explain that, if you are willing to take the time to sit down with them and let the tax conversation develop, most Sierra Leoneans will want to talk about the (lack of) taxation with regard to local mining operations. At that time, large new mining investments were flowing into the country, but the government had signed ad hoc agreements with mining companies and had granted them large-scale tax exemptions. As a result, the government was collecting very little revenue from the mining companies, either through corporate income tax or through royalty charges on the depletion of national assets. In 2010, the Sierra Leone government was seeking to renegotiate some of those contracts. Taxpayers were asking why the government was gathering taxes from poor citizens, but collecting little or nothing from the large mining firms that seemed to have a much greater capacity to pay. It was not only in Sierra Leone that this question was being asked. Then, and today, many African governments raise strikingly little direct revenue from mining operations (Chapter 5). Samuel said that most taxpayers had neither the interest nor the expertise to discuss details of mining tax design, but they had a strong sense of fairness and they believed that the current system was not delivering it. The powerful were not paying their fair share, while those lacking political connections and international links were picking up the bill.

If you sat for longer with local taxpayers, Samuel explained, the conversation would likely get around to a more general question: 'Why should I pay taxes when I don't seem to get anything in return?' Many people in Sierra Leone, and across the continent, lack access to electricity, running water, consistently passable roads or decent health and education facilities. And surveys suggest that in many countries tax and customs authorities themselves are viewed as corrupt (Chapter 6),[1] while taxpayers have little confidence that the revenue that reaches the government will be used productively (Aiko and Logan 2014; Jibao et al. 2017; van den Boogaard et al. 2018; Paler et al. 2017; Fjeldstad and Semboja 2001). As Samuel explained, it is small wonder that there is little active public support for, or interest in, increasing taxation.

There is mounting evidence that while effective enforcement is important to ensuring tax compliance, so too is perceived fairness, reciprocity and accountability in the collection of taxes – and in the spending of tax revenues (e.g. Ali et al. 2014). Talking with taxpayers, Samuel explained, makes clear the need for stronger links between what people pay and what they receive in return. Many tax collectors have similar views. They lament that, although they bring in the money, they are not in a position to make their own job easier by influencing how that money is used. Reliable surveys suggest that most Africans believe that governments have the right to collect taxes and that, in principle, citizens have a duty to pay them (Aiko and Logan 2014). But there is widespread mistrust of the claims that taxes will be translated into viable services, or that public opinion affects how the money is spent.

Concerns about fairness, equity and reciprocity are thus pervasive among taxpayers. Yet popular initiatives to improve tax systems have been rare, both in Sierra Leone and elsewhere. This seems to reflect a broad sense among taxpayers that the failures of national and local tax systems are firmly rooted in the realities of power and politics. It is commonly believed that powerful individuals do not pay the taxes that they owe – be they income taxes, corporate taxes, trade taxes, property taxes or others – because of the political influence that they enjoy. Official data almost everywhere seems to confirm this story. While taxation is often presented as a highly specialist, technical and rule-bound enterprise, taxpayers themselves often have a visceral sense that politics explains much of what occurs in practice.

Finally, Samuel stressed that to fully understand taxation in Africa it is also necessary to consider history, and especially colonial history. A central point of reference for the tax history of Sierra Leone is the Hut Tax War of 1898. The British had recently established the protectorate and had introduced a new tax on dwellings. Led by a coalition of chiefs, local forces launched armed resistance that lasted nine months. It ended after the British resorted to 'scorched earth' policies (Abraham 1974). In the minds of Sierra Leoneans, the Hut Tax War is not ancient history. Rather, it is a significant influence on how they understand the world today. At the time when Samuel and Wilson were having this conversation, the government had been proposing to introduce a property tax to provide a revenue source for local councils in smaller towns. This new tax was introduced successfully, but during the process critics often referred to the Hut Tax War. Again, it was said, the government in Freetown was trying to extract revenue from rural areas without making any effort to consult, create consensus, or offer reciprocal benefits. This awareness of the extractive character of colonial taxation is widespread across the continent (Chapter 2).

Underlying Samuel's history of tax was a broader understanding that taxation is not only about the (tedious, technical) practicalities of raising revenue, but also about questions of power, accountability and effective, legitimate government. On the one hand, the Hut Tax War illustrates the coercive face of taxation, and the ways in which, even before the colonial period, rulers have flailed around to raise revenue. On the other hand, it also demonstrates both the depth of popular convictions that taxation ought to be legitimate and accountable and the consequent potential for tax policy failures to become springboards for popular political action. Samuel explained that, in the aftermath of a decade of civil war between 1991 and 2002, the Sierra Leone tax system was neither fair nor accountable. But many Sierra Leoneans understood that improving it was very much about changing politics, and closely connected to the task of strengthening governance more broadly.

Taxing Africa: what are the big questions?

Samuel is one of many people contributing to a mounting level of debate in Africa about how tax systems might be transformed for the better, so that they are more fair, equitable, reciprocal and accountable, and contribute to development more broadly. This book aims to capture this emerging set of ideas and debates and to open them up to new audiences. What are the overarching ideas that we seek to capture?

The diversity of tax experiences

The first idea relates to the diversity of tax experiences, and the importance of making public the relatively untold story of how tax impacts on most Africans.

Academic and policy accounts of taxation in Africa focus on central government taxes – personal income tax, corporate income tax, value-added tax, customs duties and taxes on natural resources. These taxes provide the bulk of government revenue. As we explain at various points in this book, African governments are not novices at the business of collecting these taxes. They do so more effectively than governments in some other low-income parts of the world, and they are making consistent, gradual progress in improving their revenue systems and in capturing a higher proportion of national income for public purposes. But the majority of people who pay taxes in Africa have no direct contact with the organisations that raise revenue for central governments – (autonomous) revenue authorities and customs and internal revenue departments of ministries of finance. Instead, most Africans who pay taxes hand their money over to local governments or to one of a range of organisations that levy what we term *informal taxes* on behalf of non-state actors. Information on the amounts of money raised by local governments and informal tax collectors is scarce and unreliable. Overall, the amounts are very much smaller than central government revenue collections. Conversely, they often account for quite a high proportion of the incomes of poor people. They face a diverse array of *small taxes*, of varying and often ambiguous degrees of formality. They almost always meet the tax collector face to face. Sometimes collection is accompanied by an element of threat or coercion. Collusion with tax collectors to reduce the agreed tax bill is common. A significant share of the revenue handed over to formal tax collectors never appears in government accounts.

There are many different tax worlds in Africa. At one end of the spectrum, a small number of large transnational companies, which provide much of the revenue collected by some African governments, interact with revenue authorities through formal procedures that would be familiar to Her Majesty's Revenue and Customs in the UK. The other end – the world of *small taxes* described in Chapter 7 – is much less formal and more diverse. Less money flows through it, but it impacts directly on more taxpayers. It is easily overlooked by people not directly involved, but it is critical to local livelihoods and the links between taxation, decentralisation and state-building.

Fairness, equity and inequality

With economic inequality increasing in much of the world – including, it seems, in Africa – more attention is being paid to the potential redistributive role of tax systems. This is actually a reversion to an earlier situation. In the 1960s and 1970s, in Africa and elsewhere, tax regimes and tax reforms were widely conceived and rationalised as means of redistributing income from rich to poor (Kaldor 1963). In practice, they failed. Africa did not have revenue administrations with the resources, commitment or political backing needed to effect change. The perception of failure helped justify the shift in the 1980s towards a less ambitious agenda for tax collectors, one that focused more on simplifying and improving tax administration at the nuts and bolts level – and on introducing the new VAT, which is a tax on consumption, not on income. The pendulum is now swinging back, towards a middle ground. For example, taxes on property, having been almost entirely ignored or relegated to the terrain of local government financing, are now being taken more seriously – by national governments in Africa, and internationally by the International Monetary Fund (IMF) and others.

The discussion over redistribution has sometimes been reduced to a simplistic debate over the relative merits of (putatively progressive) direct taxes and (potentially regressive) indirect taxes. The underlying intuition is clear and, in very general terms, mostly correct. Direct taxes on income and wealth are more likely to harvest revenue from the relatively wealthy than are taxes on sales, imports or value added. But in any specific country at any moment in time, the real policy choices will be more diverse and complex. Some taxes on sales, imports or value added might be good ways of 'soaking the rich'. Even regressive taxes can have redistributive effects if they fuel progressive patterns of public spending.

More important perhaps in much of Africa are the implications for fairness and equity, not just of the law and formal tax schedules but also of the ways in which they are implemented by revenue administrations. Personal income taxes are only redistributive if wealthy people actually pay them; in practice, many – probably most – wealthy people in Africa do not (Chapter 6). Similarly, the property taxes that in principle could raise significant revenues from wealthy people, especially in the light of a series of booms in property prices in many African cities, generate very little money

(Chapter 7). Either the legislation is not in place or it is not implemented – or even implementable. Larger corporations often benefit from excessive and unjustified tax exemptions granted by governments, and from their ability to exploit international tax rules to their own advantage (Chapters 3, 4 and 6). Meanwhile, the *informal taxes* mentioned above appear to fall disproportionately on those with lower incomes.

Tax systems that are visibly unfair and regressive do not only exacerbate inequality. They also threaten to undermine tax compliance and the legitimacy of governments more generally.

Linking the international, national and local

In recent years, we have learned a great deal about the many ways in which the international tax system facilitates tax avoidance and evasion by transnational companies and wealthy individuals. We know that African governments lose revenue. But how big is this problem in relation to other tax challenges facing the continent? And what can be done about it?

The basic narrative advanced by tax justice campaigners is correct. The evolution of the system for taxing trans-border economic activities over the past century was shaped by richer, capital-exporting countries in their own interests. In recent decades, various kinds of 'tax havens' have developed to become major players. They comprise both the small islands that feature strongly in popular images of tax havens and, in varying degrees and in different ways, rich Organisation for Economic Co-operation and Development (OECD) countries such as Ireland, the Netherlands, Luxembourg, Singapore, Switzerland, the UK and the US. Capital and potential tax revenue are systematically extracted from low-income countries. There is no shortage of examples of transnational enterprises, particularly in the extractive industries (Chapter 5), paying little of the tax that they would otherwise owe by siphoning profits to tax havens overseas. Similarly, we know a great deal about how Africans who possess great wealth – and especially those who came by it illicitly – hide it offshore beyond the reach of their national tax and judicial authorities.

We know that the current international system drains potential tax revenues from Africa. We do not know precisely the size of the revenue loss. More importantly, we do not understand with certainty how African governments should best respond. Should they, collectively, put a great deal of effort into trying to change the rules of the international tax game? If, individually or collectively, they were to focus their energies on more closely monitoring and auditing the local subsidiaries of transnational corporations, how much addition revenue could they generate in the long term? Or would they scare off potential investors? Should they instead try to close the many loopholes found in their domestic tax systems? And might new approaches to combatting international tax challenges be more successful than those adopted in the past? This book does not answer these questions, but attempts to provide analysis and information that will help African authorities and campaigners to think through what is most effective in their specific circumstances. Here are some of the issues that they might need to bear in mind:

- No individual African government can do much about the rules of the international tax system. Collective action is required to change the rules.
- There are, however, considerable opportunities for governments to reduce their trans-border tax losses by implementing the current international rules more rigorously.
- The same is true of internal taxation. From a technical perspective, there is a great deal of scope to collect more revenue.
- It is not obvious that efforts to strengthen the collection of domestic taxes will reduce either the motivation or the capacity to tax trans-border activities more effectively. There may be more synergies than conflicts.
- Lobbyists for transnational companies, especially those engaged in sectors such as tobacco or alcohol, are persistently telling

African ministries of finance that trying more effectively to tax transnational activities is a mistake. Beware of lobbyists.

Politics, and the challenge of reform

Underpinning all the issues listed above is the reality of power and politics. Many of the shortcomings of African tax systems could be remedied, in whole or in part, if there were determined and effective political leadership. This may sound obvious. Taxation involves extracting resources from taxpayers with no guarantee of any kind of corresponding benefit. It is, of course, deeply political. That in turn vindicates analysing tax challenges through an explicitly political economy lens. Economists, lawyers and accountants all have much of value to say about tax. But political economy should help us address the question of how to mobilise the political support necessary for reform.

For example, the low yields from personal income tax collection in so many African countries cannot be boosted simply by recommending measures such as improved audits or wider use of data from 'third party' sources – banks, property registers or passport offices, for instance. Without political support, tax auditors may feel unable to question the tax returns submitted by influential citizens. Similarly, standard tax administration procedures for recording, collating and cross-checking data about individuals may fall into abeyance because no one in authority shows interest in them. Effective reformers need both to identify appropriate technical, organisational or procedural changes and to identify or construct political support. That may mean building political support among national elites, among tax administrators themselves, in the private sector, or among a broader public. Each case is likely to have unique political dynamics and require tailored strategies for overcoming resistance.

This message recurs in various ways throughout this book. While property taxes are poorly collected almost everywhere, we present evidence that the technical capacity for improved performance is relatively easily constructed. The problem lies in finding strategies to overcome political resistance. Similarly, the pervasiveness at local levels of *small taxes* that fall heavily on low-income people reflects politics, including the unwillingness of local elites to agree to more efficient local taxes and dysfunctional relationships between central and local levels of government. If tax reformers do not take these political considerations into account, progress is likely to be very slow.

Taxation, accountability and state-building

Currently, in Africa and among its aid donors, there is much emphasis on increasing total tax collection, with frequent suggestions that governments should aim to collect no less than 15% of gross domestic product (GDP) in taxes – and, in some cases, suggestions of targets as high as 20%. This is argued to be the minimum needed to finance public goods and service – sometimes equated with achieving the UN's Sustainable Development Goals. However, the use of such targets has prompted an important objection: expanded revenue collection is worthwhile only if that revenue is translated efficiently into valuable public goods and services. Yet we know that this often does not happen, and the use of revenue targets could, at worst, motivate and validate more coercive forms of tax collection.

Arguments in favour of the expansion of taxation are often linked to a belief in the potential of such an expansion to contribute to state-building and increased government accountability. A particular narrative about these links has become relatively widespread in recent years. This narrative holds that states that rely heavily on taxation to fund their activities – as opposed to relying on natural resource wealth or foreign aid – are more likely to build strong state structures and become accountable to their taxpayer citizens. A government seeking to collect its own tax revenue will be forced to build more effective public sector organisations to collect that revenue; this will include, for example, a wider use of meritocratic hiring and promotion practices, improved business and land registries, stronger law enforcement and judiciaries. Meanwhile, the expansion of taxation may prompt processes of 'tax bargaining' and the construction of new 'fiscal social contracts' as taxpayers resist taxation, make demands for reciprocity and enter into constructive interaction with governments. This narrative is grounded in the history of taxation and state-building in early modern Europe, but appears to be supported by the results of recent research in Africa and elsewhere in the developing world.

However, while the causal links set out in the narrative are potentially powerful, they are also seductive and can easily be over-simplified and robbed of necessary nuance, complexity and local content. There is clear evidence that taxation can be, and has been, a driver of expanded political responsiveness and accountability, and a spur to constructing new state capacity. However, it is equally clear that these positive connections are not guaranteed. Taxation is, everywhere, in large part an exercise in the use of coercive power, as states extract resources from citizens. Whether that process leads to state-building and accountability depends on the broader characteristics of the state doing the taxing, the nature of the polit-ical resources possessed by taxpayers, and the characteristics of tax systems themselves. The big questions are thus not about whether taxation can in principle be a spur to improved state–citizen rela-tions and accountability, but about when and how such connections are likely, and how these positive processes might be supported. It is on these latter questions that we focus much attention – especially, but not only, in Chapter 8.

The shadow of history – and a distinctive African future?
Finally, underpinning the discussion in this book is an effort to place contemporary African tax debates, structures and policies in histor-ical perspective. In many respects, the history of taxation in Africa is a story of external imposition of tax policies and practices, and of the influence of the global tax system and of the ideas of global epistemic

communities of tax specialists. The origins of some contemporary tax practices lie in the colonial period, when the tax system was not only imposed externally but was fundamentally oriented to extraction and control. After independence, governments retained some of the features of colonial tax systems while introducing new and more 'modern' taxes from abroad. Two decades later, the period of structural adjustment brought major tax reforms dictated largely by the IMF and World Bank – including the introduction of VAT – with very little public debate. These external models were not always perfectly suited to local needs. In recent years, it has become increasingly clear that African countries are substantially – and negatively – affected by international tax rules over which they have no effective say.

More recently, there have been encouraging signs that African governments, civil society organisations and researchers are becoming more active and assertive in seeking to shape the future tax agenda on the continent. This is reflected in the creation of a new pan-African network of tax administrators, the African Tax Administration Forum (ATAF); in the development of closer tax cooperation in Southern and Eastern Africa; in the rise of civil society organisations and business associations that are increasingly engaged in shaping national tax debates; in African governments and civil society organisations finding a voice in international tax debates for the first time; and in the emergence of a distinctively African discussion of tax policy and administration dealing with issues as diverse as the taxation of small informal firms, approaches to more effectively taxing elites, and the use of mobile technology to improve taxation. The strength of local dialogue around tax reform appears to us to be an essential part of any account of taxation in Africa – and to be pivotal in the potential for longer-term improvements.

This book

This book is broad in scope and light on the technical details of tax policy and administration. Those details certainly matter. We highlight them where they are particularly important. We are, however, more focused on the realities of how tax systems function in practice, and on their broader societal and political implications and consequences. We present what we think we know about these larger issues, indicate where big and important questions remain unanswered, and highlight the implications for thinking about development challenges in Africa. The book does not aim to be prescriptive – that is, to tell people such as Samuel what should be done – but to contribute to engaging new audiences with these debates, and thus creating space for locally led strategies and solutions to take root.

Bearing that in mind, in Chapter 2 we present a broad overview of the history of taxation on the continent. The emphasis is on the changes since the colonial period in the ways in which African governments have financed themselves. Over the last two to three decades, they have become more dependent on taxes for revenue, and more effective as tax collectors. Their tax systems have increasingly come to resemble those of most other countries in the world. In Chapter 3 we explain how the international tax system impacts on Africa, especially on the ability of African governments to raise revenues domestically. Chapter 4 follows on directly: what can African governments do to either change the international tax system or operate more effectively given the constraints that it imposes? The extractive sector – oil, gas and mining – features prominently in many African economies and accounts for a high proportion of the value of exports from the continent. The sector in general – and the mining subsector in particular – poses major tax challenges for governments. Those challenges are explored in Chapter 5. Chapter 6 addresses the question of how well national revenue collection systems in Africa are performing. Our summary includes a mix of achievements and some significant deficiencies.

These national revenue collection systems barely touch directly the great majority of people and taxpayers in Africa, who are much more affected by *small taxes* – a diverse, and often perverse, mixture of local, informal and small-scale taxes that we survey in Chapter 7. Chapter 8 provides a more in-depth exploration of the connections between taxation, state-building and accountability. Drawing on the material in the preceding chapters, we seek to ground abstract ideas about taxation and governance within the diverse realities of Africa today. The central question we address is not whether taxation can be a spur to improved governance, but when and how this is likely to happen in practice – and what we can confidently say about how such positive dynamics can be encouraged. Chapter 9 speaks for itself: the way forward.

Most of the arguments in this book are supported by citations or statistics. Where that is not the case, it is intentional. We have been preparing to write this book for a long time. We – the three authors – collectively have several decades of experience in researching, advising and teaching on tax in low-income countries, predominantly in Africa. Equally importantly, since 2010 we have had the privilege of managing the ICTD. This has enabled us to encourage, support and participate in a wide range of research projects on taxation in Africa. We have enjoyed access to the work of many researchers, including people whose main jobs are in tax administration or in academic research – or, like Samuel Jibao, squarely at the intersection of the two. In making occasional claims that cannot be supported by reference to published literature, we feel that we are on solid ground.

Finally, a note about 'Africa'. Is this a book about those elements of the taxation story that are common to the very diverse countries of sub-Saharan Africa, or is it a study of that diversity? It is both. We have tried to strike a balance: to make useful generalisations about 'Africa' without denying the diversity. Some bias has crept in. In particular, we have not paid a great deal of attention to some of the most populous countries in the region:

- The taxation system of Nigeria, the most populous country (186 million people), began to crumble in the 1970s when oil became a major source of public revenue and focus of political attention. The fiscal statistics are poor. It is likely that total public revenue now accounts for only about 7% of GDP, which is about half the figure for Ethiopia, the second most populous country. Partly because of the strength of Nigerian federalism, tax systems are quite diverse in practice. Unlike in most of Africa, the outsourcing of tax collection to private (but politically well-connected) agents is widespread. Nigeria is also home to the single most impressive 'tax turnaround' in recent African history: large-scale mobilisation of new revenue by successive governors of Lagos state in exchange for new public services (Cheeseman and de Gramont 2017; de Gramont 2015).

- Because it has always lacked many of the institutional and political attributes of a modern state, the Democratic Republic of Congo (79 million people) has never had a modern taxation system. We know that the great majority of the revenues raised by agents of the state never feature in government accounts (Chapter 7). To a much greater extent than Nigeria, information on public revenues is rare.

- By contrast, the taxation system in South Africa (56 million people) is of OECD standard and information is abundant. The South African Revenue Service (SARS) collects a great deal of data, analyses it, and makes it publicly available. We make little use of it in this book because of the ambiguities about how far South Africa can usefully be classified with the other countries of sub-Saharan Africa.

Because Africa's national tax systems have been created through intense interaction with the wider world – first with colonial rulers, then with aid donors, and more recently with the IMF, the OECD and a wide range of international organisations – they have a great deal in common. We can make more useful generalisations about

Africa's national tax systems than about its economies, its forms of governance, or, as we shall see in Chapter 7, the taxation experiences of ordinary citizens. But, of course, generalisations remain just that, and individual circumstances certainly vary. The best solutions are likely to arise when the broad debates and challenges highlighted here are then addressed with reference to the specific histories, constraints, capacities and objectives of individual countries.

Chapter 2

A NEW TAX ERA
IN AFRICA?

In Nairobi the posters proclaim '*Tulipe Ushuru, Tujitegemee*'; in Kigali it is '*Qui Paie Ses Impôts Bâtit Sa Nation*'; and in Accra 'Be a Part of Nation Building. Pay Your Taxes' or 'Have You Paid Your Income Tax This Month? Little Drops of Taxes Make a Mighty Nation.' In these and other African cities, the core message is the same: paying taxes helps build free and independent nations.

These poster campaigns are not signs of governments in financial distress. Most African government budgets have much less red ink in them today than at any point since independence around half a century ago. When they were in greater need of money, African governments typically did not bombard their citizens with these kinds of messages. Why are they doing so now? And why are they appealing to patriotism when so many other governments urge citizens to pay taxes out of self-interest: 'Your taxes built this road' or 'Pay your taxes to educate your children'? These slogans are not carefully crafted motivational messages. Many taxpayers find them irritating. Rather, they are signals of the interest of government elites, rooted in the fact that, for the first time since independence, African taxpayers and taxes collected in Africa are becoming the dominant source of income for most governments on the continent. That claim might sound curious. Surely taxes and governments are inseparable? Not always, and not entirely. We show in this chapter that it is only after half a century of experimenting with other ways of funding themselves that African governments have become primarily dependent and focused on the taxes they collect themselves. We tell this story by sketching out four stages in the revenue history of contemporary Africa: the financing of colonial governments; the extractive era; the aid era; and the tax era.

Financing colonial governments[1]

Scholars and politicians still dispute the exact mix of motives that led to the European colonisation of Africa. A contrast with India is useful. The British colonial conquest of India in the eighteenth and early nineteenth centuries was driven largely by the prospect of loot or profitable trading opportunities. India was relatively rich and exploitable. Even the agricultural population was taxable. The population was sufficiently dense and settled that the British colonial authorities, building on foundations laid by previous rulers, were able to establish a system of land records that permitted them to collect up to a third of the value of agricultural production through land taxes. Those land records were written, maintained and continuously updated locally. In principle at least, for most of the subcontinent they contained information on the size, productivity and ownership of every piece of cultivated land. Land revenue was the dominant source of public finance for the early Raj, and was only overtaken in value by customs duties in 1920 (Naseemullah and Staniland 2016).

Economic motivations played a smaller role in the colonisation of Africa; geopolitical concerns were more prominent. Once the notorious 'scramble for Africa' was initiated in the 1870s, the Belgian, British, French, Italian, German, Portuguese and Spanish governments hastily claimed and occupied territory in part to pre-empt their rivals, or to protect their existing colonies and borders. Much of this newly acquired territory was of little material value to its new rulers. The British occupation of Somaliland was an exemplary case. The principal purpose was to protect the shipping lanes through the Suez Canal to India. By occupying the coast of Somaliland and formally claiming the interior, the British shut out the rival governments and the pirates who might otherwise have controlled the ports along the southern shore of the Gulf of Aden. The intention was never actually to rule the interior, which would have cost money. Because it was so difficult to tax a territory populated mainly by itinerant pastoralists, imposing a more standard form of colonial rule would have implied permanent subsidies from London.

Compared with India, Africa was less of a cornucopia for colonial administrators and their accountants. Nevertheless, considerable wealth was generated in many parts of the continent: in the areas of white settlement in South Africa, Kenya and Southern Rhodesia (Zimbabwe); in the gold, diamond, copper and iron ore mines of the Congo, the Gold Coast (Ghana), Guinea, Mauritania, Northern Rhodesia (Zambia), Southwest Africa (Namibia), South Africa and Sierra Leone; in those areas along the West African coast and elsewhere where cash crop production (of cocoa, coffee, cotton, groundnuts, palm oil, sisal and tobacco) was attractive to African small farmers; and in the ports through which external trade was channelled – Dakar, Banjul, Conakry, Freetown, Monrovia, Abidjan, Cape Coast, Accra, Lomé, Cotonou, Lagos, Port Harcourt, Calabar, Douala, Libreville, Luanda, Cape Town, Durban, Lourenço Marques (Maputo), Beira, Dar es Salaam, Zanzibar and Mombasa. In these locations, colonial administrations could finance themselves adequately, mainly by taxing international trade. Levies on imports and exports were the main single source of colonial government revenue. In the 'labour reserve' economies of Eastern and Southern Africa, colonial governments ensured that large proportions of African males were mobilised and organised to work on European-owned farms and mines. These relatively intrusive colonial states were relatively effective at raising taxes (Mkandawire 2010). But in much of Africa, especially the areas of sparse populations, pastoralism, hunter-gathering and subsistence agriculture, colonial administrations struggled to raise revenue at all.

There were two significant consequences. One was that considerations of 'economy' – the need not to spend much – shaped colonial policy and administration in Africa to a high degree. The other was that, where there were few visible tax 'handles', colonial rulers resorted on a large scale to the most elementary and provocative instruments in the tax collector's book: taxes levied on people and their dwellings. Under both so-called 'direct' and 'indirect' systems of rule, colonial administrators were preoccupied by the question of how best to organise the collection of 'head (or poll) taxes' levied on individuals – typically adult males – and 'hut taxes' levied on housing units. Their varied and changing answers shaped their systems of territorial administration. The costs of getting it wrong were high. In low-income rural environments where income flows were highly seasonal and unpredictable, these kinds of direct taxes are almost inevitably perceived as arbitrary and unfair, and collected with more than a degree of coercion and corruption. There were few systemic checks on self-enrichment on the part of collectors, regardless of whether they appeared in the guise of public officials (as was more common in French colonies) or 'chiefs' (more usual in British colonies). Taxpayers avoided and evaded where they could. Where they could not, they sometimes revolted. The 1898 Hut Tax War in Sierra Leone is one of the more notorious instances. Colonial administrations were aware of the incendiary nature of these revenue practices. Organised coercion was expensive. Like tax agencies everywhere, they sought ways to soften the blow. Most British colonial administrations aimed to move through a developmental sequence. Hut taxes, which were based on enumerating buildings, were to be replaced by head or poll taxes on individuals. Those in turn were differentiated to try to reflect the relative capacity of different categories of people to pay. But the transition was often incomplete. Taxation remained a running sore.

The Indian colonial land revenue system was certainly not popular. The payment burden was heavy, partly because it supported an elaborate and expensive infrastructure of land records, land administration and land law. But that infrastructure had some positive features. Tax burdens were predictable and – to a degree – equitable: liabilities were permanently recorded and calibrated to the potential productivity of each field. Land revenue was levied on a durable productive asset, not on the mere existence of people or houses. There was a basis for appeal against individual assessments. And the revenue collected supported a public administration that had the capacity to verify the existence and extent of droughts or other extreme weather events and grant tax remissions village by village.

Box 2.1 Hut and poll tax rates in Tanganyika

In the 1920s, the hut and poll tax rates in Tanganyika were equivalent to one or two months' wages at prevailing wage rates. In 1945, the tax levy in Rufiji District represented 25% of gross income per taxpayer. Tax defaulters were required to labour on public works, including grass clearing along roads and serving as porters for safaris. As late as 1950, compulsory labour consumed an average of ten days per person per year in some regions.

Source: Fjeldstad and Therkildsen (2008).

The hut and head tax systems of colonial Africa generally lacked such compensatory features. Further, as far as we can tell from inadequate data, the colonial tax systems were probably extremely regressive. In particular, rural Africans paid much higher proportions of their incomes in tax, both direct and indirect, than did resident Europeans (Young 1994: 172–3). Taxes became associated with brutality, and provided tinder and fuel for anti-colonial movements in many parts of the continent. At independence, substantial hut and head taxes constituted the taxation experience of most Africans. Independence was expected to bring liberation from taxes as well as from coercive administrative practices more broadly. Africans of the independence generation are often puzzled by the sentiments underlying the slogans with which this chapter opens. How can taxes build nations or liberate peoples? Historical memories imply the very opposite – as indeed do the contemporary experiences of those many people in rural Africa today who are subject to heavy 'informal taxation' (Chapter 7).

After independence, in most cases hut and head taxes were formally abolished, allowed to wither away, reassigned to subnational governments, or appropriated by more or less informal 'traditional chiefs'. Even without formal reassignment, subnational governments – and the various kinds of more or less informal and more or less heavily armed groups that sprang up to exercise local territorial authority in places where central rule was weak – began to assert the right to collect a wide range of revenues, often on road traffic and at border crossings. As we explain in more detail later, a new kind of dualism between tax systems began to emerge in much of sub-Saharan Africa. In the colonial era, the main contrast was between: (1) the customs organisations that collected international trade taxes at ports; and (2) the more pervasive, diverse and dispersed mechanisms for levying head and hut taxes. In contemporary Africa, the more significant dividing line is between: (1) relatively coherent and formal central government systems that dominate the more promising tax bases, especially larger companies and most international trade (Chapter 6); and (2) the more fragmented, diverse, unregulated – and often informal – local systems that collectively raise much less money but probably touch more people (Chapter 7). The consistent factor is that, for most Africans, now as under colonial rule, taxpaying typically involves a face-to-face interaction, often with a known person, in a context in which coercion is an ever-present possibility.

The extractive era

From the 1960s in particular, as colonial rule began to disappear, both Western and Soviet bloc governments began to compete to provide development aid to Africa. But the volumes on offer generally were not great, and most African governments faced a financing problem. On the one hand, their fiscal wants were high. Colonialism had left them with costly public administrations, especially salaries at levels that had allowed British staff to retire in comfort to Eastbourne or Tunbridge Wells, and Frenchmen to do the same to Paris. The new governments did not cut these salaries. More importantly, their developmental ambitions were elevated and expensive. A mixture of nationalist, socialist and developmentalist ideas pointed towards large public sector capital investments, in manufacturing, in infrastructure and in mechanising agriculture. On the other hand, the scope for raising tax revenue was as limited as it had been under colonial rule. Indeed, the unpopularity of colonial direct taxes on heads and huts – and the fact that so many countries quickly fell under military or autocratic rule – made it especially unlikely that African governments would imagine funding development by offering their citizens any kind of 'tax for development' deal: *you consent to pay more taxes, and we will deliver development.*

The most obvious source of additional revenues for the newly independent governments – so obvious that even the colonial government of the Gold Coast (later Ghana) was tapping into it before independence – was the commodity export economy. The international market prices of products such as cocoa, coffee, copper, cotton, diamonds, gold, groundnuts, palm oil, sisal and tobacco had soared in the mid-1950s during the Korean War, offering false hope about future market potential. Starting with Ghana, which was first in line for independence in 1957, independent governments set about capturing for themselves a larger share of what they would often term the 'surplus' from commodity exports. To capture that surplus, they used combinations of three main mechanisms (see especially Bates 1977; Lipton 1977; Bezemer and Headey 2008). Only the first was a tax instrument, in the normal sense of the term: (increased) taxes on commodity exports. The other two mechanisms were:

- overvaluing their national currencies, while maintaining foreign exchange controls – this automatically transferred resources from exporters to importers, who were often public sector industrial and trading enterprises; and
- creating state monopoly marketing organisations through which agricultural commodity producers, who were nearly all smallholders, were obliged to market their produce.[2] The monopoly purchasing organisations often paid the producers a low price and sold on at a much higher price. Some became notorious for inflated budgets and inefficiency. They racked up losses and large bank overdrafts, and often failed to provide the promised 'surplus' to the public treasury.

The main burden of these surplus extraction policies fell on the agricultural sector. Large-scale mining existed in only a few countries, notably the Congo (now Democratic Republic of Congo), Northern Rhodesia (now Zambia) and South Africa, and to a lesser extent in Angola, Sierra Leone and Southern Rhodesia (Zimbabwe). The combination of political disorder in the Congo – from independence in 1960 until today – and declining international market prices for commodities such as copper (from a peak in 1970 to a trough in 2003) meant that there was little surplus for governments to extract from mining in Africa until early in the current century, when, especially between 2004 and 2014, mining investment, production and exports blossomed again. Oil was insignificant in sub-Saharan Africa until Nigeria and – with much smaller volumes – Gabon became oil exporters in around 1970. The Republic of Congo (Congo-Brazzaville) joined the oil exporters' club in 1973, and Cameroon in 1979. The only new entrant in the

1980s was Angola. Until the widespread new oil and gas discoveries and investments in the current century (Chapter 5), there were few petrostates in Africa. In the 1960s and 1970s, attempts by governments to extract more from the export sector were directed mostly at agricultural commodity exports.

We have no reliable numbers on the volume of economic resources channelled, invested or wasted through these mechanisms for extracting economic surpluses from agricultural producers. It is likely that the incidence of extraction peaked in the 1970s or early 1980s. The subsequent decline was the result of the interaction of four main factors:

- After peaking in the early 1970s – and fluctuating widely in the short term as they always have – global market prices for most of Africa's agricultural commodity exports tended downward. There were fewer surpluses for governments to capture.
- Extraction was a decreasingly effective way for governments to raise money. Farmers responded to low prices by cutting back planting and production. Traders responded by smuggling export commodities across borders to neighbouring countries where market prices were less depressed.
- Development aid became an increasingly viable alternative source of funding for African governments. Western aid budgets were growing and being refocused away from middle-income countries towards low-income economies, i.e. towards Africa. Total aid to sub-Saharan Africa grew rapidly in the 1980s (Figure 2.1). For the average country in the region, aid amounted to less than 12% of GDP in 1980, and peaked at almost 19% in 1994 (see Figure 2.2).
- Increased Western aid was in part tied to the adoption of structural adjustment programmes promoted by the World Bank and the IMF, and, more broadly, to a shift from state-centric to more market-centric development strategies. Most state commodity marketing boards lost their monopolies or were

abolished. More strikingly, most African governments accepted Washington's advice to radically reduce tax rates on imports and exports. Producers of commodities such as cocoa, coffee and cotton experienced some price liberation. Governments were persuaded that, if they were to introduce the new value-added tax (VAT), within a few years they could make up for lost revenue (Chapter 6). In the meantime, they had more aid to plug the budget gap.

Figure 2.1 Total official development assistance (ODA) to sub-Saharan Africa, 1970–2015

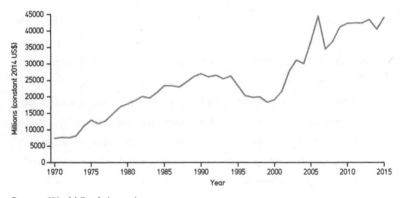

Source: World Bank (2015a).

In some cases, the mechanisms used to extract surplus from agricultural commodity producers were formally abolished. In other cases they withered. But they did not always disappear (Bezemer and Headey 2008). As in the earlier case of colonial head and hut taxes, a statement from central government that a tax was slashed or abolished provided an opportunity for other revenue hunters. For example, when the Tanzanian government abolished export taxes on traditional export crops such as coffee, tea and cashew nuts in 1985–86, local governments then imposed high taxes of their own. The coffee 'cess' levied by councils in some coffee-producing areas could be as high as 60% of the farm gate price. This provided incentives for the smuggling of crops across local authority as well as national borders. Councils in areas that did not produce coffee typically did not levy a coffee cess, so, within their jurisdictions, coffee could be sold without incurring a tax. Roadblocks manned by armed police and other 'authorities' checked most of the lorries transporting goods into Dar es Salaam. At border posts across Africa, truck owners still have to make payments to people claiming the authority of three or more public agencies: customs, the police, the border police, the army, or the phytosanitary (plant disease) inspection authority (Amin and Hoppe 2013; Cantens et al. 2014; Cuvelier and Mumbunda 2013; Titeca 2009; Twijnstra et al. 2014).

Figure 2.2 Tax revenue as % of GDP and ODA as % of GDP. Averages for all sub-Saharan Africa countries, 1980–2014

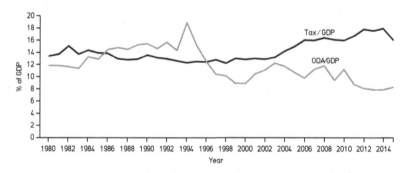

Sources: World Bank (2015a); ICTD/UNU-WIDER (2017).

The aid era

All African governments have been aid recipients from the point of independence until today – with, of course, large variations. Some have been heavily dependent on aid for their income, and some remain dependent.[3] But there was only a brief period of 'big aid' to Africa as a whole – i.e. when the average African government received more money from aid donors than from its taxpayers. It lasted about a decade, from around the mid-1980s to the mid-1990s (Figure 2.2). That claim might surprise people working inside the aid business, who are likely to have a perception of almost continuous growth in aid. Having fallen back in the late 1990s, the total volume of aid to Africa grew particularly fast from 2000. By 2006 it had more than doubled (Figure 2.1). However, at various points in the 1990s or early 2000s, several larger and more important economic variables also began to grow steadily: average rates of economic growth in African countries; world market prices of most of Africa's major export commodities (oil, gas, minerals, and many agricultural commodities); the volume of mining production in Africa; levels of tax revenues collected; and levels of non-tax revenues collected (in particular because of royalties and similar levies on oil, gas and mining activities). Africa's economy expanded, and an increasing proportion of that expanding economy was captured by the tax collector. For present purposes, the most telling figures are the changing ratios between tax revenue and aid as percentages of GDP for the average Africa country (Figure 2.2). From 1980, aid grew, exceeding tax to GDP in 1986 and peaking with the Rwandan genocide in 1994. But thereafter the figures diverge. From 1996, where the lines cross, tax to GDP ratios increased steadily while aid decreased, so that, by 2014, average tax revenues were more than double average aid revenues as a percentage of GDP.[4] This marks the transition from the 'aid era' to the 'tax era'.

The tax era

The international image of sub-Saharan Africa is still somewhat poor. The continent is associated with violence, corruption, weak public institutions, poverty and bad governance. There is a large academic literature, much of it produced in the 1990s, devoted specifically to explaining why governance is – or recently has been – so bad in Africa (Bayart 1993; Bayart et al. 1999; Chabal and Daloz 1999). Since raising revenue is a core function of governments, we might then expect to find that African governments simply have not been collecting taxes. There are certainly examples of this. Tax collection collapsed in Uganda and Rwanda during their extended civil conflicts in the 1980s and 1990s – only to bounce back once peace was restored. The central governments of the Democratic Republic of Congo, Somalia and Somaliland have never been able to collect much revenue. Once Nigeria began to export oil in significant quantities in the early 1970s, revenue collection from other sources dwindled – apparently permanently.[5] The government of South Sudan, formally in existence since 2011, has very little capacity to collect taxes on anything but oil – and even that is in question. But these cases are not typical. Most African revenue systems have functioned continuously since the end of colonial rule. A range of indicators suggest that currently they perform relatively well:

- A very basic measure of performance is total revenue collection (comprising both tax and non-tax revenue) as a proportion of GDP. The figures in column (a) of Table 2.1 indicate that, on average, sub-Saharan African tax collectors perform almost as well as their peers in the much wealthier environment of Latin America, and appreciably better than in South Asia.[6]

- A more sophisticated measure of revenue collection performance is 'tax effort' – the ratio between the actual revenues that a government collects and the amount one might expect it to collect after taking into account various features of the structure of the national economy. For a range of reasons, reliable estimates of tax effort are rare. According to one reliable series, based on data for the period 1991–2006 but covering only a limited range of countries, the average tax effort in Africa was high relative to South Asia and Latin America.[7] A more recent set of estimates, covering 120 developing countries for the period 1990–2012, also takes into account the potential depressing effect of economic vulnerability on tax collection. The researchers conclude that, compared with other low-income regions, the average level of tax effort in sub-Saharan Africa is 'outstanding' (Yohou and Goujon 2017: 1).

- One might reasonably object that we should not evaluate tax systems purely – or even mainly – on the amount of money they manage to extract from taxpayers. A somewhat more equity-oriented performance measure is provided in column (d) of Table 2.1: the proportion of tax revenue that comes from *direct taxes* (i.e. taxes on income, property and other assets). Broadly speaking, a higher dependence on direct taxes indicates a more progressive tax system, in which people with income and assets pay more than the poor and those without property. In the OECD countries, 55% of tax revenues are from direct taxes, while the equivalent figure for sub-Saharan Africa is only 31%.

Table 2.1 Government revenue collection as a percentage of GDP, regional averages, 2011–15

Region (number of countries covered)	Total revenue collected as a percentage of GDP	Tax revenue collected as a percentage of GDP	Direct tax revenue collected as a percentage of GDP	Direct tax revenue as a percentage of tax revenue
	(a)	(b)	(c)	(d)
Sub-Saharan Africa (49)	21	17	6	31
South Asia (8)	16	12	4	25
East Asia and Pacific (30)	29	20	9	35
Middle East and North Africa (20)	35	14	7	25
Latin America and the Caribbean (34)	22	20	7	30
Europe and Central Asia (51)	38	32	20	48
North America (2)	36	28	22	63
OECD (35)	41	34	23	55

World Bank regional classifications used.

Source: ICTD/UNU-WIDER (2017).

As we explain in Chapters 6 and 7 in particular, African governments do under-tax their own wealthy citizens, and they should
raise more revenue from direct taxes – rather than from *indirect*
taxes such as customs duties, VAT and other sales taxes, and
excise duties. However, rather than the OECD countries, the
relevant comparators for Africa are in Asia and Latin America.
Again, as we see in column (d) of Table 2.1, sub-Saharan Africa
does not perform badly: its dependence on direct taxes (31%) is
not much lower than that of the (much wealthier) East Asia and
Pacific region (35%); just above that of (much wealthier) Latin
America and the Caribbean (30%); and considerably higher
than that of (wealthier) South Asia (25%) and the Middle East
and North Africa (25%).

- The World Bank publishes annual estimates by country of one
measure of the tax compliance burden: the number of staff hours
consumed in the typical medium-sized company in dealing with
taxes. On average, tax collectors in sub-Saharan Africa impose
a slightly lower compliance burden on companies than their
South Asian equivalents – and a much lower burden than the
Latin Americans (World Bank 2012: 31; 2016d: 31).

- Globally, there is an excessively high rate of job turnover among
heads of revenue administrations, which affects performance
adversely. For the five years from 2009, the turnover rate for
the Africa region was about the same as for Europe and for the
Middle East and Central Asia region, and considerably lower
than for Latin America and the Caribbean and for the Asia
Pacific region (IMF 2015: 33).

- On two of the measures mentioned above, African tax collectors have been improving their average performance since 1990,
the first year for which we have adequate reliable data. Total
revenue collections have slowly crept up, from an average of
16% of GDP in 1990–95 to 20% in 2010–15. Further, the contribution of direct taxes to total revenue has also increased, from
24% in 2005 to 33% in 2015 (Figure 2.3).

- There is evidence that, over the past decade, tax reforms have led to an increase in the proportion of Africans who believe that governments have a right to tax them.[8]

Figure 2.3 Government revenue as a percentage of GDP, sub-Saharan African averages, 1990–2015

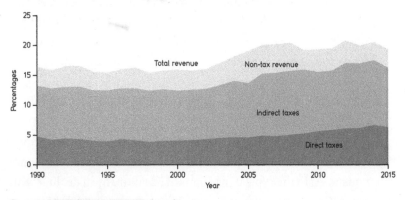

Source: ICTD/UNU-WIDER (2017).

It would certainly be desirable for some African governments to collect more revenue to finance much-needed public health, education and infrastructure programmes. It is, however, a recurring theme in this book that the more urgent challenges are around who pays taxes, how they are collected, and how governments use the revenue. It would be a mistake to view the African tax policy agenda as principally a matter of helping under-resourced governments to raise more money. They are already fairly good at that. When, after independence, African governments resorted to coercive, extractive mechanisms to finance themselves, it was not so much because they were short of money in an absolute sense, but because they were trying to construct the relatively elaborate and expensive infrastructure of modern states with economies that in many cases were not sufficiently productive or taxable to support such burdens. In the last two decades, those economies have become more taxable. The distinctive feature of the 'tax era' is not that

African governments are raising significant tax revenues for the first time. Most have been doing that continuously for decades. It is rather that tax is now the dominant source of public revenue, and the focus of increased attention from government elites. Those elites have reformed their revenue systems to bring them closer to the global norm. Most contemporary African governments are now financially dependent on much the same mix of taxes as prevails in the rest of the world: VAT; corporate and personal income taxes, including personal income taxes collected from employers through PAYE (pay as you earn); import duties; and excise taxes on tobacco, liquor and fuel.

We conclude this chapter where we began: 'Tulipe Ushuru, Tujitegemee' ('Pay Your Taxes and Set Our Country Free'). Posters and advertising campaigns linking taxpaying to patriotism reflect the fact that, as taxation has come to dominate over alternative sources of government income, Africa's rulers pay it more attention. They are increasingly finding that a naira of tax revenue can be worth more than its face value. A robust and effective tax system allows a growing number of governments to borrow money commercially. Compared with governments dependent on aid, they can more plausibly promise to repay capital and interest 10 or 20 years down the line. Before 2006, the South African government was the only one in sub-Saharan Africa to borrow commercially through sovereign bonds. By the end of 2014, another dozen had done so (World Bank 2016c). Historians classify regimes that can access commercial borrowing in this way as *fiscal states*. In the contemporary world, fiscal states have scope to say 'thank you, but no thank you' to the IMF, the World Bank, aid donors and other sources of official external financing – and then to pick and choose among commercial lenders. That is the vision of independence that many influential Africans have in mind when they suggest that taxes help set countries free.

From where will those additional tax revenues be collected? Principally from African individuals and companies, and not least from the fast-growing ranks of wealthy Africans who pay very low taxes on their incomes and properties (Chapter 6). But there is also scope to tax more effectively the profits of the transnational companies that have such a dominant position in many African economies. The global tax system has a major influence on the capacity of African governments to raise revenue from transnational corporations and, directly and indirectly, from African-registered companies and Africa's rich individuals. We now move, in Chapters 3 to 5, to look at the effects of the international tax system on revenue raising in Africa.

Chapter 3

IS AFRICA THE VICTIM
OF GLOBAL FORCES?

Introduction

On 25 March 2014, people in Abuja, Nigeria witnessed a surprising scene: a public protest, outside a meeting of the African Union finance ministers, to highlight unfair international tax rules that were holding back African development. Why would anyone bother to try to ignite public debate about such a dull, remote and technical issue? While protests *against* taxes are not unusual, the demonstrators were calling for *more* taxes – on transnational companies. The subject might be complex, but the core of their argument was straightforward: international tax rules have allowed wealthy individuals and multinational enterprises, aided and abetted by global tax havens and the accountants and lawyers that support them, to evade and avoid their obligations to the societies from where they draw their incomes and profits. Cracking down of these abuses would help finance development and combat inequality and corruption.

The protestors were tackling complex issues far removed from the everyday lives of most citizens, and impinging on space traditionally closed to popular participation. However, their presence was not an aberration. The protest was part of a growing movement of civil society actors – supported by journalists, academics, policymakers and others. Following the report of the High Level Panel on Illicit Financial Flows from Africa led by Thabo Mbeki (UNECA

2015), the 'Stop the Bleeding' campaign was launched by a group of civil society organisations across the continent. In some places, the impact of international tax rules on national development has even begun to emerge as a mainstream political issue. In February 2015, for example, the Economic Freedom Fighters party of South Africa – a populist rival to the ruling African National Congress – opted to make rules about international tax abuse a priority for their parliamentary agenda. Only a few years previously, a focus on such an obscure and technical subject would have been highly improbable.

In South Africa, as in many other countries, the narrative of large-scale international tax evasion, facilitated by the abuse of power by internationally connected elites, shapes popular understandings of the causes of growing inequality. This emerging 'tax justice' movement argues that unfair international tax rules have undermined the public finances of low-income countries by facilitating tax evasion and avoidance by wealthy companies and individuals. Existing international tax rules have created, either by accident or by design, a system characterised by extensive secrecy, excessive complexity and widespread loopholes. It is increasingly difficult for national tax authorities to tax mobile wealth. The most striking manifestation of this system has been the growth of a global system of offshore financial centres – better known as 'tax havens' or 'secrecy jurisdictions' – which have offered a destination for both wealthy individuals and multinational corporations (MNCs) seeking to minimise their tax payments and disguise their wealth. While most governments find that their potential revenues are being hijacked in this way, the outflows are especially high from Africa and other low-income regions: there is limited capacity to implement effectively the complex rules and procedures that might stem the revenue leakages.

Tax evasion and avoidance by MNCs and wealthy individuals have seriously dented tax revenues in Africa. As we explain towards the end of the chapter, we do not know the precise size of the tax losses – except that they are big. But tax evasion and avoidance do wider damage. International tax rules have not offered opportunities for evasion and avoidance equally, but have almost exclusively bene-fited wealthy individuals and MNCs. They have thus contributed to reinforcing and deepening existing inequality, potentially distorting economic competition in favour of international companies, and creating downward pressure on the rates at which governments can levy taxes on wealthy individuals and transnational corporations. The same rules have generated new opportunities for corruption, through the complex structures of transnational enterprises, tax havens, secret bank accounts, and secretive legal arrangements to obscure the real ownership of assets.

For some, the inequity of the international tax system fits squarely within broader narratives about the ways in which an unfair global political and economic system systematically disad-vantages poorer countries. That narrative shifts the analytical lens away from national policy and pins much of the responsi-bility for Africa's development difficulties on international actors and the institutions they create. However, as with many narratives that attribute national problems to perverse external forces, the reality is complex. International rules are clearly disadvantageous to African countries, and largely outside their control. But African decision makers are not powerless in the face of an unfair interna-tional system. They are also part of that system: they have some scope to shape the ways in which it impacts on Africa, and are also sometimes complicit in enabling – or directly benefiting from – the opportunities for tax avoidance that it permits.

Against this background, this chapter sketches the challenges for Africa posed by international tax rules, while Chapter 4 considers the potential for changing them. The remainder of this chapter looks first at the general challenges of the international tax system, and then turns to exploring in more detail the dynamics surrounding, first, the taxation of wealthy individuals, and then of taxing MNCs. The latter topic has received the bulk of international attention in recent years, but the discussion to follow makes clear that tax evasion and avoidance by wealthy individuals pose a similarly serious threat to developing countries.

Complexity, secrecy and tax havens

The basic tax challenges faced by governments of low-income countries in the international arena are little different from those facing tax collectors anywhere. Governments are keen to tax the profits of corporations and the earnings of wealthy individuals according to national laws, while many of these potential taxpayers aim to disguise and hide as much profit and wealth as possible. The challenges of taxing international economic transactions are distinct because of the complexity of the global tax system. In a world in which capital (money) can flow freely across national borders, wealthy individuals and multinational companies have many opportunities to disguise and hide their wealth from national governments. In principle, effective international cooperation could overcome these challenges. In practice, cooperation has been limited. In the strict sense of the term, there is no international tax *system*. There is rather a network of (overlapping) national arrangements; bilateral treaties; principles endorsed by international organisations, above all the OECD; international agreements; and custom and practice. Some of the resultant 'rules' are soft, implicit and contested; others are firmer and legally binding. Their effectiveness depends largely on willing compliance. Among the actors with the power to enforce compliance, the government of the United States is most prominent. There is no global tax organisation – not even one with limited powers like the World Trade Organization. The international tax system has come to be characterised by unequal decision-making power, escalating complexity and the emergence of growing secrecy, with potentially serious developmental consequences. Various scholars have explained the historical processes leading to this situation (Sharman 2006; Palan et al. 2010; Shaxson 2011; Picciotto 2013). Here, we briefly summarise the history and key current features of the global tax system.

Unequal global rules

The 'rules' governing international taxation have largely been made by the more powerful states. Unsurprisingly, they have been broadly designed to benefit their creators – or powerful interests located within them. Early debates about who had the right to tax the profits of companies operating internationally centred on the distinction between 'residence countries' and 'source countries': that is, between the place where a company was owned ('residence') and the place(s) where it did business and thus sourced its profits ('source'). At the time, most companies undertaking foreign investment were resident in one of what later became known as the OECD countries – or were subsidiaries of such companies. The rules were implicitly designed to enhance the taxing rights of those OECD/residence countries. A similar pattern emerged in the international arrangements for taxing very wealthy individuals. Wealthy individuals in both richer and poorer countries increasingly sought to place their wealth in foreign bank accounts, at least in part to avoid the reach of national governments. The owners of that wealth were often politically powerful. Provided that most of their wealth continued to move to and between bank accounts located in OECD countries and their dependencies,[1] little effort was made to monitor or control these movements.

Over time, OECD countries increasingly entered into bilateral tax treaties, which established additional rules about how the right to tax MNCs would be divided among signatory countries. These treaties were initially primarily between OECD countries, but tax treaties between OECD and developing countries became increasingly common. Formally, these treaties were designed to reduce the risk that the profits of an MNC would be taxed twice, first in the source country and then in the residence country – *double taxation.* However, the risk of double taxation is now much reduced: the tax authorities of most residence countries allow companies incorporated there to deduct corporate income taxes paid in source countries from their final corporate income tax bill at home. Instead, the primary role of tax treaties has been to shape the respective taxing rights of resident and source countries, either by setting explicit limits on the taxes that can be levied by source countries, or by creating loopholes and grey areas that are open for abuse (Hearson 2013; 2015).

Secrecy, and the global system of tax havens

In most cases, international rules, however unequal, do not directly authorise tax abuse. Instead, either by design or by accident, they create spaces for potential abuse. Since the 1960s in particular, this space has been filled by an ever more complex network of offshore financial centres (OFCs) – more popularly known as 'tax havens' or 'secrecy jurisdictions' – designed in large part to facilitate secrecy, tax avoidance and evasion. These are legal jurisdictions offering a combination of low tax rates for foreign individual and companies, limited regulation, and extreme secrecy about the ownership of registered corporations and individual assets. This secrecy has been achieved, among other means, through national bank secrecy laws designed to prevent the sharing of information about clients, even with national authorities, and by making it easy to register 'shell corporations' – that is, legal corporations that have few or no substantive activities in the country. These policies are designed to attract 'offshore' – that is, foreign – wealth and corporations by disguising the identities of their owners, and by moving them beyond the reach of national authorities.

This, in turn, has been a fundamentally beggar-thy-neighbour strategy. Financial service providers within secrecy jurisdictions achieve economic gain by offering services to foreign capital, but do so by undermining tax laws elsewhere in the world. From a societal perspective, the costs certainly outweigh the comparatively modest economic benefits to tax havens themselves. While the term 'tax haven' generally evokes images of small Caribbean islands, there is a growing recognition that this is misleading. If the focus is on countries that employ secrecy and idiosyncratic benefits to attract foreign companies and wealth, the primary culprits are, in fact, members of the OECD. The largest recipient of offshore financial wealth remains Switzerland, with London, New York, Luxembourg, Singapore and others close behind. Meanwhile, research by Findley, Nielson and Sharman (2014) has found that the easiest place globally to create a secretive corporate entity is the US state of Delaware.

Complexity and loopholes

While the network of tax havens has provided the infrastructure for international tax abuse, that abuse has thrived on the complexity of the global tax system. Notwithstanding a bias in favour of wealthier countries, international tax rules are, for the most part, formally intended to ensure that individuals and corporations pay appropriate taxes in the jurisdictions where they live and operate. However, the complexity and imperfections of those rules have created scope for lawyers, accountants and advisers to find loopholes through which their wealthy individual and corporate clients are able to minimise their tax payments. While tax havens have provided a *destination* for individuals and MNCs seeking to avoid taxation, complexity, grey areas and loopholes have provided the *facilitating environment* that has allowed funds to flow into tax havens. Unsurprisingly, then, when efforts have been made to reform the international tax system, calls for simplification have often been met with fierce resistance by those who benefit from existing arrangements (Chapter 4).

Collectively, these features of the international tax system pose challenges for *all* countries. However, these challenges are particularly acute for governments of low-income countries. They have had little say in developing the rules. The complexity of those rules means that national tax agencies require highly specialised accountancy and legal skills if they are to fight their corner. But these skills are in limited supply everywhere – and particularly in most African states. Multinational firms and wealthy individuals – supported by transnational accounting and professional services firms[2] – typically employ teams of lawyers and accountants that are larger and much better paid than those working in national tax agencies. Against this background, we can now look at the challenge in more detail, focusing first on tax avoidance by wealthy individuals, and then on equivalent efforts by MNCs.

How do international tax rules benefit HNWIs?

Although the tax activities of MNCs have received the most critical publicity in recent years, there is mounting evidence that tax losses arising from tax avoidance and evasion by wealthy individuals may be of a similar size. The key actors are so-called high net worth individuals (HNWIs): individuals with at least $1 million in financial wealth. While few in number, they control a large and growing share of national income in most countries. According to the Global Wealth Report (Credit Suisse 2017) there are 36.1 million millionaires in the world, making up 0.7% of world adults and accounting for a total of $128.7 trillion, or 45.9% of the world's wealth. While this share is rising almost everywhere, it is estimated to be rising significantly faster in Africa than in any other region in the world (Bird 2015). Of the 20 countries whose ultra-wealthy ($30 million or more in net assets) populations are estimated to have grown most rapidly over the last decade, 11 are in Africa (Knight Frank Research 2017). All told, one recent estimate is that there are 145,000 HNWIs in Africa, who control about $800 billion of total wealth (New World Wealth 2017) – though even this is likely an underestimate, owing to the large proportion of wealth held offshore (Zucman 2014).

It is difficult to tax HNWIs because: (1) they are mobile internationally; (2) much of their income is in the form of capital gains on investments; (3) they can employ expensive advisers to assist them in developing complex tax avoidance strategies; and (4) they often have influence with and cooperation from political elites (Fjeldstad and Heggstad 2014). Unsurprisingly, there are indications that efforts by HNWIs to avoid taxes have accelerated with the spread of globalisation. Recent studies in South Africa, Kenya and Uganda have suggested that the lists of HNWIs held by tax authorities may capture fewer than 10% of those they should (Forslund 2012; Kumar 2014; Kangave et al. 2016).

Perhaps the most revealing illustration of the magnitude and brazenness of tax evasion and avoidance by HNWIs came in early 2015, when a list of clients of HSBC bank with secret accounts in Switzerland became public. The leaked documents revealed that, in 2007, and in just one bank in one country, people resident in sub-Saharan Africa held over $6.5 billion in secret accounts. This accorded with earlier stories of powerful Africans with vast and mostly illicit wealth held overseas. Perhaps the most famous is the case of Sani Abacha, who is estimated to have stolen between $2 and $5 billion, and possibly more, during his five years as president of Nigeria (Barry 2015). These and similar stories are a reminder that this is not merely a story about tax evasion, but also about the ways in which secrecy in the international system reinforces inequality, facilitates political corruption, and undermines democracy.

How do HNWIs hide wealth offshore?

While the details of international tax evasion and avoidance by HNWIs can be complex, the core of most strategies is straight-forward: transfer personal wealth – whether legally or illegally acquired – into secretive bank accounts or asset holdings abroad, where they can avoid scrutiny by tax officials. Such secrecy can serve entirely legal purposes. However, tax evasion is pervasive among those involved in illicit activities, including corrupt public officials, and it is popular among wealthy individuals seeking to avoid taxes as well as to disguise the extent of their wealth. Recent studies estimate that at least 80% of wealth held offshore goes untaxed (Zucman 2014).

In simplified terms, moving money offshore begins with transferring wealth overseas without the knowledge or scrutiny of national tax authorities. In some instances, this is easy: various types of income may be paid directly into offshore accounts, particularly where that income comes from offshore sources. More elaborate schemes can see money moved offshore through payments to shell companies that are designed to look like legitimate commercial transactions. These more sophisticated strategies are supported by specialist legal, financial and accountancy firms, whose activities have been highlighted through a recent series of data leaks.[3] It is difficult for tax authorities in OECD countries to monitor these transfers. It may be near impossible for many African administrations, which often lack the capacity to keep track effectively of the assets and incomes of their own HNWIs and the political support to do so. Most illicit international transfers arrive in bank accounts protected by bank secrecy laws, designed to prevent banks from revealing the identities of account holders – or, more precisely in this case, to ensure that national tax authorities cannot identify money held offshore by their taxpayers.

This, however, is only the beginning of strategies for tax evasion and avoidance. Others involve shell companies and other complex legal structures to further disguise the identity of the person who effectively controls the assets – their 'beneficial owner'. For example, rather than transferring funds directly into a secret bank account in Switzerland, a wealthy tax evader from Kenya might transfer the money to a shell company in the Cayman Islands, or in the US state of Delaware, which would then deposit the funds in a Swiss bank account under the company name. Alternatively, the shell company might not use a bank account at all, but may instead purchase financial assets, property or luxury goods, which can make tracing ownership still more complicated.[4] The wealthy tax evader might seek to ensure that there is no verifiable connection between herself and the shell company by, for example, appointing her overseas lawyers as the only company directors. Additional layers of deception might be added, each involving a further anonymous account or shell company. The goal is to ensure that, even if the Kenyan tax authorities were formally to ask the Swiss bank about assets held by the wealthy tax evader, they would find nothing. The bank would first refuse to share information about their clients – unless, perhaps, there was pre-existing evidence of wrongdoing. However, even if they did share that information, it may lead only to other anonymous accounts or to shell companies designed to complicate any effort to trace the funds.

To be clear, while secrecy laws are technically legal under international rules, the use of structures that fully disguise the identity of the beneficial owner of wealth held overseas is, in many cases, technically illegal. Banks, financial institutions and company registries are generally required to know the identity of the beneficial owner. However, in practice, these safeguards are frequently ineffective. Studies have demonstrated that rules requiring the identification of the beneficial owners of shell companies and assets are easily avoided (Sharman 2010). Even if the ultimate beneficial owners are known, the maze of anonymity, legal barriers and complex structures can make it very difficult for African tax administrations to produce sufficient legal evidence to prosecute tax avoidance and evasion. The persistence of these loopholes is not surprising. The financial institutions, lawyers, accountants and national governments that attract this overseas wealth have a strong interest in seeing it continue.

What is the scale of the problem – and what are the potential benefits of addressing it?

While the broad problem is widely recognised, estimates of the magnitude of wealth held overseas remain imprecise. Most of it is intentionally hidden, and scattered across a vast network of secrecy jurisdictions. Table 3.1 shows the top 40 jurisdictions ranked in the Financial Secrecy Index (FSI). The FSI value is calculated using a secrecy score (a qualitative measure based on an assessment of 15 key financial secrecy indicators reflecting the jurisdiction's laws and regulations, international treaties, etc.) and a quantitative weighting to take into account the jurisdiction's size and overall importance in the global market for offshore financial services (Tax Justice Network 2015).

Table 3.1 Top 40 jurisdictions in the Financial Secrecy Index

Rank	Jurisdiction	FSI value	Rank	Jurisdiction	FSI value
1	Switzerland	1,590	21	Canada	426
2	USA	1,298	22	Macao	425
3	Cayman Islands	1,268	23	United Kingdom	424
4	Hong Kong	1,244	24	Cyprus	404
5	Singapore	1,082	25	France	404
6	Luxembourg	976	26	Ireland	388
7	Germany	769	27	Kenya	378
8	Taiwan	743	28	China	373
9	United Arab Emirates (Dubai)*	661	29	Russia	361
10	Guernsey	659	30	Turkey	354
11	Lebanon	644	31	Malaysia (Labuan)*	335
12	Panama	626	32	India	317
13	Japan	624	33	South Korea	314
14	Netherlands	599	34	Israel	314
15	Thailand	551	35	Austria	310
16	British Virgin Islands	503	36	Bermuda	282
17	Bahrain	491	37	Saudi Arabia	279
18	Jersey	438	38	Liberia	277
19	Bahamas	429	38	Marshall Islands	275
20	Malta	426	40	Philippines	270

Notes: Jurisdictions shaded in dark grey are overseas territories and crown dependencies where the Queen is head of state; powers to appoint key government officials rests with the British Crown; laws must be approved in London; and the UK government holds various other powers. Jurisdictions shaded in light grey are British Commonwealth territories whose final court of appeal is the Judicial Committee of the Privy Council in London.

*These jurisdictions may be ranked higher than warranted due to the lack of subnational data.

Source: Tax Justice Network (2018).

While we know with some confidence that Switzerland remains the largest destination for overseas financial wealth, it is still only one of many. The size of bank accounts can mislead: much of the wealth is held overseas in the form of stocks and bonds, as well as in tangible assets including property, art and other luxury goods that are particularly difficult to track.

However, despite these challenges, there is mounting consensus about the broad scope of the problem – and the numbers are extremely large. The most robust estimates come from Zucman (2014), who estimates that $8 trillion of personal financial wealth is held in offshore accounts. This figure is intentionally very conservative. It captures only financial wealth, excluding tangible assets such as property, jewellery or art works. Other estimates of total wealth held overseas are as high as $32 trillion (Henry 2012; Ryle et al. 2013). That would imply that roughly 20% of total global wealth is held offshore. The plausibility of this higher figure is supported by mounting evidence of massive sums of foreign wealth flowing into international property markets in particular, often through shell companies.[5] Meanwhile, Zucman argues that the share is even higher for Africa. He estimates that Africans hold $500 billion in financial wealth offshore, amounting to a staggering 30% of all financial wealth held by Africans – and, again, this is a conservative estimate.

What does this mean in terms of tax revenue lost by African governments? Most studies assume that 80% to 95% of offshore wealth goes unreported to governments, implying that financial returns in the form of interest, dividends or capital gains go untaxed by national authorities. Based on standard assumptions about the rate of return on financial assets held abroad, Zucman (2014) estimates that African governments lose roughly $15 billion annually. The inclusion of non-financial wealth, or a reliance on higher estimates from the literature, could push this figure as high as perhaps $45 billion annually. And this is only part of the story. It is also likely that much of the wealth offshore went untaxed when initially earned and transferred abroad; and that a meaningful portion was originally stolen from the public purse. While these estimates are inherently imprecise, they offer a sense of the magnitude of the issue – and the potential benefits of addressing it.

What has been done?

In many ways this type of tax evasion and avoidance by HNWIs is shocking precisely because of its relative simplicity and brazenness – and the sense that it should be straightforward to combat. All of the strategies described here depend on the complicity of financial institutions, lawyers, accountants and their regulators overseas. But, most basically, they depend on official, state-sanctioned secrecy, which prevents tax administrators from accessing the information that they need – and which is, in principle, available – to enforce national tax laws.[6]

The primary mechanism for uncovering – and taxing – wealth held overseas has been a network of bilateral tax information exchange agreements (TIEAs). The core premise of these agreements has been straightforward. If a citizen from country A has assets held in country B, then country B should report that information to the tax authorities in country A, thus eliminating secrecy and facilitating tax enforcement. The expansion of these TIEAs was a central goal of an early OECD campaign to curb tax abuses in the late 1990s. However, the notional appeal of such agreements was matched only by their ineffectiveness in practice. The expanded network of treaties still covered only a small subset of all bilateral relationships, and almost entirely excluded low-income countries. In any case, even small gaps in coverage can offer a destination for tax-avoiding funds. The exchange of information remained 'on request': this meant that, in order for a tax authority to request information, it often needed to be able to request a specific type of information, about a specific person, along with a clear justification. Needless to say, this proved problematic. Even African governments that manage to sign treaties are largely unable to request information on bank accounts or other assets held overseas because they have insufficient information to make a precise request. Even when requests are made, the recipients often respond slowly, if at all. Anecdotal evidence suggests that major tax havens have not even been cooperative with one another.

The bottom line is that even the very limited measures actually adopted to curb international tax evasion and avoidance have achieved little – and African countries have been largely excluded from even these meagre opportunities. While these failures have been attributed to technical and legal complexity, it is difficult to avoid the conclusion that complexity is principally an excuse for inaction. The greater problem is much simpler. The existing system has benefited powerful individuals who have placed funds in offshore accounts, powerful service providers that profit from the system, and powerful countries that have been the recipients of this wealth. Contrary to popular public images of small island tax havens, much of this wealth has in fact flowed into OECD countries. Indeed, perhaps the greatest illustration of weak international commitment to addressing the concerns of African states comes from efforts to repatriate stolen wealth held abroad through the Stolen Asset Recovery Initiative (StAR). Even where funds held abroad have been identified and linked to corruption and public fraud, only a fraction have been returned, and cooperation by OECD states is reported to have been limited (Gray et al. 2014).[7]

How do international tax rules benefit MNCs?

The complex strategies that wealthy individuals (HNWIs) use to avoid paying taxes are often either illegal, of very doubtful legality, or abusive. Changes in laws, if enforced, would greatly reduce the ability of HNWIs to evade taxes. The strategies that transnational companies use are sometimes abusive, and probably occasionally illegal. However, their success depends largely on the remarkable complexity and ambiguity of existing international tax rules. Tax law and practice are even more complex in relation to MNCs, owing to more extensive grey areas in the law and the challenges of dividing taxing rights across the many countries in which individual MNCs often operate. As a result, it is particularly difficult to estimate how much potential tax is lost to African governments or to determine the best ways of stemming those losses, which are certainly very large.

At the root of most corporate strategies to avoid and evade taxes is a simple goal: to shift profits out of high-tax jurisdictions and into low-tax jurisdictions. To understand this basic objective, it is useful to imagine a hypothetical corporation in order to clarify the logic of corporate tax strategies. We will label this corporation MNCCo, with operations in three countries – Residentland, Sourceland and Havenland. It has annual pre-tax profits of \$1 billion. If the three countries in which MNCCo operates all had the same corporate profit tax rate, the company would likely pay taxes in each country in proportion to the value added by its activities there. But if one of the three countries, Havenland, has a dramatically lower tax rate – or perhaps no corporate taxes at all – then MNCCo will have a powerful incentive to make it appear that it is making most of its profits in Havenland, to reduce the overall taxes it pays – even if, in practice, it has virtually no physical presence there.

Table 3.2 illustrates the tax savings that can result if MNCCo is able to engage in profit shifting to a low-tax jurisdiction. It correspondingly faces powerful incentives to do just that – 'creative'

Table 3.2 The effect of profit shifting on corporate tax payments

Extent of profit shifting	Profits in Residentland (30% tax rate)	Profits in Sourceland (30% tax rate)	Profits in Havenland (0% tax rate)	Total taxes paid	Tax 'savings'
No profit shifting	\$500 million	\$500 million	\$0	\$300 million	\$0
↓	\$333.33 million	\$333.33 million	\$333.33 million	\$200 million	\$100 million
Aggressive profit shifting	\$250 million	\$250 million	\$500 million	\$150 million	\$150 million
	\$0	\$0	\$1 billion	\$0	\$300 million

accounting has the potential to increase after-tax profits by as much as $300 million. It is thus easy to understand why companies have invested heavily in accountancy and legal services to facilitate this kind of outcome. However, while the motives for profit shifting are straightforward, intuition suggests that it should be difficult for companies to do this. Surely profits are the result of identifiable economic activities conducted in specific locations? Governments should then be able to tax profits generated within their borders. Unfortunately, this is far from easy. Indeed, it is often, and increasingly, impossible.

The entities we call 'multinational corporations' typically comprise dozens, or often hundreds, of separate corporate entities and subsidiaries, scattered across the world, each contributing a small part of the overall business. To some extent this proliferation of subordinate legal entities – typically subsidiaries or affiliates of some other company in the corporate group – has a substantive purpose, reflecting the globalisation of production processes. However, in other cases subsidiaries and affiliates exist largely for legal and tax purposes. The globalisation of production itself makes it increasingly difficult to decide where profits are actually created. Imagine a car sold throughout Europe and the Middle East that is assembled in Germany, from parts imported from China, Thailand, Malaysia and several European countries, using technology partly developed in Japan. Imagine also that the process is all coordinated by an office in the United States. It would be a challenge even for a totally sincere and scrupulous team of accountants and economists to say what part of the total profit was earned in which country. Then add some formal transactions among different subsidiaries within the MNC made for legal and accounting purposes. For example, some of the most valuable technology might be owned by a company based in the Bahamas. The engineers who oversee production in Germany might be paid by a company based in the Virgin Islands. And drive shafts manufactured in Thailand might be purchased first by a company based in Luxembourg before being sold to the German assembly firm. The question of where the profit actually originates then becomes an extremely complex – and inescapably political – question.

The arm's length principle and existing international rules

Understanding the strategies used to reduce tax payments – and the threat that this poses to low-income countries – requires first understanding the international tax rules currently used to allocate profits across multinational firms. These rules, in fact, reflect a complex variety of international agreements, treaties and norms, comprising both 'hard' and 'soft' law.[8] Their foundation is the *arm's length principle.*

The arm's length principle seems straightforward. When two subsidiaries within the same multinational group engage in an economic transaction, the price at which the transaction is booked in company accounts is known as the *transfer price.* According to the arm's length principle, the transfer price should be as close to a genuine market price as possible. It should be the price that would have applied if the transaction had been at 'arm's length' – i.e. between two 'unrelated' entities both seeking the best value in a competitive market. If all economic transactions between the individual entities comprising an MNC were to be priced and valued in this way, 'the market' would in effect decide where profit was being earned. In practice, this simple principle is sometimes useless, for linked conceptual and practical reasons.

The conceptual problem is that, in reality, multinational companies do not constitute a bundle of separate units that happen to do a great deal of business with one another across international borders. Multinational enterprises emerge because of the synergies that can be created by, for example, marketing and promoting Coca-Cola in 200 separate companies – or by designing computers in California, locating the production of the components in China, Malaysia and Taiwan, undertaking the final assembly in Indonesia, and marketing them from Singapore. These are not 'arm's length' transactions, and they are not understood as such by the people who manage the companies. Integration and synergy between the many units are central to business and investment strategies, and to management accounts. The decision to transact is typically made in light of the collective interest of the corporate group, rather than reflecting a market relationship between individual units.

The related practical problem is that it is often very difficult for tax authorities – or anyone else – to estimate what transfer prices should be applied for the purposes of calculating the profits of individual companies within a transnational group. When they are making their declarations to customs at the point of import and export, and when they are preparing their accounts, companies normally declare that they are using arm's length prices for these intra-group transfers. But the revenue agency – and any other third party – may find it hard to verify those claims. The arm's length principle demands the availability of a 'comparable' market trans-action that can be used to establish an appropriate arm's length transfer price. While this appears simple in principle, it is hugely complex in practice. It works for some bulk commodities: for example, it is possible to find out the reference market price for Grade 1 Harrar C coffee beans within Ethiopia on any given day. If one Ethiopian subsidiary of a multinational commodity-trading company sells a tonne of Grade 1 Harrar C to another subsidiary based in the Netherlands, there is little scope to declare a transfer price that differs significantly from the reference price on that day. But that is unusual. Most transnational economic transactions have their own characteristics, and may even be unique. The circuit boards produced by one Vietnamese company for one type of tele-phone system may differ significantly from those produced by the same company for another system. From the perspective of the tax accountant, they are not perfect 'comparables'. Perfect comparables are rare. Even adequate comparables may not be available much of the time (TUAC Secretariat 2015). Reflecting this problem, a senior Chinese tax official declared to an OECD tax meeting that the arm's length principle is ineffective, as she is never able to find 'true comparables' in assessing multinational accounts (MNE Tax 2015).

These issues become significantly more complex when we move from the realm of physical goods to that of so-called 'intangibles', including intellectual property, management and consulting services, debt and other financial transactions. The trade in intangibles within an MNC does not require any physical movement of goods or individuals. There are no standard prices. Actual or potential *transfer mispricing* – i.e. choosing transfer prices with the intention of shifting accounting profits across borders for tax purposes – is a bigger problem and challenge to tax agencies in relation to intangibles than in relation to physical goods. If a subsidiary of an MNC employs technology owned by another subsidiary of the same MNC, how much should it pay for using it? If one subsidiary provides 'consulting services' to another subsidiary in another country, how can tax authorities possibly check whether the reported transfer price reflects an acceptable arm's length price? Alternatively, if one subsidiary lends money to another subsidiary of the same MNC, how can tax authorities judge whether the charges for the loan are reasonable – given that they are typically wrapped up in financial derivatives and given a risk rating by the lender?

The bottom line is that the theoretically straightforward arm's length principle is characterised by major practical difficulties in practice. The fact that the principle still formally drives the pricing of most related party transactions – which are now estimated to comprise more than two-thirds of all international trade (WTO 2013: 54) – creates space for MNCs to engage in aggressive profit shifting designed to reduce tax liabilities.

Profit-shifting strategies

The strategies employed by MNCs to shift profits offshore and to reduce their tax payments are highly varied and complex, and far beyond what can be covered here.[9] What follows thus aims to introduce simplified versions of the most common strategies, for purposes of illustration – and to set the stage for a discussion of potential responses.

Transfer mispricing

The most common means of shifting profits overseas is also the simplest: the mispricing of goods or services sold between two parties.[10] Building on the earlier example, if an MNCCo subsidiary in Sourceland wished to artificially transfer profits to Havenland, it would underprice the goods it sells to the Havenland subsidiary of MNCCo (to reduce revenue in Sourceland) while overpricing the goods it buys from the Havenland subsidiary (to increase costs in Sourceland). The subsidiary in Havenland can reap profits simply by acting like a post office. It can re-sell the goods bought cheaply from the subsidiary in Sourceland at a higher price in global markets, while similarly profiting from selling goods purchased on global markets to the Sourceland subsidiary at an inflated price. The goods need go nowhere near Havenland. The transactions may occur entirely on paper, with the goods transiting directly from the source country to the market. Actual cases of transfer mispricing are generally more complex than this simple example, owing to both the complexity of global production chains and a desire to disguise any abuse. But the basic logic is as simple as that described here. A real-world example is described in Box 3.1.

The tax benefits of mispricing transactions within an MNC can be multiples of the extent of mispricing. Table 3.3 provides a simple mathematical illustration: a case in which a 10% under-reporting of actual export revenues results in a 30% reduction in taxes. Such relatively modest levels of mispricing are very hard to prevent. To combat transfer pricing effectively, revenue authorities require either detailed knowledge of each business that they audit, which is extremely difficult, or access to price information on near-perfect comparables, which is scarce. MNCs invest vast resources in developing legal and accounting techniques and expertise to make the task of the revenue authorities more challenging. Even if a revenue

Box 3.1 Transfer mispricing in Kenya's flower industry

In 2012, a tax dispute over transfer mispricing arose between the Kenya Revenue Authority (KRA) and Sher Karuturi, an Indian multinational company in the business of growing and exporting flowers. The KRA found that Karuturi (Kenya) was selling roses to Flower Express, a related party based in Dubai, on 'free-on-board' terms at the Jomo Kenyatta International Airport in Nairobi. However, before the flowers left the airport, some were re-sold by Flower Express to third parties at substantially higher prices for export to Europe and other markets. Kenyan newspaper The Standard found that, for a stem of roses, about 5 cents were paid to the Kenyan company, while almost a dollar was charged to third-party companies.

The KRA used the difference in price to make an adjustment to the price between Karuturi Kenya and its sister company Flower Express. This adjustment resulted in $10.7 million in additional taxes owed, equivalent to almost 1% of Kenya's total tax collection in 2012. Karuturi filed an appeal in 2013, and although the case is still unresolved, it has been reported that Karuturi negotiated the tax bill from $20 million down to $4 million.

Sources: Waris (2017); Michira (2014).

authority suspects transfer mispricing, proving it can be difficult, time consuming and costly when the limited resources of developing country tax administration are pitted against the resources of large multinationals. Tax authorities generally attempt to use whatever leverage they have to ensure that profits are reported locally. For tax authorities in most African countries, this leverage is limited.

Table 3.3 The impact of reduced revenue on the profits and taxes of the export company

Extent of profit shifting	'Market' price of goods	Sales price claimed by MNC	Quantity sold	Total revenue in source country	Total profit in source country	Total tax payment in source country (30% tax rate)	Trade mispricing (%)	Decline in taxes (%)
No profit Shifting ↓	$10	$10	30,000,000	$300 million	$100 million	$30 million	0%	0%
	$10	$9	30,000,000	$270 million	$70 million	$21 million	10%	30%
Aggressive profit shifting	$10	$8	30,000,000	$240 million	$40 million	$12 million	20%	60%

Transactions in intangibles

As noted earlier, while combating the mispricing of trade in physical goods is difficult, these challenges are much greater for trade in intangibles. In turn, the expanding role of intangibles in the modern global economy presents a growing challenge to national tax administrations.

The logic is again straightforward. When a multinational company possesses valuable expertise or intellectual property, it can be legally assigned to a subsidiary or affiliate company based in a tax haven. Rights to use that intellectual property may then be sold or licensed to other subsidiaries of the same multinational group located elsewhere. In this way, profits are shifted away from the subsidiary (the 'related party') that is 'buying' the intellectual property in the source country, and to the 'owner' of that intellectual property in a tax haven. This occurs irrespective of the fact that they are all part of the same multinational enterprise, and that there may be very little substantive activity in the tax haven beyond a mailbox to hold intellectual property, or a very small staff. An illustrative example is in Box 3.2.

Box 3.2 Profit shifting via intangibles in Ghana

In 2010, ActionAid conducted an investigation into London-based SABMiller, at the time the largest brewing company in Africa and the second largest in the world. The report found that SABMiller was using payments for two types of intangibles to reduce the profits, and thus the tax liabilities, of its African subsidiaries.

Royalty payments
The company's African beer brands, such as Castle Milk Malt, Stone Lager and Chibuku, are owned by a Rotterdam-based sister company called SABMiller International BV, taking advantage of the Netherlands' rules that enable companies to pay next to no tax on royalties. Between 2007 and 2010, the Ghanaian subsidiary Accra Brewery Limited paid 1.33 million in royalties to this company for use of its brands. Over that period, this arrangement saved Accra Brewery an estimated 210,000 in corporate income tax, which is charged at 25% in Ghana.

Management fees
The Ghanaian subsidiary also paid substantial fees to another sister company called Bevman Services AG, based in the Swiss town of Zug, which offers tax incentives to management companies so that corporate income tax can work out at only 7.8%. Accra Brewery paid this company 932,000 per year for 'management' services, despite no Ghanaian staff being aware of Swiss involvement in running the firm and a Swiss employee saying that they didn't do international human resources or marketing, as they were 'just the European head office'. These payments led to an estimated tax loss of 160,000 per year for Ghana.

From 2007 to 2010, Accra Brewery paid a total of 4.57 million in management fees and royalties, representing 6.7% of the company's turnover and nearly ten times its operating profit.

> *Despite controlling 30% of Ghana's beer market and earning 63.3 million in revenue over this period, the company managed to make an overall pre-tax loss of 3.07 million. Accra Brewery's tax bill for the four years amounted to only 216,000, with the company paying no corporate income tax at all for three of the four years. By contrast, SABMiller made profits before tax of 16% worldwide in 2009.*

Source: ActionAid (2012).

Derivatives contracts

While firms may misprice 'standard' transactions in goods and services to shift profits offshore, they also employ more complex financial transactions to achieve similar goals. One such option is the use of derivatives contracts to achieve a more complex form of transfer mispricing.

Imagine an oil firm interested in minimising its tax liability in Sourceland, where the drilling takes place. A simple strategy for doing so is to artificially reduce the price at which the oil is sold internationally to a subsidiary in Havenland – which will then re-sell it on the world market at a profit. But how to artificially reduce the sales price of the oil, when global oil prices are widely reported and comparatively easy to verify?

One option is the use of a derivatives contract – that is, an agreement to buy and sell products in the future at a predetermined price. In this case the subsidiary in Sourceland may enter into a contract with the subsidiary in Havenland to sell oil at a fixed future price. The trick is to set a future price that is, in fact, below the expected actual future price. In this way, a below market price is 'locked in' but is disguised within a complex derivatives contract. Tax administrations are confronted with the challenges of both identifying the abusive transaction and proving that the intention is tax avoidance rather than a genuine desire to manage risk.

Thin capitalisation

Finally, MNCs may seek to shift profits among members of the group through the use of inter-group loans. Again, the core strategy is straightforward. In order to shift profits from Sourceland to Havenland, the MNC could have the Havenland subsidiary make a large loan to the Sourceland subsidiary. This needs to be repaid, with interest. This could be a fully legitimate transaction, reflecting a financing need in the Sourceland subsidiary. But the subsidiaries of MNCs often lend much more to each other than is needed for financing purposes. Naturally, they charge higher rates of interest

Box 3.3 Tax avoidance in Zambia via an intra-group loan

In 2013, ActionAid published a report on the tax avoidance strategies of Associated British Foods, an FTSE 100 company and the largest sugar producer in Africa. One of the strategies identified was a 'dog-leg' loan.

In 2007, Zambia Sugar plc borrowed $70 million from Citibank (US) and Standard Bank (South Africa), at an interest rate of over 17%. Despite the loan being denominated in Zambian currency (kwacha), secured on Zambia Sugar's assets, and repaid via a bank account in Lusaka, the banks in fact made the loan to Illovo Sugar Ireland, which then made an identical loan to its sister company Zambia Sugar. This allowed the multinational to take advantage of the Zambia–Ireland tax treaty, which denies Zambia the right to tax interest payments.

The loan generated $29.4 million in interest payments. The ActionAid report argued that by routing the loan through Ireland and preventing Zambia from levying its usual 10% to 15% withholding taxes, Associated British Foods deprived the Zambian government of up to $3 million in tax revenue.

Source: ActionAid (2013).

than would be charged on a purely commercial transaction, so that they can thereby shift profits from the subsidiary that is borrowing money to the one that is lending – or vice versa. This strategy is known as 'thin capitalisation', in reference to the fact that the recipient firm is financed disproportionately by debt rather than capital. As with the other strategies described here, national tax laws frequently contain provisions against these strategies, and national tax authorities attempt to prevent them. However, enforcement again is challenging. The lender may charge 1% above the apparently 'normal' interest rate, but defend that on the grounds that the loan is being used to fund a particularly risky activity. If the subsidiaries of an MNC lend enough to each other, the profits shifted by adding 0.876% here and 1.124% there can add up to a great deal of profit shifting. Inter-group financial transactions are a major mechanism for profit shifting globally.

The challenge facing low-income countries

While all of these profit-shifting methods are in principle well understood, decades of experience have revealed that combating them is exceptionally difficult, and particularly so for low-income countries. OECD governments and tax administrations have invested heavily in strengthening policy and enforcement practices to curb the worst abuses. They also have comparatively ready access to relevant data, either directly from MNCs or though collaboration with other OECD tax authorities. However, despite these advantages, they have at best enjoyed mixed success in curbing tax abuses – indeed, most research suggests that abuses expanded through the 1990s and 2000s (Cobham and Jansky 2015). The struggles of OECD tax authorities therefore serve to highlight the enormous challenges faced by the tax administrations of lower-income countries. They lack the technical expertise and resources enjoyed by OECD governments. Owing to their small size and their economic and political weakness, they have struggled to gain access to data from tax authorities overseas. The problems created by the complexity and secrecy of the international system are amplified for lower-income countries. They have a particularly strong interest in simplification and transparency (Chapter 4).

How much revenue is lost to Africa?

It is a common mistake to confuse two very different things: the tax revenues lost to Africa from the use of the profit-shifting techniques discussed above, and levels of capital flight from Africa. Capital flight refers to any wealth leaving the continent, for any reason. Not all capital leaves to avoid tax; only a fraction of the capital that flees would ever be owed as taxes.

Here, we focus on tax losses. The concept is relatively clear. Estimates of the magnitudes are, however, diverse.[11] This is partly because it is genuinely difficult to estimate the effect on tax collections of highly complex and opaque tax evasion and avoidance strategies. It is also because different estimation methods are used, and the researchers sometimes focus on rather different issues. Some dramatically large estimates, based on questionable methods, have been widely promoted and officially cited.[12] Some of these headline figures are aggregate estimates of total tax losses across *all* developing countries. These can be misleading, especially in relation to Africa. The bulk of aggregate tax losses are incurred by middle-income countries, especially China (Forstater 2015). As these issues gain increasing global attention it is very important to use carefully the inadequate data we have – and, of course, to improve it – lest the problem be overstated, or its causes oversimplified.

Despite these caveats, researchers seem to be moving towards a rough consensus about the scale of the problem, which remains undeniably large. Recent studies suggest that, on a global scale, the activities we have discussed above – now officially labelled *base erosion and profit shifting* – have led to lost revenue of about 1% of global GDP. This percentage is probably somewhat higher for developing countries, at perhaps 1% to 2% of GDP (Crivelli et al. 2015; Cobham and Jansky 2015). In sub-Saharan Africa this would be equivalent to about \$18 billion to \$36 billion in 2015. These estimated revenue losses would amount to 6% to 13% of total government tax revenue in sub-Saharan Africa, and 33% to 67% of total development assistance from OECD countries to Africa in 2014.[13] In many countries, the tax losses are equivalent to 50% or more of national health budgets, which averaged 2.5% of GDP across sub-Saharan Africa in 2015. There would also be important equity benefits from measures that could reduce total tax losses, including fewer privileges for MNCs in relation to local firms that operate in only one country, and increased overall confidence in the equity of African fiscal systems.

Conclusions

It is, of course, important to keep the numbers above in perspective. They are large. But even with stricter tax rules and better enforcement, African governments would be able to collect only a portion of these missing revenues. The more effective the enforcement, the greater the chances of adverse effects on investment and thus economic growth. However, any opportunity to close these large tax gaps should certainly be seized, as the potential benefits to African governments could be substantial.

For many observers, these international tax challenges are consistent with a broader historical narrative of Africa's marginalisation from international rule making and exploitation by international interests. On a broad historical level, this narrative is undeniable. An enormous amount of wealth, and tax revenue, is lost to Africa every year owing to the policies and activities of actors based overseas, led mainly by OECD countries. However, there is also a danger in focusing too narrowly on a narrative of exploitation – and, by extension, helplessness – when the reality is more complex. As discussed in the next chapter, in recent years growing attention has been given to the concerns of developing countries.

Meanwhile, a potential consequence of a narrative of exploitation is an excessive focus on tax avoidance and evasion by multinational firms, at the expense of attention to the costs of the tax avoidance activities of Africa's elites.

While Africa has undoubtedly been disadvantaged by global rules, Africa's leaders are neither entirely helpless nor entirely without responsibility. African political leaders and tax administrations have not always done all that they can to combat tax abuses – and they have sometimes been complicit in them. There are significant options available to African governments, some of which have emerged through recent reform efforts at the international level. It is to these options that we now turn.

Chapter 4

WHAT CAN AFRICA DO IN THE FACE OF INTERNATIONAL TAX CHALLENGES?

Introduction

While the international tax challenges discussed in the previous chapter have only recently begun to attract significant attention within Africa, they have long been recognised within the OECD. The OECD launched its first major campaign against what it labelled 'harmful tax competition' in 1999. The campaign began aggressively, with threats to blacklist countries facilitating tax avoidance and evasion. The case for reform seemed compelling: there was mounting evidence of widespread personal wealth held offshore, and of corporations sharply reducing tax payments through the manipulation of international tax rules. Yet the campaign collapsed quickly. This failure holds at least three lessons for contemporary reform efforts. First, the campaign revealed the powerful influence of those who benefited from the status quo: not only tax havens themselves, but also wealthy individuals, many MNCs, banks and financial institutions, the big transnational accounting and professional services firms – and, of course, those OECD countries that benefited by attracting foreign wealth. Second, the campaign was undermined by accusations of hypocrisy, as it targeted small island nations that acted as tax havens, but failed to directly acknowledge and confront the tax haven activities of many OECD governments. Third, while the reform programme was framed as 'multilateral' it was in reality initiated and led by a handful of OECD countries. Developing countries played no significant role (Sharman 2006).

The 2008–09 global financial crisis helped put international tax issues back on the global policy agenda. OECD countries were confronted by mounting fiscal deficits; civil society was increasingly active in the wake of the crisis and signs of growing income inequality; and there was accumulating evidence that international tax evasion and avoidance were expanding rapidly because of digitalisation and globalisation. Critically, and for the first time, the connections between international tax rules and development in poor countries began to gain significant traction, spurred both by the efforts of civil society groups and by the increasing sophistication and assertiveness of some developing countries.

This confluence of factors resulted in the endorsement by the G20 group of the more powerful countries of the Base Erosion and Profit Shifting (BEPS) action plan in July 2013, and the launch of a series of bilateral and multilateral initiatives to confront international tax avoidance and evasion by both individuals and MNCs. While initially greeted by significant scepticism, these processes collectively emerged as perhaps the most ambitious re-evaluation of international rules in decades. However, the old concerns remained. The day-to-day leadership of these reform efforts fell to the OECD, thus raising concerns about the representation of developing countries in consultations and negotiations. Meanwhile, powerful actors who were invested in the current system lined up against reform.

Ultimately, these reform efforts resulted in some important steps forward. There are new rules to expand multilateral information sharing about wealth held abroad by individuals, and to increase transparency surrounding the global operations and tax strategies of MNCs. Yet, on balance, most observers, especially in low-income countries, have viewed the results as a disappointment. Efforts were made by the OECD to include lower-income countries in consultations. Yet the short timeline, acute differences in technical capacity and relative newness of the issues meant that, in practice, lower-income countries had a limited voice. Their concerns were often marginalised. This chapter explores the implications for African countries of this failure to achieve more thoroughgoing reform. We first assess the efforts to reform the taxation of HNWIs. Then we do the same for the taxation of MNCs, and conclude by looking at the options now available to African governments.

Efforts to tax high net worth individuals

Most tax avoidance and evasion by HNWIs rests on a simple logic: hiding wealth overseas where it cannot be identified by national authorities. The foundation for most proposed solutions is equally straightforward: the sharing of information *among* national tax authorities from around the world, in order to reveal the location and ownership of offshore wealth and allow it to be taxed.

This was the approach adopted in the OECD's 1999 campaign against harmful tax competition. Countries were pushed to sign bilateral tax information exchange agreements (TIEAs), through which they would share information about wealth held within their borders by foreign nationals. However, this proved almost entirely ineffective in practice. The coverage of the treaty network was far too limited to confront the extreme mobility of capital (Elsayyad and Konrad 2012); it was difficult to access the information needed; and low-income countries were almost entirely excluded.

This remained the situation until the reform initiatives that followed the 2008–09 financial crisis. The push for reform in turn accelerated amidst persistent leaks of information that revealed the extent of secretive offshore wealth held abroad.[1] Recognising the limitations of the existing system of TIEAs, the governments of developing countries, and their supporters elsewhere, sought a system that would be universal, transparent, automatic and effective.

Automatic exchange of information

The cornerstone of reform efforts targeting HNWIs was a push for the creation of a multilateral agreement on the automatic exchange of information for tax purposes (AEOI). Unlike bilateral TIEAs, for which access to information was available only on request, AEOI would see countries automatically share information about bank accounts held abroad by foreigners. For example, if an Indonesian held a bank account in Switzerland, information about that account would be automatically shared with Indonesian tax authorities. While it initially seemed unlikely that existing tax havens would accept such an agreement, support for AEOI expanded rapidly amidst active civil society campaigning and growing recognition of the need for reform. This culminated in October 2014 with the ratification of a new OECD standard for AEOI, and the signing of a multilateral competent authority agreement (MCAA) to implement AEOI among all signatories, with initial exchanges occurring between 'early-adopter' countries beginning in late 2017. While this has marked an important step forward, South Africa is the only African country so far to have participated in exchanges. For remaining African countries the devil will lie in the details in assessing the eventual impact. Four questions remain unanswered:

1. *Will the bar for participation in the agreement be achievable for lower-income countries?* Countries participating in AEOI have justifiable concerns about the need for strong data controls and protection, and about ensuring that data is used fairly. However, these concerns can easily become a barrier to lower-income countries being able to participate and benefit from the new initiative.

2. *Will data be provided in a way that is usable by low-income countries, taking into account their more limited technical and organisational capacity?* AEOI can potentially involve the transmission of very large quantities of data, which, unless planned appropriately, could overwhelm tax administrations in lower-income countries.

3. *Will OECD countries be proactively supportive of improved enforcement in Africa?* AEOI agreements may serve to grant African countries access to data on wealth held abroad by their residents and citizens. However, effective action to curb tax abuses may require subsequent cooperation: for example, the sharing of additional and more detailed information, or, where there is evidence of illegality, a willingness to block bank accounts or repatriate wealth. However, OECD jurisdictions have historically offered only limited cooperation with, for example, the Stolen Asset Recovery Initiative (Chapter 3).

4. *Will African countries themselves summon the political will to participate actively in the initiative?* The damage done to African tax collection is not attributable only to problematic international rules, but also to the complicity of some African governments and officials in facilitating tax abuse. Many African elites – including some political leaders – hold significant wealth offshore. Their influence may lead African states not to join the initiative at all, or to fail to use the information they do obtain.

At the time of writing, the answers to these questions are uncertain. As of April 2018 only five African countries – Ghana, South Africa, Nigeria, Mauritius and the Seychelles – had signed the agreement, let alone demonstrated the ability use data effectively. Meanwhile, the rules governing the eligibility of low-income countries to join the agreement remain somewhat murky. There is a general requirement that they have effective systems in place to ensure data security, but how this rule is applied will remain an important question. If the bar is set too high, or if low-income countries are not supported in their efforts to build capacity, they may find themselves unable to benefit from the new rules (Financial Transparency Coalition 2017).

Similarly, there is little evidence that African political leaders are entirely ready to tackle tax avoidance practised by their own wealthy citizens. In 2015, 'Swiss Leaks' revealed that almost 5,000 clients from 41 sub-Saharan African countries held over $6.5 billion in Swiss HSBC accounts (see Figure 4.1). Despite this, inquiries with the International Consortium of Investigative Journalists (ICIJ) and news reports suggest that investigations were launched in only a handful of countries, and that, with the exception of South Africa, to public knowledge no African governments have received the data or recovered funds using it.

Despite these limitations, the adoption of an AEOI agreement marks an important step forward, as it recognises the scale of the problem and the need for multilateral solutions. Much more information on its substantive impact – and key challenges – will become available in the years ahead as implementation begins.

Figure 4.1 The top 20 countries in sub-Saharan Africa, by amount of money (in $ million) held by nationals in Swiss HSBC accounts, 2006–07

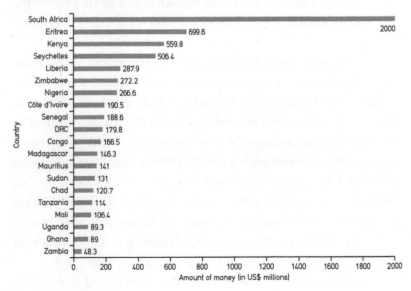

Source: ICIJ (2015).

Strengthening beneficial ownership rules

In addition to effective information exchange, taxation of individual wealth held abroad is dependent on parallel efforts to strengthen rules relating to the beneficial ownership of assets. Assets cannot be effectively identified and taxed without knowing who owns them.

In principle, relatively strong rules on beneficial ownership have long existed as part of recommendations from the Financial Action Task Force (FATF), a G20-mandated body to combat money laundering (FATF 2012). However, in practice those rules have long been poorly enforced. Research has consistently revealed the relative ease with which shell companies and other structures can be established to disguise beneficial ownership of assets (Findley et al. 2014). In response, the 2013 G8 summit, which focused on tax evasion and transparency, endorsed a set of core principles on beneficial ownership that are consistent with FATF standards. The following year the G20 followed suit and published 'High-level Principles on Beneficial Ownership and Transparency'. Both groups called for central national registries of beneficial ownership and timely sharing of data, and suggested that at least some data be made public.

Progress in taking the practical steps needed to realise these official promises has been slow.[2] Ownership registries accessible to the public would greatly improve transparency, and allow activist organisations to put pressure on national authorities to take action in cases of abuse – something that is important everywhere, but particularly in lower-income countries that have historically been reluctant to effectively tax national elites. Yet support for public access to registries of beneficial ownership has been very limited, seemingly signalling the power of sectional interests and a lack of concern for the particular needs of lower-income countries. Progress in this area seems urgently needed.

Efforts to reform the taxation of multinational corporations

Taxing HNWIs more effectively requires more multilateral cooperation; the same is true of efforts to more effectively tax MNCs. In both cases real progress has been made. But in both cases the results of recent reforms have ultimately been disappointing, particularly from the perspective of lower-income countries.

The BEPS process, which brought together officials from across the OECD and more broadly, was launched in 2013. It was impressive in scope, with the overarching goal of ensuring 'that profits are taxed where economic activities occur and where *value is created*' *(OECD 2015b)*. Despite doubts that it would be able to produce a major reform programme within the two years allocated, the OECD delivered a final set of reports detailing the BEPS recommendations in October 2015. These recommendations enjoyed expressions of high-level support from the G20 in particular. In the view of many observers, the proposals amounted to the most extensive reform of international tax rules in a generation, including a range of useful new tools for combatting tax avoidance and evasion. However, as the dust settled, it became increasingly clear that the proposals had made only limited progress in addressing the core concerns of lower-income countries – and had left fundamental questions about the overall design of the global tax system unaddressed.

The concerns about the BEPS process from the perspective of lower-income countries reflect their particular needs and circumstances, with four interconnected issues standing out:

1. *Urgency*: The revenue losses from international corporate tax avoidance and evasion are believed to be significantly larger for low-income countries (Chapter 3). As such, there is greater urgency for low-income countries, and stronger incentives to consider more ambitious reform.

2. *Simplicity*: Developing countries have much less organisational capacity to combat complex international avoidance and evasion, and have a correspondingly greater interest in simplifying existing rules, in order to make them more enforceable.

3. *Transparency*: Most large MNCs are located in richer countries. The tax administrations of those countries, through a variety of more or less formal channels, have access to quite a lot of information that helps them design and implement tax regimes for MNCs. By contrast, tax administrations in low-income countries depend more heavily on the information that could be made available through more formal transparency in tax-related issues.

4. *Inclusiveness*: Developing countries have more reason to favour fully inclusive multilateral agreements, whereas OECD countries may prefer agreements that include economically 'important' countries, but exclude the rest.

In practice, the BEPS process has tended to produce reforms that favour OECD interests and/or fail to address the particular concerns of lower-income countries. The final BEPS recommendations increase, rather than reduce, the complexity of international tax rules. They are backed by more than 10,000 pages of technical documentation. Even if the reforms are technically desirable, in practice this expanded complexity risks increasing the enforcement gap between wealthier and lower-income countries. Meanwhile, some of the most important proposals imply low levels of transparency and inclusiveness. Documentation related to beneficial ownership and country-by-country reporting of company financial accounts appears likely to be held privately, rather than publicly, and will be available only to revenue authorities and other government agencies that have a specified 'need to know'. Finally, the OECD has effectively rejected more fundamental reform proposals advanced by developing countries. They continue to be marginalised in the process of shaping global tax policy, and their needs have not been taken sufficiently seriously. This can be usefully illustrated in relation to two key aspects of the new rules: reliance on the arm's length principle and country-by-country reporting.

Arm's length pricing and the alternatives

As described in Chapter 3, the bedrock of the existing system of international tax rules is the arm's length principle. This involves observance of the legal fiction that the companies within a transnational group are separate entities, rather than components of a single enterprise that is integrated financially, economically and managerially. Cross-border transactions among those companies are treated as if they were undertaken at arm's length, by unrelated businesses. Reflecting the key concerns of OECD countries, much of the BEPS process has focused on how to strengthen the application of the arm's length principle – that is, how to ensure that recorded transactions between different components of multinational groups are legitimate economic transactions that are appropriately priced, to ensure the proper allocation of profit between different tax jurisdictions. To this end, the BEPS process has introduced a variety of new rules designed to combat various forms of abuse.

However, these new rules – and the overall focus on strengthening the application of the arm's length principle – look very different from the perspective of developing countries: the arm's length principle is at best highly imperfect, and at worst fundamentally flawed. As described in Chapter 3, governments of developing countries have argued that, while the arm's length principle may appear desirable in the abstract, in practice it can be close to impossible for them to implement it effectively. This is particularly true for the trade in so-called 'intangibles' and for interest payments flowing from developing country subsidiaries to parent companies abroad. Calls for greater flexibility and openness to alternatives to the arm's length principle were largely sidelined during the BEPS process.

Most of the alternatives to the arm's length principle that are on the table are designed to be implementable by tax administrations in countries at all income levels. In different combinations, the most ambitious such proposals share a common starting point: allowing tax authorities to treat MNCs as *integrated enterprises*, and then dividing their *combined profits* in proportion to the estimated value created in each location. For many people this approach is conceptually attractive because it starts from the reality that MNCs are, in fact, single, integrated, economic entities; and it is practically appealing because it might simplify the tax collectors' task. Implementing the arm's length principle involves policing the accuracy of a huge range of recorded transactions, for many of which there are no 'comparables'. By contrast, variants of a *profit-split approach* can, in principle, achieve the same ends on the basis of analysis of a much smaller range of data – notably data on 'allocation factors' such as employment, assets and sales in each country.

There is a range of suggestions for sharing the right to tax the profits of MNCs among national tax administrations. They can usefully be understood as ranging from relatively complex, case-specific approaches, to simpler, more generalised approaches. At one end of the spectrum are firm-specific 'profit-split' approaches, which are permitted under limited circumstances within current OECD rules. In essence, individual tax administrations are permitted to use this profit splitting to help assess the profits of the local subsidiaries and affiliates of transnational corporate groups when the application of the arm's length principle is simply impossible.[3] At the other end of the spectrum are calls for the implementation of a global system of formulary apportionment, or 'unitary taxation', in which all MNCs would be treated as unitary entities, with their profits allocated across countries according to a commonly agreed formula.[4] Such an approach has been endorsed, for example, by an important group of international tax lawyers and economists from the developing world (ICRICT 2015). Lying between these extremes are options that apply a relatively common apportionment formula, but only to some, rather than all, MNCs (see, for example, Durst 2015a).

The case-specific profit-split approaches that are allowed – though strongly discouraged – by the OECD are analytically relatively precise, and offer a useful option for low-income countries. However, they remain comparatively complex to implement. While they obviate the need to identify comparables, the tax authorities would require a sophisticated understanding of the overall economic operations of the firms concerned. By contrast, methods based on relatively standard formulas for allocating profits across borders are more easily implementable. However, they would be less precisely calibrated to the characteristics and circumstances of particular firms. In consequence, it would be difficult to achieve agreement between two or more governments claiming the right to tax the profits of the same MNC. The most important barrier to a shift towards any kind of apportionment formula is getting agreement among governments.

There may not be a single or simple 'best' option. However, there seems little doubt that openness to alternatives would offer lower-income countries greater options, and leverage, in seeking to ensure fair tax payments by MNCs operating within their borders.

Country-by-country reporting

One of the major outcomes of BEPS was a commitment to introduce country-by-country financial reporting for multinational firms. Under existing global accounting rules, MNCs are not required to report financial information, including profits and taxes paid, for every country in which they operate. They may simply present aggregate accounts on a regional basis. The absence of this information can obscure the overall structure of multinational firms, and the distribution of profits and tax liabilities across their operations. This, in turn, makes it more difficult for tax agencies to identify possible abuse.

The logic of country-by-country reporting is straightforward. Every multinational company should report key financial information for every country in which it operates. This will be collated into a master file, which would be available to tax administrations in every country concerned. This would provide much greater transparency about the operations of multinational firms, and would help tax administrations identify areas of risk. For example, access to the master file might reveal that an MNC is reporting no profits in one jurisdiction, but that a connected subsidiary in a tax haven is reporting large profits.

Country-by-country reporting is particularly attractive to developing countries because it has the potential to meet the triple objectives of simplicity, transparency and universality. It potentially provides data that is easily understandable for developing country tax administrations and reduces their disadvantages in accessing international data on the corporations that they are seeking to tax. Meanwhile, the data contained in country-by-country reports, if shared with researchers, would allow for far more accurate estimates of the scope of potential international tax losses and the effectiveness (or ineffectiveness) of recent reforms. For these reasons, the decision to introduce country-by-country reporting was widely viewed as an important victory for developing countries.

However, the details of the final BEPS recommendations, which are now being carried forward, on country-by-country reporting were disappointing. First, only MNCs with annual revenues of at least €750 million would need to produce country-by-country accounts. This excludes many mid-sized MNCs that are of limited concern to larger countries but may be very important to low-income countries. Second, country-by-country reports are to be submitted to tax authorities in the residence country of the parent MNC – overwhelmingly in OECD countries – rather than being submitted in all countries in which the MNC operates. Those residence countries *may* share the reports with other countries in which the MNC operates, but they are not required to do so. While other countries retain the right to request country-by-country reports directly from MNCs, their ability to access the data will not be guaranteed – with particular risks to low-income countries. Finally, data from the country-by-country reports will not be made publicly available – even in anonymised form. This will undermine the potential for public pressure where governments do not act, and make it difficult for researchers to investigate the extent of abuses and assess the effectiveness of existing rules.

These new arrangements for country-by-country reporting might evolve to meet the needs of developing countries eventually. The hope is that low-income countries will be successful in accessing the master file data in the short term, and in pushing for expansion over the medium term. Meanwhile, greater transparency will remain a demand among civil society more broadly. However, as it stands, it appears that MNCs – and OECD residence countries that potentially benefit from weak tax enforcement in low-income countries – may continue to prevent the governments of low-income countries from having reasonable access to information, at least in some cases.

Future reform and alternatives to multilateralism

Evaluating the likely overall impact of reform efforts is difficult. Recent initiatives have certainly brought some benefits to low-income countries. Though limited, AEOI and country-by-country reporting may offer access to new and valuable data to at least some African tax administrations. Stronger international rules on beneficial ownership and marginal increases in openness to the adoption of alternatives to the arm's length principle may also bring benefits over time. New tools for combating transfer mispricing, and for reforming tax treaties, should support some improvement in tax enforcement. Yet it remains unclear how successfully African countries will be able to access newly available data, how able they will be to employ that data to curb abuses, and, indeed, whether there will be the political commitment necessary to confront politically and economically powerful tax evaders. Perhaps as importantly, the reform process appears far from over. There have been conflicts between the US and Europe over the implementation of BEPS rules, while the US discussed – though ultimately did not pursue – its own radical reform of corporate taxation designed to address the problems of transfer mispricing by introducing destination-based cash flow taxation (DBCFT). Meanwhile, increasingly proactive engagement from China has added another potential voice for broader reform, while even the IMF has raised questions about the adequacy of recent reforms (Keen 2017). All of this suggests that the BEPS process may be the beginning, rather than the end, of significant international corporate tax reform.

Notwithstanding the potential for future reform, there remains a general feeling that efforts so far have yet to deliver significant benefits for African countries. Access to data on individual wealthy taxpayers remains somewhat uncertain, and may not be used effectively even where it is available. African governments still have few new and practically useful tools to confront abusive transfer pricing, or to curb profits moving offshore through interest payments and service fees. BEPS similarly does not directly address inequalities embedded in African states' existing tax treaties, the erosion of tax revenue through tax competition (Chapter 6), or the frequent inability of states to effectively tax capital gains on the sale of assets based in Africa (including natural resources) but sold offshore between international parent companies (Chapter 5) (Michielse 2016).[5]

Part of the challenge moving forward will undoubtedly lie in continuing to push for greater attention to these concerns. But outcomes are likely to remain uncertain: African countries continue to exercise a relatively limited global voice on these issues, and they remain in the early phases of efforts to build regional platforms for engagement.[6] Gaining the ability to shape global outcomes more actively is clearly important, but this will probably take time. In the interim, global rules are likely to continue to reflect continuing debates among OECD countries and, potentially, the growing voice of larger and wealthier developing countries such as China and Brazil. These latter countries share some of the same concerns as lower-income states in Africa, and they may be important allies. For example, both China and Brazil have been champions in the past of simplified approaches to transfer pricing, which diverge somewhat from the arm's length principle. They have also championed efforts to make the negotiation of international tax rules more inclusive,[7] and to support research and capacity-building efforts led by developing countries. On the other hand, both countries are increasingly important foreign investors in Africa, and China has aspirations to become a global financial centre. In these respects, their interests may diverge from those of lower-income African states (see, for example, Li 2012).

Yet while African governments have undoubtedly been disadvantaged by international rules – and are likely to continue to be disadvantaged – they are not powerless, nor are they without immediate options. African leaders enjoy a range of potential domestic options for addressing international tax challenges while working within existing rules. At a basic level there is scope, with international support, to expand efforts to enforce rules against transfer mispricing through both policy reform and more assertive administrative. Recent, though poorly documented, experiences in a range of countries are suggestive of very large returns to investments in expanded enforcement. These efforts should almost certainly continue to be expanded, as should international support for them. There is also a range of additional options that are significantly broader than is often recognised. We briefly summarise some of these less widely discussed options here.

While the BEPS process left intact the supremacy of the arm's length principle, the OECD nevertheless permits governments some scope to apply alternatives where the arm's length principle simply will not work, or is judged too complex to be applied effectively.[8] Formally, under OECD rules, countries are seriously constrained as to the conditions in which they are permitted to apply these methods, and the analytical complexity that is expected in applying them. This has made them extremely difficult to employ in practice. However, it is not inconceivable that, over time, African governments could opt to apply simplified versions of these methods, even at the risk of pushing the limits of OECD guidelines. The most likely option would be the transactional net margin method (TNMM), which effectively applies a fixed profit margin on top of a measure of local business activity, such as sales or costs, in order to sidestep the problem of establishing accounting profits. At present, the barriers to applying this method under OECD rules are high: countries are expected to use (often non-existent) comparables and additional analysis in order to establish an appropriate margin. In practice this has proved to be near impossible. However, one could imagine governments opting to apply more simplified approaches, less reliant on the use of comparables. Indeed, Brazil in particular – benefiting from its relative economic strength – has done precisely that. To date, African countries have almost universally avoided using these alternatives, owing, it appears, to their lack of negotiating power relative to the OECD and MNCs. However, this may also reflect a lack of awareness of the options. African tax administrations may find the selective application of alternative methods to be an increasingly viable and useful strategy, possibly while trying to draw on support from large emerging market economies.

African tax administrations may similarly be able to make use of a wider variety of 'second-best' approaches to taxing income and profits more effectively. With respect to individuals, some observers have long advocated a greater focus on taxing visible assets, such as property or luxury vehicles, which are often more readily observable than income. At a minimum, African governments could better use information on ownership of these assets to identify tax avoidance and evasion. This is particularly relevant given evidence that wealthy Africans, many of whom pay very few taxes (Chapter 6), are investing heavily in lightly taxed local property (Goodfellow 2015).

In the same spirit, various observers have suggested the potential for expanded reliance on withholding taxes and taxes on revenue rather than profits – including alternative minimum taxes (Durst 2015a; BEPS Monitoring Group 2016). All of these approaches share an emphasis on taxing comparatively easily observable transactions and revenues, rather than profits, which are more easily manipulated and disguised. Under most withholding tax regimes, so-called 'withholding agents' – generally the government or some large firms – withhold taxes from those with whom they do business when a transaction occurs. They then remit that revenue directly to the tax authorities. This acts as a prepayment of taxes by the firms that do business with 'withholding agents', and serves to bring them into the tax net and reduce the scope for evasion.

Meanwhile, while standard corporate tax regimes focus on taxing the profits of firms, these profits (and thus taxes) can be minimised by artificially reducing revenues or increasing costs, through transfer mispricing or simple misreporting. Taxes based on total revenues require less information, and thus reduce the scope for evasion by reducing the potential space for manipulation by firms. The most common forms of such taxes are revenue-based royalties levied on extractive industries and alternative minimum taxes based on revenues, which are levied if reported profits fall below a certain minimum threshold.[9] Such strategies would need to be used with caution, in order to avoid deterring potential investors. However, in the context of the existing highly imperfect international tax system – and the weakness of tax administration more broadly – recent research has suggested that revenue-based taxes in particular, used selectively, could potentially improve both revenue collection and fairness (Best et al. 2015). The more coordination among African countries in exploring, testing and developing alternatives, the more likely they are to be effective.

Tax treaties are another issue on which African governments can take action without waiting for external support or agreement. There has been growing recognition that many existing tax treaties unfairly limit the ability of developing countries to tax particular economic activities, and open loopholes for international tax avoidance and evasion.[10] The BEPS process has resulted in the creation of new model provisions to prevent such abuse: the 'Multilateral Convention to Implement Tax Treaty Related Measures to Prevent Base Erosion and Profit Shifting' (the 'Multilateral Instrument'). However, the onus will be on African countries to review and renegotiate their existing treaties, to move towards either new international model provisions, or, for example, to Africa-wide model provisions that reflect the specific needs of the continent. There is already clear precedent, with Rwanda and Uganda – alongside various other developing countries[11] – already having begun to renegotiate the most problematic treaties bilaterally.[12] Less optimistically, there have also been recent cases of governments exploring tax treaties that appear more likely to harm domestic tax collection – such as a widely contested tax treaty between Kenya and Mauritius ratified in 2014 (Guguyu 2016).

Finally, African states can ensure that they are not contributing to exacerbating the problem or undermining tax collection among their neighbours through tax competition. Over the past 15 years, a variety of African states have explored the possibility of becoming offshore financial centres, with the implicit goal of attracting foreign wealth. The government of Botswana launched an international financial service centre (IFSC) in 2003. A similar process was initiated in Ghana in 2004 with the support of Barclays bank, and was only stopped after significant resistance from the public and from other African states, following unfavourable media coverage (Dogbevi 2016). More recently, the Kenyan government has been exploring the creation of an offshore financial centre, which might undermine efforts to strengthen tax collection being made by other African governments (Ngugi 2016; Mwanyumba et al. 2017).

Conclusions

To observers of African development, the broad contours of the story told here are familiar. International taxation is far from the only area of international policy in which African countries have been marginalised and disadvantaged. Current debates reflect complex, technical questions, but they equally reflect easily recognisable power politics. African countries are small fish in the larger pond of international taxation, and the reform proposals that might benefit them most are not priorities for the bigger fish. In many ways, the progress made so far in putting the concerns of developing countries on the table has been a welcome surprise, but there remains much that is unfinished.

It is important that African states – hopefully collectively and in partnership with regional organisations representing other developing countries – continue to push for the further reform of international rules to better reflect their needs. However, a narrow focus on international reform is likely to be both misguided and incomplete: misguided in that history suggests that, while progress is possible, international reform to fully address African priorities is unlikely in the short term; incomplete in that African governments are not powerless, but in fact enjoy significant scope for immediate domestic action to combat the challenges of taxing international transactions and offshore wealth. Recent pilot efforts to deploy new tools for combating transfer mispricing in Africa – often with international support – have enjoyed significant successes in identifying corporate misbehaviour and raising new revenue. These efforts should undoubtedly be continued and expanded.

While international tax rules are deeply important for African states, and their inequity deeply troubling, it remains the case that the greatest potential for improving outcomes still lies in strengthening domestic tax systems on the continent. International tax rules and MNCs present easy and attractive targets for criticism by advocacy organisations. In recent years, these criticisms have been very effective in broadening awareness of the issues and encouraging some reform. But there remains a risk that a focus on international tax issues may distract attention from major domestic challenges, which African leaders have sometimes been slow to address. For every MNC evading taxes internationally, there is also a domestic firm benefiting from unjustified tax exemptions (Chapter 6). For every wealthy African with assets hidden overseas in Switzerland or Luxembourg, there are several others avoiding taxes at home in relatively plain sight and without repercussions. There is thus a risk of increased attention to international challenges distracting from equally urgent local challenges. Both are needed, and they are complementary.

We now turn towards these domestic challenges and opportunities by examining a tax issue that is particularly problematic and important for sub-Saharan Africa. It lies at the intersection of 'international' and 'domestic' taxation. How can African governments obtain significant revenue from the transnational corporations that dominate what has become a major component of the economy of the continent: the extraction and export of oil, gas and minerals?

Chapter 5

EXTRACTIVES AND EXTRACTION: TAXING OIL, GAS AND MINERALS[1]

Let us begin with a good film: *Zambia: good copper, bad copper* (Public Eye 2012). Made in 2012, it contains some powerful campaigning material: large numbers of former mine workers who cannot find jobs in highly mechanised contemporary mining operations, yet suffer because the industry poisons their air and water; a transnational mining company (Glencore) that pays little tax on its Zambian profits; and the callous indifference of some of the people enjoying these profits – the notoriously wealthy residents of Zug canton in Switzerland. You might also watch *Stealing Africa – Why Poverty?* (Guldbrandsen 2013). It tells a similar story. In fact, online there are dozens of video clips and countless blog and news items about the exploitation of Zambia and Zambians by mining companies. Try, for example, the video in which Anil Agarwal, the boss of Vedanta, one of the world's largest natural resources companies, is boasting to Indian business colleagues about how he obtained his original mining concession in Zambia in 1994 with little money, modest effort, petty deception, and few future tax obligations (Das 2014). The returns on his investment have been sky-high.[2] Or look at the wealth of commentary on Chinese-owned copper mines in Zambia, such as China Nonferrous Mining Corporation (CNMC), Non-Ferrous China Africa (NFCA) and Sino Metals.

Why, in recent years, have journalists and video-makers been so interested in Zambia's copper mines, so critical of the mine owners, and so attentive to the question of how little tax they seem to be paying to the Zambian government? The answer comes in several parts. Two are specific to Zambia. First, it is one of the largest mining economies in Africa. Second, there has been a great deal of open controversy over mining between Zambians: strikes, protests, and electioneering around employment conditions in the mines, environmental pollution and the small contribution of mining companies to Zambia's tax revenues. Global advocacy organisations have certainly helped stoke the controversies. But the controversies are rooted in Zambia's history and politics. During the colonial era, Northern Rhodesia, as Zambia was then known, was one of the few African countries to host a large mining industry. Its Copperbelt was urbanised, and its trade unions powerful. The unions were weakened, however, after the mining sector was nationalised in 1969, international copper prices declined dramatically in 1975, and most mines were mothballed in the 1980s. By the mid-1980s Zambia was one of the most indebted nations in the world, relative to its GDP. Following privatisation, the mines were reopened on a small scale in the 1990s. At that point few people expected copper prices to recover to historic levels. There were, however, sufficient residues and memories of trade union power that the new mining companies – many of them Chinese or Indian – faced continual political challenges. The companies paid very little for their mining rights and began to profit very handsomely when world copper prices started to increase early in this century. Partly because the new mining arrangements were subject to so much political scrutiny and criticism, the Zambian government has revised the ways in which it taxes the mining companies several times – but sometimes it has been forced to retreat in the face of threats from the companies that they would cut back on investment and production.

When the international media go to the Copperbelt, they are reporting on issues specific to mining in Zambia. But Zambia also exemplifies a range of issues relating to the extractive sector – i.e. the business of digging stuff out of the ground – that are character-istic of Africa more broadly:

- Extractives are very important to Africa. They are the contem-porary equivalent of the exports of cocoa, coffee, cotton, groundnuts, palm oil, sisal and tobacco that played such a major role in the regional economy in the last century (Chapter 2). Although Africa is only a minor supplier of oil, natural gas and minerals to the global economy,[3] extractive industry accounts for a much larger proportion of economic activity in Africa and is the dominant earner of export revenues.[4] What happens in the extractive industry has a big influence on rates of economic growth in Africa and on the amount of tax collected by governments.
- It is challenging for contemporary African governments to tax the extractive sector because, unlike the agricultural commodity export economy that they taxed so heavily in the 1960s, 1970s and 1980s (Chapter 2), mining and energy are dominated by foreign transnational companies. The companies are respon-sible for almost all exploration and most production.[5] They may import almost all their production requirements, including equipment and skilled labour, and export 100% of production. In almost all cases, they purchase their imports from and sell their product to 'related parties' – that is, other companies belonging to the same multinational group. This provides generous opportunities to reduce tax liabilities by engaging in the transfer mispricing activities outlined in Chapter 3.
- In fact, it is particularly difficult to effectively and sensibly tax foreign transnational companies operating in the extractive sector, and even more challenging to tax companies involved in mining than those extracting energy (oil and gas). The reasons are many and complex. One purpose of this chapter is to explain them. The results are that, in Africa as elsewhere in

the world, while energy companies might be somewhat under-taxed, mining companies typically are greatly under-taxed. Indeed, it is only a slight exaggeration to say that, with a few significant exceptions, notably Botswana's diamond mines, mining in Africa is barely taxed at all. One reliable source indicates that contemporary African governments collect about 55% of the total value of energy production in tax revenue, but only 3% of the value of mining production.[6] Bear in mind that, when they collect revenue from extractive activities, governments are not just taxing value added as they do when levying corporate income taxes on transport companies or shoe manufacturers. Governments are also selling national assets: oil, gas or minerals that might otherwise stay underground and remain part of a nation's wealth for future use. That figure of 3% suggests that, in practice, at least some African governments are not selling national assets to mining companies. They are giving them away.

• The gross under-taxation of mining became especially visible to many observers as a result of the 2002–10 boom in global commodity prices. The index of global metal prices, expressed in constant US dollars, almost tripled between 2002 and its peak in 2006 (World Bank 2016b: 1). While prices of copper and other commodities soared, African governments' revenues from mining activities increased much more slowly. 'While the third raw materials super cycle increased the global turnover of the mining sector by a factor of 4.6 between 2002 and 2010, the tax revenues from the non-renewable natural resource sector earned by African governments only grew by a factor of 1.15' (Laporte and Quatrebarbes 2015).

There are particular reasons why the Zambian mines attract so much attention. But the underlying problems in taxing the extractive industries are common across Africa – and, indeed, in lower-income countries generally. In this chapter, most of our examples and illustrations relate to mining, and not to the other major component of the extractive sector: energy (oil and gas). The reasons why under-taxation is especially severe in the mining sector lie in political economy. We explain below that, while the political economy of the mining and the energy sectors are similar in some important respects, there are some particular features of the mining sector that make it even more vulnerable to under-taxation.

Box 5.1 Sub-Saharan African countries where extractives accounted for 70% or more of gross exports in 2015–16

Angola (crude petroleum); Botswana (diamonds); Burkina Faso (gold); Chad (crude petroleum); Congo-Brazzaville (crude petroleum and copper); Democratic Republic of Congo (copper and copper alloys, base metals, diamonds, crude petroleum, and other ores and concentrates); Equatorial Guinea (crude petroleum and petroleum gas); Eritrea (copper ore and concentrates, gold, and other ores and concentrates); Gabon (crude petroleum); Guinea (gold and aluminium ores and concentrates); Mali (gold); Niger (radioactive chemicals and gold); Nigeria (crude petroleum); Sierra Leone (diamonds, iron ores and concentrates, titanium and aluminium ore); South Sudan (crude petroleum); Sudan (gold and crude petroleum); and Zambia (copper and copper alloys).

Source: Growth Lab (2016), using data from United Nations Comtrade.

Controversy, secrecy, manipulation and uncertainty

Taxation instruments and outcomes are very variable from one extractives project to another (Laporte and Quatrebarbes 2015). Tax arrangements are subject to frequent, destabilising change. And, as we explain towards the end of this chapter, the choice of tax instruments is often wrong. However, bad technical choices do not principally reflect ignorance or inexperience. They are intimately related to the poor governance of the extractive sector more broadly. There is evidence that extractive industries are particularly poorly governed in sub-Saharan Africa.[7] But mining is worse than oil and gas. Why?

Mining activities in Africa are mostly intensely politicised: there is political conflict over mines, from the exploration stage, before precise locations are even identified, to the end of their useful life. These conflicts involve shifting combinations of presidents and ministers, ministries and other public agencies, exploration companies, mining companies, managers of ports and railways, individual politicians and bureaucrats, wheeler-dealer local and international businesspeople and 'political' fixers', grassroots political activists, small-scale (artisanal) miners and their representatives, local bandits, lawyers, tax advisers, civil society organisations, and local and international media. Their tools and tactics are complex and variable mixtures of secrecy, stealth, public campaigning, bribery, principled claims, bluff, manipulation, threat, lawsuits, misinformation and intimidation.

Anyone who combines an interest in the extractive sector with a taste for drama will relish the ongoing story of Simandou.[8] Simandou is a mountain range in the deep interior of Guinea. It comprises so much high-grade iron ore that geologists have given its peaks names such as Iron Maiden and Metallica. Rio Tinto, the British-Australian mining multinational, was granted exploration rights in 1997. Two decades later, no significant engineering work has been done. Many sceptics believe that Simandou will never be exploited. The costs of building the infrastructure needed to get the ore to the point of export – 650 kilometres of railway, tunnels, bridges, 128 kilometres of road and a new deep-water port – are estimated to be at least twice the costs of setting up the actual mine. Yet vast amounts of money have been ventured, won and lost in the course of political manoeuvring over the rights to develop Simandou. Some advance taxes have even been paid.

Rio Tinto was granted exploration rights to Simandou in 1997. In late 2008, two weeks before he died, the president of Guinea, Lansana Conté, expropriated half of Rio Tinto's rights and awarded them to Beny Steinmetz, an Israeli billionaire who had made his fortune in the diamond business. Neither Steinmetz nor his business vehicle, Beny Steinmetz Group Resources (BSGR), which is controlled by family trusts, had any previous experience in iron ore mining. Contrary to the usual practice, BSGR made no upfront payment to the government of Guinea for these rights. After about a year, BSGR sold 51% of its interest in Simandou to Vale, the Brazilian mining conglomerate, for $2.5 billion – of which only the first tranche was ever paid. There was a brief period of military rule after Lansana Conté's death, then free elections were held in late 2010. The new president, Alpha Condé, had a reputation for honesty. His government reviewed all the mining licences that Conté had awarded – for Guinea also has large reserves of bauxite and significant quantities of diamonds, gold, uranium and offshore oil. Following the review, the Simandou mining rights were returned to Rio Tinto. At that point, Rio Tinto owned 46.6% of the total rights. Chinalco, a Chinese state company, was the second largest stakeholder.

That is the outline of the plot. The play itself is much more complex and colourful. Conté's youngest widow testified that BSGR had offered her millions of dollars, jewellery, two Toyota Land Cruisers and a 5% stake in the project to persuade her dying husband to sign over the Simandou rights to BSGR. Among the supporting evidence was a contract she had signed with the head of BSGR operations in Guinea, in which she agreed to use her influence to get Simandou mining rights transferred to BSGR in return for these rewards. This contract for corruption was stamped with the BSGR corporate seal. Rio Tinto filed a case in the US courts against Vale and Steinmetz for 'racketeering', and alleged that $200 million had been paid to Conté and his ministers as bribes. The case was thrown out on a technicality in 2015. Meanwhile, Steinmetz did not give up. He variously threatened or started court proceedings for defamation against: Global Witness, the London-based advocacy organisation; Mark Malloch Brown, a former Deputy Secretary-General of the United Nations and a former UK government minister; Theresa May, the current British Prime Minister when she was Home Secretary; the UK Serious Fraud Office; and the billionaire philanthropist George Soros. Vale launched a compensation claim against BSGR. Rio Tinto, too, was proactive in asserting its rights to Simandou. In 2011, the company made a payment of $10.5 million to a former top French banker who had been Alpha Condé's classmate. When this became public in November 2016, Rio Tinto immediately dismissed two senior managers who had been involved.

Alpha Condé survived an assassination attempt, and was re-elected president in 2015. But there were serious accusations of election fraud, and his rule has been marred by violence and large-scale street protests. Unsurprisingly, both government and opposition allege that their opponents are working for foreign companies seeking either to protect their mining rights or to grab a share of those currently belonging to someone else. The latest twist is that, in October 2016, Rio Tinto agreed to sell its rights in Simandou to Chinalco, leaving this Chinese company as the dominant player.

The Simandou story is particularly colourful. But it is not unusual. Why does so much controversy, corruption and drama surround mining projects in Africa? It is better to treat that as two separate questions. First, why does so much controversy, corruption and drama surround *extractives* projects? Second, why the particular intensity of these phenomena in the *mining* sector? In both cases, part of the explanation is obvious: there is a great deal of money to be made. But that leaves much unanswered. In particular, why do the influential people involved – the governments, the transnational companies, the politicians, and the international wheeler-dealers – not find ways of peacefully carving up the profits between them more regularly, without taking so many risks and generating so much uncertainty? In fact, mutually advantageous, stable deals between powerful elites are more common in the energy sector than in mining, in Africa and globally. To answer the two questions set out above, we need to examine the structure and political economy of the extractive sector in general, and the mining sector in particular.

The structure of the extractive industry

There is no single feature of the extractives business that is not found in some other economic sector. Nevertheless, extractives exhibit such a combination of special characteristics that the political economy of the sector is quite distinctive. We list below six of these characteristics. We then detail five characteristics of the mining subsector that distinguish it from the energy (oil and gas) subsector.

1. Extractives projects are very dependent on the approval, cooperation and support of governments. Throughout Africa and in most of the world, sub-soil assets belong to the state. Without a licence from government, private agents can neither prospect for sub-soil assets on a large scale nor extract them. Without the approval and cooperation of government, the extensive infrastructure required – roads, pipelines, railway lines, ports, offshore drilling rigs, electricity and water supplies – cannot be put in place.

2. Companies that invest in extractives projects are very vulnerable to changes of policy or attitude on the part of governments. As Rio Tinto found in Guinea, this is especially true in countries where the law does not rule and where private investment is so low that governments have few concerns about further discouraging investors by behaving arbitrarily. In such circumstances, all investors are vulnerable. Investors in extractives are especially vulnerable for two reasons. One is that the gestation

periods for extractive sector projects are long. Like Rio Tinto in Guinea, companies can be exploring and planning for decades before they begin to shift any earth. There is typically an interval of several years between the initial investment and the point at which a well produces oil or a mine yields saleable coal, copper, zinc or iron ore. The second cause of vulnerability is that extractives investments are heavily 'front-loaded': the big investments – in exploration, in purchasing exploration and extraction rights, in setting up the mine or well, and in putting the associated infrastructure in place – typically are made in the early years, before the facility begins to produce and generate revenue. Governments therefore face a continual temptation to agree one set of terms with investors to encourage them to invest, and then, once they have sunk a lot of money, to offer less favourable terms, including less favourable tax arrangements. The government of Zambia has changed its mining tax regime nine times in the last 12 years (Manley 2015). This is sometimes motivated by high world copper prices and at other times by concerns that the mining companies will reduce production if taxes are not reduced. In the last resort, governments can often credibly threaten that mines will be taken over by the state or given to a different investor, leaving the original investor with huge losses and debts.

3. Natural resource extraction projects often generate large 'rents' for the people who control them: that is, 'super-profits' that are higher – and sometimes much higher – than the combined totals of all production costs and normal profits. For example, it currently costs around $35 to produce a barrel of oil in Angola (Rystad Energy 2015). When, in 2014, oil was selling at around $100 a barrel, the government of Angola was receiving about $65 a barrel in rent.[9] By contrast, in early 2016, when world market prices briefly fell just below production costs, there were no rents to collect. Rents are much larger when commodity

market prices are high. At any moment in time, rent levels can differ greatly among mines or wells producing the same product, because extraction costs will be higher in one mine or well than in another. Natural resource rents are a major feature of the economy of sub-Saharan Africa: they account for about one-fifth of GDP.[10] From a political economy perspective, rents are the surpluses that can be extracted from an activity, through the use of political or military power, without making the business unprofitable and therefore risking its closure. Politicians, criminals, bankers, generals, arms dealers, monarchs, bureaucrats, and other assorted wheeler-dealers scramble to share in these rents – either by getting control of the extraction and export processes or by wresting a payoff from the people who do control them. These predators do not scramble to anything like the same extent to share in the profits of companies assembling mobile phones or providing call centre facilities. Such enterprises typically face strong competition and do not generate very high profits. They are likely to go out of business quickly, or to move their operations to another country, if politicians, soldiers or thugs try to muscle in. By contrast, provided they can continue to make some profit, the operators of mines or oil wells will keep them in operation even if they are forced to hand over much of the rent to the predators. The Democratic Republic of Congo contains a large proportion of the world's accessible resources of coltan, the source of the excellent conductor of electricity, tantalum, that is essential for mobile phones, DVD players, laptops, hard drives and gaming devices. The violence, exploitation and massive profits associated with the business of getting coltan out of the Congo are almost legendary. Similar violent scrambles over natural resource rents have significantly shaped the contemporary history of many other countries in Africa, including Angola, Guinea, Nigeria, South Sudan and Sudan.[11]

4. World market prices for oil, gas and minerals are unstable and tend to fluctuate in long 'super-cycles' of different and unpredictable lengths. This generates major uncertainties about the likely long-term profitability of individual projects. It also tends to produce cyclical shifts in domestic public and political opinion: from anger that extractive companies are not paying more in taxes (when world market prices are high), to fears that they might close down operations entirely (when prices are low).

5. The information needed to estimate the likely long-term yields, profits or rents from extractive projects – and therefore to calculate the likely consequences of different tax arrangements – is typically scarce and unequally available to the main parties involved. There are several interacting reasons for this, in addition to the market price uncertainty mentioned above. The basic geological information is sometimes generated through private surveying and not made publicly available. Even if available, it may not be very accurate in respect of either the likely quantity or quality of the product.

6. Extractive projects are likely to intrude strongly in the lives of some groups of ordinary citizens of the host country. Some of the effects might be positive, including jobs. Historically, mining employed large numbers of manual workers. From the mid-nineteenth to the mid-twentieth centuries, South Africa's mines sucked in migrant labour from throughout Southern Africa. In South Africa and Zambia, as elsewhere in the world, large mining labour forces were often at the forefront of trade union organisation. By contrast, Africa's new mining projects, as well as oil and gas projects, are highly mechanised – and most of the oil and gas is offshore. They employ few people. Most wage rewards go to highly skilled expatriates. These projects provide few employment opportunities to compensate local populations for the disruptions they suffer, or to assuage their concerns that 'their'

resources are being taken from them without recompense. The disruptions include displacement from home and agricultural land; appropriation of scarce water supplies; pollution of land and water with chemicals, oil spills, etc.; and price inflation for food and housing in project areas. In turn, resource extraction companies increasingly engage in 'corporate social responsibility' activities to compensate local populations – or to try to ensure their quiescence. It is sometimes possible for the organisations and individuals who are constantly vying for a share of rents from extractives – competing politicians, wheeler-dealers and companies, aided by journalists and activist NGOs – to mobilise what looks like 'local support' for their case, whether that case be how much local people have benefited from oil drilling or the mine, or how much they have endured. We know, for example, that the inhabitants of the Niger Delta in Nigeria have suffered badly from oil spilled by Shell and other energy companies. But we also know that local people sometimes break pipes deliberately to steal the oil, that local politicians compete fiercely and sometimes violently for the corporate social responsibility payments from the oil companies, and that the armed gangs that rule much of the Delta often have strong links to powerful politicians (Ghazvinian 2007).

These are the main distinctive features of the extractive sector. There are then five characteristics of the mining subsector, which are not generally shared with oil and gas, that help explain why mining in particular is associated with controversy, corruption and drama.[12]

1. The risk that governments will try to renegotiate agreements in their own favour is increased because, in mining but not in the energy sector, experience and expertise in the business are not essential conditions for entry. Beny Steinmetz had no significant experience of iron ore mining when he bid for the rights

to Simandou. Vedanta, which is now a major global mining company, originated in the scrap metal business in Mumbai. Because of the high level of politicisation and conflict in the sector, some operators can be very successful on the basis of an aptitude for the politics, access to large amounts of capital, and a huge appetite for risk.

> 'It's roulette,' Steinmetz said; if you work hard, and take risks, you sometimes 'get lucky.' As a small company that was comfortable with risk, BSGR made investments that the major mining companies wouldn't. His company lost money in Tanzania. It lost money in Zambia. But in Guinea it won. (Keefe 2013)

Once entrepreneurs have control of mining rights, they can either sell them on for a profit to more established and experienced mining companies or buy in the expertise needed to open and operate mines. It would not be difficult for any government to find a private company willing to take over a functioning mine if the terms were right – and even if more established global firms declined to participate. A former minister of mines in Guinea is quoted as saying: 'When a new government comes into power, especially an inexperienced one, there's one phenomenon that never fails: every crook on earth shows up. And every crook on earth has the biggest promises, has access to billions of dollars of lines of credits, of loans' (Mailey 2015: 53).

2. Mining is more diverse than energy in terms of the range of products produced and the processes involved in extracting and processing them.[13] The energy subsector produces only oil and gas, and the range of types of each product is limited. Each type can normally be identified in terms of one of a small number of standard reference types – West Texas Crude, Brent Blend and Dubai Crude in the case of oil – for which there are

large, deep global markets and daily posted reference prices. Miners, by contrast, unearth a much wider range of products including, in sub-Saharan Africa, bauxite, chromium, coal, cobalt, coltan, copper, diamonds, gold, iron ore, lead, nickel, platinum, palladium, phosphate, soda ash, titanium, zinc and various radioactive chemicals and rare earths. Global markets are more fragmented and diverse. There is less product standardisation and less market information. Governments trying to regulate and tax mining have less access to reliable information and reliable independent consultants than do governments dealing with energy companies.

3. Some minerals, including diamonds, gold and palladium, have a high value-to-weight ratio. It is relatively easy for miners to understate production levels and smuggle product out of the country.

4. These adverse effects of the diversity of the mining subsector are exacerbated by the near absence, at least in Africa, of an organisational arrangement that is common in the energy sector: a national oil and gas corporation. These corporations employ professional staff and, in varying combinations, regulate private sector operators, own some of their equity, engage in production-sharing agreements, or undertake exploration, extraction or downstream processing in their own right. These activities give governments some insight into the logistics and economics of oil and gas extraction, and thus some capacity to regulate the activities of private companies. Some governments, including those of Botswana, Guinea, Tanzania and Zambia, own equity in companies operating mines on their territory. In principle, this is an alternative way for governments to obtain revenue from mining operations. However, there is no evidence that, by owning a minority share of the equity in a locally incorporated mining company, governments can prevent companies

from engaging in transfer mispricing and shifting their profits offshore to their parent companies. Botswana is the exception. The government owns 50% of Debswana, the main diamond producer, and is generally believed to obtain a fair share of diamond revenues.

5. Joint ventures between two or more large transnational companies (with or without the participation of the host government) are common in the energy sector but rare in mining. The energy sector is technically the more demanding. Oil and gas transnationals enter into unincorporated joint ventures with one another to share expertise. One of them is responsible for operations and has to report in detail to the others. This ensures a degree of accounting transparency and accuracy that reduces the scope for cheating the local tax administration. There are few joint ventures in the mining sector in Africa.

Taken in combination, these structural features of the extractive industry have important implications for the ways in which companies and governments relate to one another – and ultimately to the ways in which the companies are taxed. Compared with most energy projects, and even more with most non-extractive investments, it is difficult for mining companies and governments: (1) to make agreements over terms, including taxation, that both consider fair and reasonable; (2) to stick to agreements when conditions change; or (3) to trust that the other is not cheating on the deal, or likely to do so when the opportunity arises. Because of the structure of the industry, companies and governments need to coordinate closely and reach long-term agreements about taxation and infrastructure provision. Yet much of the information they would require to reach stable deals (on geology and long-term project economics, for instance) is either not available to either party or available only to the companies. Governments, possibly egged on by predatory third parties, have incentives to change contract terms to their advantage if it suits them, to the extent of threatening to make the business uneconomic. When commodity prices are high, all kinds of interested parties are tempted to employ their political resources to obtain a share of the rents, often by stirring up political controversy about some aspects of mining operations – the underpayment of taxes, environmental pollution, land grabbing, or exploitation of labour. The local operating companies, which are virtually all subsidiaries of large transnational mining groups, have wide scope to understate profits by: (1) overstating the import costs of the capital equipment, management and technical expertise, loans, and skilled labour that they purchase from related companies abroad; and (2) understating the real value of the copper, zinc and gold that they produce and sell, invariably also to related companies (see Chapter 3). The fact that transnationals in the extractive business are particularly fond of locating subsidiaries in secretive tax havens is consistent with the claim that they do not forego the many opportunities they have to engage in transfer mispricing.[14]

How, then, do governments and mining companies deal with the continual uncertainty and distrust that characterise their relationship? Part of the answer is given above: continual controversy and political manoeuvring. Another part is that they make arrangements that benefit them mutually, at the expense of other stakeholders, notably the public treasuries and the populations of the host countries. Many of the signed agreements allocating rights to explore or extract natural resources are wholly or partly confidential. The agreements are often made with little or no parliamentary or public knowledge or discussion. Sometimes governments are more insistent on confidentiality than mining companies. Arrangements for the companies to make upfront payments ('signature bonuses') may not be fully covered in written agreements.[15] Frequently, those agreements cover the ways in which individual projects will be taxed. Mines are thus taken outside the ambit of the national corporate tax code. Many governments have relatively little experience of dealing with large extractive projects: with negotiating exploration and exploitation contracts, monitoring their observance, exercising environmental and other kinds of regulation in relation to very large specialist companies and production facilities, or taxing them. Especially in low-income countries, government agencies often find that the specialist, experienced staff they need to perform these functions have been bought, directly or indirectly, by the companies they are expected to regulate.

Taxing extractives

There are three broad explanations for the under-taxation of extractives – especially mining – in contemporary Africa:

- The business is so risky that extractives companies would not invest unless they were largely liberated from the burden of paying taxes.
- The African political leaders who control extraction rights choose to enrich themselves rather than collect taxes.
- African governments are unable adequately to regulate and tax extractives because they lack the expertise, the trained and committed personnel, and the organisations that they need. They are, in effect, outgunned by the transnational extractives companies.

There is some truth in each of these explanations. It is impossible to weigh and rank them. The situation varies widely from place to place and over time: when global prices for commodities are high (and are expected to remain so), the behaviour and attitudes of the stakeholders may be very different compared with periods of declining or low prices. It is genuinely difficult to tax extractives effectively.[16] In the wrong circumstances, even a committed, capable and honest government might find itself almost powerless and face a choice between keeping quiet and seeing mines or oil wells closed. But what could committed, capable and honest governments do in more propitious circumstances? How should they set about taxing extractive operations? Here are seven pointers, starting from the more general and moving to the more specific.[17]

1. There is a wide range of techniques that governments can use to obtain revenue from extractives. They can retain ownership of the resource and contract an operating company on a fee basis. They can agree to share the value of production with the operating company. They can establish a state-owned operating company. They can go into a joint venture with one or more partners. And they can levy various kinds of taxes on operating companies, including royalties on the product extracted, taxes on the rents earned from extraction, and the more familiar corporate income taxes. These modes of obtaining revenue can be found in many combinations. The choice among them should, of course, be made after careful, independent analysis of the options. It should also take into account issues of domestic regulatory and taxing capacity. For example, if the national tax administration is weak, it may make sense for government to agree a production-sharing agreement with the operator, and focus scarce organisational capacity on ensuring that the value of production is recorded accurately.

2. It is hard to tax extractives more effectively without improving the overall governance of the extractive sector. Poor governance and ineffective taxation are closely linked, in ways that have been explored in some detail in this chapter. There are many dimensions to the governance of extractives. One of the most fundamental is the procedure for allocating exploration and extraction rights. Currently, those rights are sometimes allocated in ways that are neither transparent nor competitive. It is very reasonable, for example, for campaigners to demand that all rights to explore for and then extract sub-soil resources should be allocated through open, transparent and competitive

auctions. The Natural Resources Charter (Natural Resource Governance Institute 2014) provides very useful broad guidance on how to improve these and other aspects of the governance of the extractive sector. Similarly, international initiatives such as the Extractive Industries Transparency Initiative (EITI 2016a) have made some progress in encouraging companies and governments to adopt greater transparency in the allocation of the revenues from natural resource extraction.

3. Related to this, some significant obstacles to taxing extractives lie in failures of public administration outside the realm of tax administration. For example, the accurate assessment of the royalties due to government on extractives requires the effective monitoring of the information that companies provide on the volume, quality and timing of production and exports. That is typically the responsibility of a separate government agency. In practice, several government agencies may share responsibility. In the case of mining in Tanzania, the list includes the Tanzania Revenue Authority, the Tanzania Minerals Audit Agency, the Ministry of Finance, the Ministry of Mines and, to a limited extent, the National Development Corporation and the Office of the Auditor General. Failures of coordination, possibly encouraged by extraction companies, can create significant tax loopholes (Readhead 2016: 21–2). Similarly, if one company has more than one project in a country, the tax exemptions granted to one project – typically a new investment – might be exploited for the benefit of older projects unless their use is carefully monitored. For example, equipment nominally imported for use on the newer project might be diverted to an older one.[18] Effective monitoring implies that governments actually have control of their subordinate agencies.

4. Currently, the taxation of many extraction enterprises in Africa – especially mining projects – is governed by the

provisions in specific agreements signed, typically on a project-by-project basis, by the host government and by investors. This is an obstacle to informed and effective taxation. While new investments in extractives necessarily involve agreements between government and investors, and much of the substance of those agreements is tailored to specific cases, the taxing arrangements should be governed by the national tax code.

5. One of the most tangible single actions that many governments in Africa might take to improve their capacity to tax extractives is to review – and, if necessary, amend – their legislation relating to taxing capital gains. Mining projects in particular frequently undergo a change of ownership at a relatively early stage. A 'junior' company with a low public profile and a limited concern for its corporate reputation organises the exploration and the securing of land and extraction rights. The operation is then sold to one of the larger transnational mining companies that are more concerned about reputational issues. The sale typically takes place 'offshore', between companies domiciled in tax havens. For example, UraniumCo, a fictional company incorporated in Niger that has established rights to extract radioactive chemicals, might be sold by the Canadian company that owns it to an Australian mining conglomerate. But the transaction will be between a subsidiary of the Canadian company incorporated in the British Virgin Islands and a subsidiary of the Australian company incorporated in Mauritius. The question of whether the company making the sale should be liable to capital gains tax in the host country has been the subject of high-profile law cases, because much national legislation is ambiguous or silent on the issue. In 2015, Tullow Oil, having lost a case in the Uganda High Court, finally accepted that it owed the Uganda Revenue Authority (URA) $250 million in relation to an offshore sale of this nature. However, this is not the norm. To date, companies have more frequently been the winners. In respect of the capital

gains issue at least, there is some low-hanging fruit for African governments to harvest.

6. Governments cannot rely on the standard corporate income tax (CIT) as the sole or main channel for obtaining tax revenue from extractive projects operated by foreign investors. There is simply far too much scope for the investors to employ transfer-mispricing techniques to move the apparent profit out of the country. Over a four-year period from 2010 to 2013, the London-based company African Barrick Gold plc (now known as Acacia Mining) paid its shareholders dividends of $412 million on the profits of its gold mines in Tanzania, while simultaneously declaring losses in Tanzania. In this case, the Tanzania Revenue Authority was able to take effective action, and in October 2016 the Tanzanian court of appeal again dismissed a case brought against the authority by African Barrick Gold plc. As a result of this judgment, Tanzania gained $82 million in additional revenue.

7. Experts disagree over what is likely to be the most effective mix of methods to tax extractive projects in low-income countries. The standard advice from the IMF is to combine: (1) a CIT on profits; (2) a fixed-rate royalty, levied at a low rate of around 2% to 5% of the gross value of production/exports; and (3) a tax on the rents captured in the extraction process that is assessed through an analysis of cash flow for each project. IMF experts believe that this combination of taxes is both relatively easy to administer and is likely to be sufficiently responsive to changes in market prices for extractives products.[19] Other experts argue that the same objectives can be achieved more simply and effectively by combining a CIT with a variable-rate royalty – i.e. a royalty levied at a progressively higher percentage as world market prices for the product increase (for example, Durst 2016b). There is no single correct recipe. The effectiveness of any formula for taxing extractives projects will be very

dependent on the willingness and capacity of the host government to understand, monitor and regulate operating companies.
This is more a matter of political incentives and administrative
capacity than of economic principles.

Conclusions

Mining has been a significant economic activity in parts of Africa
since early colonial rule. Nevertheless, the commodity price boom
of the early years of this century has introduced new extractive
activities – mining, oil and gas – into areas where they had not
been seen before, and has generally expanded the importance of
the sector. Extractives now account for a large portion of economic
activity in Africa, and for most of its export earnings. They are the
dominant source of government revenue in countries including
Angola, Republic of Congo, Gabon, Equatorial Guinea, Nigeria
and Chad – although for any single government, natural resource
revenues might vary greatly from one year to the next. Extractives
may be even more important in the future. We know that Africa
has been less thoroughly searched for minerals than any other
continent. When the search intensified early in this century as
world commodity prices rose, it was Africa that yielded the greatest
returns: the ratio of mineral discoveries to exploration costs was
higher than for any other continent.[20] Africa's extractive industry,
especially mining, is very much under-taxed. In principle, vast
additional public revenues could be collected if the sector could be
taxed more reliably, consistently and effectively. The reasons to be
pessimistic about the prospects are set out above. There are also
reasons to be more optimistic: there are no great technical problems
to be overcome; improvements in the ways in which the sector is
governed, regulated and administered are well within reach; and
some experts believe that African public administrations, which are
often new to the challenges of taxing extractives, are learning from
recent experiences.

Chapter 6

TAXING AT NATIONAL LEVEL: RISING TO THE CHALLENGE?

Judging performance

In Chapter 2 we presented a range of evidence that, when compared with other low-income regions of the world, sub-Saharan African tax administrations on average perform relatively well in terms of the proportion of GDP that they collect, the percentage of revenues that come from direct taxes, and the compliance burdens that they impose on formal businesses. We can say with confidence that, when it comes to revenue collection *at national level*, Africa is not dominantly a continent of problems and crises. Considering the prevalence of deep governance challenges in the region generally, national-level taxation stands out as an area of relatively good public sector performance. Conversely, we know that, on some measures, revenue systems in Africa perform poorly. A range of pieces of information suggests that the costs of revenue administration, as a proportion of revenue collected, are high in sub-Saharan Africa, and rivalled only by those of the Middle East and North Africa. Part of the reason is that the average tax administration employee in sub-Saharan Africa is responsible for fewer active taxpayers than in any other world region. Another part is that he – and they are dominantly if decreasingly male – is relatively well remunerated (World Bank 2012: 31). In this chapter we provide evidence that VAT is used very inefficiently, that corruption in tax collection is significant, and that the technology that could help deal with some of these problems is much underused.

Our central argument is that, while national-level tax systems in Africa perform modestly well, there is great scope for improvement, especially in terms of the equity of burden sharing, efficiency, and the quality of interactions between tax collectors and taxpayers. The material underpinning this argument is organised into three main sections:

- There has been considerable **progress** in some areas of national tax administration, notably in: (1) making the procedural and organisational changes that permit improved relationships between tax collectors and taxpayers; and (2), in Anglophone Africa in particular, in giving a degree of managerial autonomy to revenue collection agencies.
- There are two issues where we can expect continuing **disagreement**: (1) the virtues and disadvantages of VAT; and (2) what can reasonably be expected of customs agencies, especially those operating in insecure border areas.
- There is evident **underperformance** in: (1) the very light taxation of the personal incomes of the growing number of rich Africans; (2) the granting of excessive and unjustified tax exemptions to investors; (3) high levels of corruption in tax collection; and (4) the failure to use the potential of IT systems to collect and analyse tax administration data to increase both efficiency and transparency.

Most of the time, we generalise about 'Africa'. To remind us of the great variety in tax policy and administration between the countries of Africa – and to underline the ways in which politics shapes this diversity – we begin with some snapshots of diverse national tax administrations.

Snapshots

Rwanda and Somaliland are both small countries. Their recent histories are in some respects similar. Both suffered severely from internal political conflict in the 1980s and 1990s; those conflicts were settled, albeit inconclusively, in the 1990s; and the governance arrangements put in place then have endured until today. Their national revenue collection systems are, however, very different.

In Somaliland, the revenue system is rudimentary in the extreme.[1] Written records are few, and computers are only now beginning to be used in the inland revenue and customs departments. Tax collection is low – possibly around 7% of GDP – and the burden falls predominantly on ordinary people. A tax levied on the import of *qat* (or *khat* – a mildly narcotic leaf chewed by a large proportion of the population) is the largest single item in the revenue accounts. More than half the money collected by the Inland Revenue Department comes from non-tax revenues, notably charges for (obligatory) administrative services. 'Registration tax', 'stamp tax' and 'administration fees' are all significant revenue sources. Staff of the Inland Revenue Department regularly man roadblocks to collect revenue from drivers who cannot prove that they have paid the two main vehicle taxes. There is no VAT, and no taxpayer identification numbers. Taxpaying is extremely unpopular, in part because the system is both extractive and extremely regressive. In 2015, the corporate profit tax accounted for a mere 1.5% of recorded revenues, and the payroll tax on private companies accounted for another 4.5%. The Inland Revenue Department, which is itself a relatively new organisation, maintains no files on corporate taxpayers. Individual senior staff 'look after' the tax affairs of wealthy individuals on a personal basis. Taxes are paid in cash.

One reason why taxes are collected in this way lies in the character of the current political settlement in Somaliland (Bradbury 2008). It is based on a relatively fragile and continuously renegoti-ated agreement between a range of powerful interests, notably the clans and big businessmen – many of whom are based in Nairobi or elsewhere abroad. There is an elected parliament, but it has limited independent influence. The public bureaucracy has little independent authority. Large businesses and wealthy individuals could quash any threat of a significant tax bill through a word in the right ear or, if that fails, a signal delivered in the form of a strike, a demonstration, or some other political disturbance.

But it also matters that, because Somaliland is not recognised by the international community, it has received very little technical assistance to build its tax system. Rwanda, by contrast, has received a great deal of support. The Rwanda Revenue Authority is in many ways an impressive organisation. A unitary authority combining customs and domestic taxation, it has steadily increased revenue collection from almost nothing during the civil conflicts of the early 1990s to 15% of GDP today. Its headquarters building in Kigali is imposing. Inside, it seems to hum with the smoothness of a large bank. Its operations are structured around IT systems. Much of its business is done online. As in other national government institutions in Rwanda, corruption seems rare. The Authority's website reports a wide range of successful initiatives in tax policy and administration. The Authority cooperates closely with a range of other public sector organisations; in 2010, it assumed responsibility for collecting contributions to the national social security and medical insurance schemes. It is also the collection agent for a wide range of public service fees, ranging from passport fees and court fines to school examination fees. In 2015, the Authority took over responsibility for collecting property taxes from local governments. There is talk of linking its electronic information systems to those of the national water and electricity companies, to make it possible to deprive tax defaulters of water and electricity. The Revenue Authority is also consciously used as a training ground for bureaucratic talent. High-flying public servants routinely serve in senior posts in revenue collection before being moved on.[2]

Just as Somaliland's rudimentary revenue system is embedded in its national political system, Rwanda's impressive-looking tax collection machinery reflects the way in which the country is governed. The dominance since 1994 of the tightly organised and highly disciplined Rwandan Patriotic Front, and the interpenetration of the ruling party and public services, enable the political elite to keep a very watchful eye over the Revenue Authority – and all other significant public institutions. The Revenue Authority needs both to perform well and to project an image of being committed, hardworking, modern and IT literate. Actual performance does not always match the image. The Authority has been struggling to increase the ratio of revenue collection to GDP.[3] Behind the continuous stream of new initiatives and advances in the use of IT, some of the basic requirements of tax administration are not met. One very important category of staffers – experienced tax auditors – resign and take posts in the private sector at a worrying rate. The registry of taxpayers is inaccurate and not updated consistently. The Authority has been unable prevent a high proportion of registered taxpayers from regularly filing returns that indicate zero tax liabilities.

If we were able to arrange Africa's national tax collection systems on a spectrum in terms of effectiveness and efficiency,[4] Somaliland's would be at the lower end. It raises little revenue; its procedures are highly informal; and it conspicuously fails to tap into the main potential sources of significant revenues: wholesale and retail transactions, corporate profits, and high incomes. Nigeria, too, would score few points, but for a very different reason. Its revenue collection system began to fall apart in the 1970s as large new oil revenues encouraged government to ignore it. At the level of the country's 36 states, revenue collection is sometimes outsourced to private companies. Elsewhere in Africa, outsourcing of tax collection is restricted to the local government level, and to revenue sources such as local market fees. A decade ago, the South African Revenue Service would have been at the opposite end of the spectrum to Nigeria and Somaliland. It was widely regarded as a model for the reform of other tax administrations in Africa. The roots of that exemplary status run deep. The pre-1994 apartheid state was an effective tax collector, not least because it had to finance the military and intelligence apparatuses needed to enforce minority rule. White South Africans were willing to pay significant income taxes to help maintain their privileges (Lieberman 2003). After the arrival of majority rule, a group of highly committed senior cadres of the African National Congress, led initially by Finance Minister Trevor Manuel,[5] set about raising the revenue needed to 'pay the social debt' incurred by apartheid. Customs and internal revenue collection were merged into the newly established South African Revenue Service (SARS). SARS underwent thorough, pragmatic and effective reforms in revenue collection, and developed an impressive capacity to investigate tax evasion and tax fraud. It became one of the most respected public organisations in the country. Sadly, after Jacob Zuma became president of South Africa in 2007, SARS appeared to have been targeted for 'capacity destruction' and became a focus of struggle between opposing factions of the African National Congress. Many senior staff were removed. Staff morale has decayed and, although SARS remains an impressive organisation, previous progress in increasing the tax take has faltered (Hausman and Zikhali 2016; Haysom 2016; van Loggerenberg and Lackay 2016).

Progress

In the 1980s, the IMF developed and articulated a coherent programme for tax reform in low-income countries (Tait 1990; Goode 1993; Thirsk 1993; Tanzi 2000; Tanzi and Zee 2000; Stewart 2002; Bird and Zolt 2003; de Mooij and Ederveen 2003; Gillis 1990: 77–8). The major components were as follows:

- Governments should desist from trying to use the tax system for purposes of social and economic engineering, i.e. to redistribute income or extract resources from agriculture to invest in industry (Chapter 2). The tax system should focus on raising revenue.

- The high dependence for revenue on import and export taxes should be greatly reduced. Export taxes should be abolished and rates of import duties should be cut radically.

- Governments should replace existing sales and turnover taxes with VAT, in the expectation that additional VAT revenues would replace those lost by cutting trade taxes.

- High marginal rates of tax, especially on income, should be reduced to discourage evasion.

- The tax system should be simplified in almost every sense of the term: fewer nuisance taxes; fewer schedules for the same tax; fewer tax rates; fewer exemptions; and clearer rules.

- Ministers of finance should pay much more attention to improving tax administration, on the understanding that poor administration, allied with excessively complex systems, was a major cause of failure to tax adequately or fairly.

This reform programme was coherent, relatively pragmatic, and well founded in an understanding of how taxation systems actually functioned. Correspondingly, it was more widely accepted than many of the other neoliberal or market-oriented ideas that 'Washington' was strongly urging on developing countries in the 1980s and 1990s. It was not without controversy, with concerns that the proposed reforms would reduce the progressivity of tax systems and questions about the viability of replacing trade taxes with harder-to-collect VAT. We discuss these debates and challenges in what follows. But, on balance, it established the broad parameters for tax reform in Africa for the next two or three decades, especially in Anglophone Africa,[6] and has had many positive effects. It was, however, not the only modernising influence. Two others have been important.

The global move towards cooperative compliance

Over recent decades there has been a substantial shift almost globally in the perception of how tax collectors can most effectively engage with taxpayers. This change can be summed up in the term *cooperative compliance*; this denotes greater cooperation, collaboration, trust and transparency in the relationship between the two parties (Aberbach and Christensen 2007; Bird and Zolt 2008; Kloeden 2011; Moore 2014). In Africa, the likely concrete manifestations of cooperative compliance would be that tax collectors would put less effort into a detailed examination of all tax returns, but instead they would: (1) rely more on various degrees of 'self-assessment' by taxpayers; (2) make it easier for taxpayers to understand the tax system and complete their own returns; and (3) focus audit activities strategically on those taxpayers who, through statistical risk analysis, are identified as most likely to be non-compliant. To put it another way, the strategy is to encourage taxpayers to comply willingly, to trust them most of the time, and to focus audit and sanctioning resources on the taxpayers who can least be trusted, to try to bring them into line. To be successful, this strategy requires organisational and procedural changes within tax authorities to minimise direct, personal contacts between taxpayers and tax collectors (or their advisers and representatives) and to clearly separate the task of assessing tax liabilities from the task of collecting the money. Historically, direct personal contacts between taxpayers and tax collectors who have the authority both to make assessments and to collect money constitute the epicentre of corruption in tax administration. There has therefore been a broad shift towards: (1) assessing liabilities from the office, on the basis of records of various kinds – including 'third party' information from business partners, banks, suppliers of electricity or other utilities, and records of ownership of real estate or vehicles – rather than through personal meetings or field inspections; and (2) either using third parties, especially banks, to receive tax payments or establishing open payment counter facilities in tax offices. Digitalisation has been central to virtually every aspect of these reforms.[7] It makes it easier, for example, for taxpayers to find out information about tax law and procedure and to file their returns online; and for revenue authorities to obtain and collate 'third party information' and to identify taxpayers for audit.

Most revenue administrations in Africa have formally adopted some variant of cooperative compliance principles. As with other dimensions of tax administration reform, there is wide scope for disagreement about how far working practices have actually changed. There is little doubt that significant progress has been made. But it is also certainly the case that face-to-face interactions between tax collectors and taxpayers have remained common in many contexts, that meaningful transparency has generally remained limited, and that IT systems remain underutilised in many places. We return to these challenges below.

Semi-autonomous revenue authorities[8]

Second only to the introduction of VAT, the most visible tax reform in Africa over recent decades, staring from the early 1990s, has been the creation of what are conventionally termed *semi-autonomous revenue authorities* (SARAs). This implies a substantial change in the organisation of tax collection, with two major components: pre-existing revenue collection organisations – typically two or three separate departments within the ministry of finance – are merged into a single agency; and this agency is removed from the direct control of the ministry of finance and given a semi-autonomous status.

SARAs are very much an Anglophone phenomenon. They have become near universal in Anglophone Africa – and have also been created in Burundi, Mozambique, Rwanda and Togo.[9] Their establishment was stimulated above all by funding and technical assistance from the World Bank and the British aid programme. The notion that central banks and other important fiscal, financial and regulatory organisations should be granted autonomy from direct government control was an element of the 'new public management' reforms that were fashionable in the Anglophone world from the 1990s.

The main claims used to justify SARAs relate to management effectiveness.[10] It is argued that a degree of autonomy allows for: the recruitment of top-level managers from outside the tax service;[11] the high salary levels needed to attract and retain staff of adequate quality, given the competition from the private sector for qualified and experienced auditors and accountants; the policy and operational flexibility required by an effective revenue collection operation; and greater freedom from political interference, particularly as it relates to tax enforcement. It is also suggested that organisations collecting revenue need to cooperate with one another rather than compete, and that cooperation is more likely if they are under common management.

The impact of SARAs continues to be debated. A number of factors complicate the debate. First, their creation did not take place in isolation. It was part of a package of reforms in tax policy and administration and was intended to facilitate those wider reforms. Second, the act of creation typically was accompanied by large salary increases.[12] Currently, SARA staff are paid much more than their counterparts in ministries of finance with whom they interact – often three or four times as much, with additional generous allowances of various kinds. These high salaries generate resentment, and help explain why the costs of tax collection seem to be so high in Africa. Third, there is no single SARA model. They are diverse organisations, and their relationships to other parts of government, notably to ministries of finance, vary between countries and over time. Arguments about their impact may involve comparing apples and pears.

So what can we conclude about the impact of the establishment of SARAs?

- In practice, they are much less autonomous than their original proponents expected or intended. To the extent that the people who run them can exercise autonomy, it is mainly in respect of (lower-level) managerial issues, including, for example, who they recruit and how, and how they deploy their staff. For major decisions, including pay structures, they are typically very much under the control of ministers of finance or presidents.[13] Likewise, they generally do not seem to be immune to political interference.

- Conversely, because their high salaries and attractive working conditions have enabled some SARAs to accumulate considerable human capital, they sometimes play an active role in issues that are formally beyond their remit, including, for example, public outreach activities to explain taxes to citizens and the tax policy analysis and advocacy activities that formally belong in ministries of finance (von Soest 2007a).

- The divergence in salaries and other forms of remuneration between SARA staff and their colleagues in ministries of finance with whom they should cooperate can become an obstacle to the effective governance of taxation more broadly (Chapter 8).

- SARAs probably did play a positive role in supporting and encouraging tax administration reforms in the 1990s and later. But those effects seem to have dissipated. Recent statistical research has failed to identify any long-term impact of the creation of SARAs on revenue collection (Dom 2017; Sarr 2016). The big debate about SARAs has little relevance to contemporary questions about tax reform – especially for Anglophone Africa, where SARAs are almost universal, and very unlikely to be dismantled.

Disagreement: VAT and customs

Value-added tax (VAT)

Value-added tax (sometimes labelled goods and services tax, or GST; see Box 6.1) attracts many critics. Consumers and tax justice campaigners don't like it because it is a tax on consumption rather than income, and therefore potentially regressive. Owners of small businesses don't like it because it requires them to keep more detailed records and, in many cases, makes it more difficult for them to evade taxes. Exporters object because they are required to pay VAT on their production inputs and then reclaim it from the tax authority once their product is exported. In many African and other low-income countries in particular, tax authorities do not pay out money easily. The bribes paid to facilitate the payment of VAT refunds are a major source of corruption in tax administration. Tax administrators have mixed views. The beauty of VAT, from the perspective of its proponents, is that it generates a large paper (or electronic) trail of data, and provides most businesses with an incentive to cooperate in providing data if they are not to pay too much tax. In principle, it is a self-reinforcing tax. But it may not work according to the book when, as in most of Africa, tax authorities have limited capacity to collate or analyse all the data that is generated.

Box 6.1 What is value-added tax?

VAT is a consumption tax. Key features of VAT are that it is a broad based tax levied at multiple stages of the production or supply of goods and services, with taxes on inputs credited against taxes on outputs (and refunded when the former exceed the latter). The design and implementation of VAT differ across countries.

In theory, VAT falls on final consumption and is neutral on production decisions. Therefore, it targets a large tax base and is growth friendly. In practice, this quality depends largely on the design features of VAT, such as the number of rates, the prevalence of exemptions, the level and number of registration thresholds, and the limitations on refunding excess VAT credits.

It is common to have low or no VAT on essential goods or services such as food, healthcare, water, power and services relating to homes. Without such social reliefs, VAT would be a regressive tax, falling heavily on those who can least afford it.

The main supporters of VAT globally are governments – and the IMF. In countries with good written or electronic records of economic transactions, VAT can be an efficient means of extracting a great deal of revenue. Since it was first launched in France in 1948, VAT has been introduced in more than 150 countries (Ebeke et al. 2016). After India finally passed the necessary legislation in 2016, the United States was left as the only large country without VAT at a national level. Currently, around 80% of the countries in sub-Saharan Africa levy one, typically raising about one-quarter of all tax revenue (Keen 2012: 11). Nevertheless, VAT has significantly underperformed as a revenue collection tool in Africa. It was introduced, mainly at the urging of the IMF and in the context of structural adjustment programmes in the 1980s and 1990s, to replace revenues that would be lost through large cuts in import and export duties (Gillis 1990: 77–8), but it has not yet replaced those lost revenues (Baunsgaard and Keen 2009). VAT is not used very efficiently in Africa. The productivity of the tax – the ratio of actual to potential collections – is much lower for sub-Saharan Africa than for any other continent.[14] Probably because VAT was in some degree imposed on African governments, the legislation was often badly prepared, allowing too many loopholes and exemptions. These were then actively defended – and sometimes expanded – through lobbying by the beneficiaries (Keen 2009; see also Chapter 9).

The record of VAT in sub-Saharan Africa is mixed and controversial. We comment on three of the main controversies below.

How does VAT affect equity?

The most widespread criticism of VAT is that it is regressive. It is a tax on consumption. A housemaid in Lomé and her wealthy employer both pay the same 18% VAT on imported toothpaste. Since we generally expect poorer people to consume a higher proportion of their income than rich people, it seems obvious that the burden of VAT will fall disproportionately on the poor. Reality is more complex. One reason is that many governments that levy a VAT, including the government of Togo, give reductions or exemptions for basic consumption items, especially food, and sometimes medicine. Another is that poorer people are more likely to purchase from the smaller, informal firms that are below the threshold for paying VAT (Keen 2009). Our Lomé housemaid might use one of many indigenous alternatives to toothbrushes and toothpaste, and may not pay any VAT on many of her purchases. The research evidence suggests that, to date, VAT on average has not contributed significantly to changing the distribution of income in poor countries (Keen 2012). Bird and Zolt (2005) find that, if VAT is regressive, it is less regressive than the trade taxes it has replaced. The most important point is that, from a policy perspective, it makes little sense to judge the impact on income distribution of VAT, or of any other single tax, on the basis of statistics about which population groups bear the burden at any moment in time. First, we have to consider the counterfactual. What is the realistic alternative? If a mildly regressive VAT has effectively replaced a very regressive set of import duties, then it is progressive, at least in a restricted sense. Second, policymakers need to know the overall impact of governments' taxing and spending activities if they are to try to use the fiscal system to improve the distribution of income. The knowledge that a particular tax appears regressive when examined in isolation is no basis for deciding to abolish it. If it were abolished, if government spending were reduced in consequence, and if the burden of spending cuts were to fall on poorer people, then the total fiscal system might become more regressive. In a study on Ethiopia, Muñoz and Cho (2003) conclude that the net impact of VAT is progressive when the higher revenues are allocated to poverty-reducing spending, especially education and health.

The 'obvious' conclusion is that tax policy decisions designed to increase equity should only be taken after a full analysis of the distributional impact of the combined effects of governments' taxing and spending activities. Unfortunately, that is a very challenging task that requires large amounts of detailed data. Except for South

Africa, and perhaps one or two other countries, the data is simply not available for most of sub-Saharan Africa. Arguments about the alleged regressive character of VAT will continue.[15] Most likely to be useful, in our view, are focused studies of the potential public benefits of targeted zero-rating of certain kinds of goods consumed in large quantities by the relatively poor.

Is VAT too complex for Africa?

The IMF is very committed to the success of VAT globally. It was the IMF, supported by aid donors, that was principally responsible for its rapid spread into low-income countries (Keen 2009). The IMF remains the guardian of VAT today, especially in low-income countries, and is eager to offer assistance to 'clean up' VATs that function poorly, feeling perhaps that its reputation is at stake.

From an administrative perspective, VAT is very demanding for both tax collectors and taxpayers. Does that make it suitable or unsuitable for low-income countries with low organisational capacity in both the public and private sectors? The debate on that question has become rather stylised. Critics say that the complexity of the tax undermines the potential benefits. The IMF continues to assert the intrinsic superiority of VAT over the alternative ways of taxing transactions in goods and services, and to suggest that problems with VAT stem from the influence of lobbying and interest groups on design and implementation. Further, the IMF tends to claim that the demanding nature of VAT administration is positively beneficial to countries with weak tax systems, because it forces systemic improvements that would otherwise not take place (Kloeden 2011). Since we have very few reliable measures on the performance of revenue agencies in Africa, there is no way of resolving this dispute using direct evidence.

There is, however, a major systemic problem with VAT that is especially damaging in Africa: the need for a refund mechanism – i.e. for revenue authorities sometimes to repay VAT to taxpayers. In practice, this applies almost exclusively to exporters. VAT is designed to tax, at the same rate, the value that is added at each stage of the production chain. VAT is (normally) collected on imports. If it were also levied on exports, it would become a tax on foreign trade. So the standard procedure is for exporters to claim a refund of all the VAT that has been paid in the production chain of a good or service once that item has been exported. The refund claim is made on the basis of documentary evidence of export, and this can be the 'Achilles heel' of VAT. Fraudsters claim refunds for exports on the basis of false documentation, either for totally fake transactions or for what is sometimes termed 'carousel fraud' (moving the same high-value, low-bulk items, like mobile phones, repeatedly across borders, claiming export refunds each time). These problems are widespread in OECD countries, despite their relatively good documentation systems (Carter 2013). In Africa, concerns about the possibility of false claims sometimes mean that tax authorities make long and detailed checks, lasting up to a year, before repayments are made. In addition, governments may be tempted to delay paying refunds when their budgets are under pressure, thereby creating serious cash flow problems for businesses.[16] Meanwhile, the bribes paid to facilitate the payment of VAT refunds are a major source of corruption in tax administration in Africa. Knowledge of this problem in turn motivates foreign investors to demand complete exemption from VAT. Overall, issues around VAT refunds infuriate many businesses in Africa and undermine the integrity and credibility of tax administration.

Is VAT achieving its revenue potential?

From the perspective of African governments, VAT has not lived up to the promise on which it was sold to them by the IMF and aid donors: that it would replace all the revenues they were going to lose by slashing import and export duties as they adopted structural adjustment programmes (Baunsgaard and Keen 2009). One reason, as explained above, is that many of these governments have allowed so many exemptions and loopholes that, on average, the revenue productivity of VAT is unusually low. Nevertheless, VAT is now a mainstay of revenue collection throughout sub-Saharan Africa, and is probably the most important single tax in the region. That somewhat surprising outcome ultimately reflects failures to tap more effectively into the main alternative tax bases: individual and corporate incomes, and the extractive sector (see above and Chapters 3, 4 and 5). The implication for many governments is that, if they were willing and able to clean up the structure and improve the administration of their VAT, they would have a very powerful revenue collection instrument in their hands.

It is possible that the IMF forced the introduction of VAT into some countries where it was inappropriately complex. It is possible that this mismatch between the administrative demands of VAT and normal business practices is part of the reason for the low productivity of VAT in Africa. Equally, it is possible that the discipline of implementing VAT has indeed helped improve revenue administration more broadly.[17] Either way, the answers to these questions have no direct implications for tax policy today. VAT in Africa is there to stay. It is highly unlikely that any government would want to relinquish a tax that has such a high revenue collection potential.

Customs collection in insecure environments[18]
In the late colonial and early independence decades, customs was often the largest single source of government revenue. Control of customs was essential to effective statecraft. Recent trends in tax policy have to some degree undermined that dominance. Not only have most export taxes been eliminated (Chapter 2), but, as we explained at the beginning of this chapter, from the 1990s onward rates of import duty were severely reduced in most cases, with VAT introduced to make up for the consequent revenue shortfall. And a key aspect of the creation of SARAs has been to bring domestic tax collection and customs under one organisational umbrella.[19]

However, customs generally remains politically and organisationally powerful. They may collect much less revenue through import duties than two or three decades ago, but they typically account for a large proportion of VAT collection.[20] As ever, and as in most of the world, customs staff are in a strong position to extract illegal payments from cross-border traders, who may be operating on credit and keen to move their goods quickly. Customs staff are obliged or empowered to physically inspect consignments. Reasons to delay clearance are easy to find. That power is slightly threatened by the current transition to electronic pre-clearance of all cross-border trade consignments. When such systems are in place, consignments in principle should be stopped and physically inspected only on an occasional and purely random basis, or if there is a valid reason for suspicion. But 'suspicion' needs little justification in an environment where there is abundant illicit trade, especially in drugs, arms, tobacco and migrants (Ahmad 2017). These, too, can become significant sources of illicit earnings for customs staff. Corruption in customs is often hierarchically organised: subordinates may 'bid' for postings according to the expected size of informal earnings and be required to remit a substantial proportion to their superiors – who may in turn have to make large regular payments to senior politicians. Meanwhile, particularly in smaller, trade-dependent countries, customs administration can offer an avenue for higher-level officials to direct important trading benefits to their business allies, or to impose costs on their opponents, thus informally shaping economic competition. Control of customs remains an important lever of statecraft.

However, it would be a mistake to view customs staff simply as venial rent collectors. They often operate in highly informal, competitive and dangerous environments. They have security as well as revenue collection responsibilities, and sometimes they have to deploy considerable skill to collect revenues. First, and especially along the coast of West Africa and on many inland borders, individual customs posts in effect have to compete with others close by in terms of rates charged and services provided. For example, shippers have a choice about whether to unload their goods in

Cotonou (Benin), Lomé (Togo) or Tema (Ghana). Truckers, too, have a range of choices when moving goods from Burkina Faso to Mali. Second, at border points themselves, customs staff often have to negotiate their charges with those levied by other parts of the state apparatus, like the army, border guards, immigration officers and environmental inspectors. Third, they may employ local 'gangs' of various kinds to provide intelligence on smuggling and to intimidate traders who fail to observe the local rules (Titeca 2009). Fourth, they often continue to operate during armed conflicts, variously cooperating with the official armed forces, trying to protect and maintain trade to ensure some revenue for (local) governments, and even providing local services such as electricity and telephones to try to generate local political support for the central state (Cantens and Rabelland 2017).

Judged by formal standards of efficiency and probity, customs organisations are likely to continue to disappoint for a long time. They are simultaneously perceived as corrupt and generate much less revenue for government than they should. Indeed, the 'deals' that they – and other border operators, including the police, the army, border guards and immigration agencies – offer to traders are often so advantageous that traders pay less in total than they would have to pay if it were simply a matter of paying the legal border charges (Amin and Hoppe 2013). From other perspectives, the behaviour of customs organisations and staff may be viewed as constructive efforts to exercise public authority effectively in the face of major challenges.

Under-performance: personal income taxes, tax exemptions and corruption

Personal income taxes

In the 1960s and 1970s, the standard expert advice to governments, in Africa and globally, was to tax incomes and wealth more effectively both to raise revenue and to improve income distribution

(Kaldor 1963; Gillis 1990). Considerable efforts were put into developing progressive personal income tax systems. In most of Africa, as in low-income countries more broadly, this programme yielded few results. Personal income tax (PIT) accounts for less than 10% of all tax revenue in most low-income countries,[21] compared with an average of more than 25% in OECD countries (Keen 2012: 10). Direct social security contributions – which, in effect, are a second PIT – are rare in sub-Saharan Africa. Revenue from PIT is collected almost entirely through PAYE ('pay as you earn' – or withholding arrangements) from the salaries paid to the employees of public sector organisations and a few large private enterprises. Revenue from taxes on income from professional self-employment (e.g. lawyers, private doctors, consultants, accountants and architects) and from property and other investments – the main income sources of the rich – is tiny by comparison.[22] Commonly, less than 5% of the African population pay PIT, compared with nearly 50% in developed countries. Bird and Zolt (2005: 1656) characterise the current PIT regime as follows: 'The global progressive personal income tax long advocated by tax experts as it has operated in most developing countries is in fact neither global nor progressive, nor personal, not often even on income.'

PIT is not a major revenue source for most African governments. The main exception is a small cluster of countries in Southern Africa: South Africa, Malawi, Zambia and Zimbabwe. This in part reflects the employment of large numbers of African men on white-owned mines and farms, especially in South Africa, in the earlier half of the twentieth century. This resulted in a higher administrative capacity to tax labour earnings and to tax in general (Frankema 2011; Mkandawire 2010). But the grandchildren and great-grandchildren of those migrant labourers mostly do not have formal sector jobs. Like the great majority of Africans, they work in the informal sector. The fact that they neither pay PIT nor make social security contributions is not itself a major policy problem. No government should try to collect direct income taxes from very poor people. The problem arises from the fact that, hiding behind the weak design and enforcement of PIT, are large and growing numbers of wealthy Africans who pay little or no income tax at all.

The number of African billionaires is few, but apparently fast growing (Bird 2015). More important for present purposes are the actual and potential millionaires. We have no reliable figures on their numbers, incomes or tax payments. We know from personal observations and abundant anecdotes that there are many of them, and that they seem to invest much of their new wealth in real estate. We know that, in some African cities, real estate prices can be very high (Chapter 7). And we know that rich Africans generally do not pay PIT. We have some very illuminating information about the situation in one country – Uganda – thanks to researchers at the Uganda Revenue Authority (Kangave et al. 2016). Here are a few facts relating to the financial year 2013–14:

- Only 5% of company directors in Uganda remitted any PIT.
- Of the four individuals who paid more than 1 billion shillings in customs duties, only two made any PIT payments. None of the 12 individuals who paid between half a billion and 1 billion shillings in customs duties paid any PIT.
- Among a sample of 60 of the top lawyers in the country, 17 paid PIT.
- Among 71 top-ranking government officials, who owned enormous assets, including hotels, private schools and media houses, only one had ever paid PIT.
- Only 13% of individuals registered as taxpayers with the Revenue Authority made any tax payments.

The researchers also reported on the various ways in which the Uganda Revenue Authority could change its procedures to collect more income tax. Their work resulted in the creation of a special unit to tax HNWIs. Within six months, the unit had identified 89 'individuals of interest' and had collected from them more than

$5 million in additional taxes.[23] More than half of this came from previously undeclared income on property rentals – widely believed to be a major income source for African elites, especially in capital cities. There is no reason to believe that Uganda's experience of underpayment of PIT by high earners is in any way unusual in Africa. While explanations for low collection of income taxes on the wealthy often focus on the difficulty of identifying the sources of their income, the Uganda experience suggests that the existence of political commitment is much more important.

Tax exemptions

When we talk here of tax exemptions, we refer to measures directed at investors that provide for more favourable tax treatment of certain activities or sectors compared with what is available to the general industry. There is a large variety of types of tax exemption (Box 6.2).

Especially if they are intended to address regional economic inequality within a country, tax exemptions may be targeted to special locations. These 'economic zones' have gained popularity across the developing world over recent decades. In 2007, the International Labour Organization (ILO) estimated that 3,500 economic zones were operational in 130 countries, compared with only 176 in 46 countries 20 years earlier (IMF et al. 2015).[24] Incentives available to investors in economic zones generally include non-tax benefits, such as good infrastructure and cheap utilities, as well as tax reductions for customs duties, income taxes and other (local) taxes and fees. Successful economic development in China, Singapore, South Korea and Taiwan has often been credited in part to economic zones (Wang 2013). These East Asian successes have inspired many other developing countries to adopt economic zones of various kinds, and China has eagerly promoted the 'Chinese model' in Africa. Experiences from East Asia have certainly inspired some African governments, including Ethiopia and Rwanda, to use tax incentives as an important part of their industrialisation strategies.

Box 6.2 Varieties of tax exemptions

Tax holiday: *Temporary exemption of a new firm or investment from certain specified taxes, typically at least corporate income tax. Partial tax holidays offer reduced obligations rather than full exemption.*

Special zones: *Geographically limited areas in which qualified firms can locate and thus benefit from exemptions of varying scope from taxes and/or customs and other administrative requirements. Zones are often aimed at exporters and located close to a port. In some countries, such as Tanzania, however, qualifying companies can be declared 'zones' irrespective of their location.*

Investment tax credit: *Deduction of a certain fraction of the value of an investment from the liability to pay corporate income tax.*

Investment allowance: *Deduction of a certain fraction of the value of an investment from taxable profits (in addition to depreciation). The value of an allowance is the product of the allowance and the tax rate. Unlike an investment tax credit, its value will vary across firms, unless corporate income tax is paid only at a single rate.*

Accelerated depreciation: *Depreciation allowances (against corporate income tax) at a faster schedule than available for the rest of the economy. This can be implemented in many different ways, including higher first-year depreciation allowances, or increased depreciation rates.*

Reduced tax rates: *Reduction in a tax rate, typically the corporate income tax rate.*

Exemptions from various taxes: *Exemption from certain taxes, often those collected at the border such as tariffs, excises and VAT on imported inputs.*

Financing incentives: *Reductions in tax rates that apply to providers of funds, for instance reduced withholding taxes on dividends.*

The inspiration from Asia is only one of several forces driving the mushrooming of tax exemptions in Africa. The grant of exemptions by one government may encourage others to follow suit, and this process of tax competition can cause a race to the bottom, with all countries ultimately ending up with lower tax revenue. According to Abbas and Klemm (2013), this has happened in Africa. Effective tax rates have fallen to almost zero in industries where special regimes are in place, with no noticeable positive impact on investment. Weak intra-government coordination also contributes to disappointing results. In Ghana, for instance, at one point as many as ten government agencies had the authority to grant exemptions (Amegashie 2011). The existence of multiple, poorly coordinated agencies allows investors to 'shop around' and to try to bid up the levels of exemptions on offer.

Proponents argue that, given the generally poor investment climate in Africa, it is imperative to provide tax incentives (i.e. exemptions) to attract investors. Exemptions may have played a role in attracting investments to Mauritius, for example (Bolnick 2004). However, such positive cases are the exceptions rather than the rule. This is no surprise, as we know that attracting (foreign) investment is only one of the reasons why governments grant tax exemptions. They are also widely used to reward political allies, to provide leverage over potential political opponents, and to raise money, both for private pockets and to fund elections and other political activities (Moore 2015). Therkildsen (2012) argues that the increasing competitiveness of elections has been a major driver for the multiplication of tax exemptions in Tanzania. A recent study by Zeng (2015) concludes that tax exemptions have generated little additional investment in most African countries. The IMF, the OECD, the UN and the World Bank have produced a joint statement detailing their excessive use in low-income countries (IMF et al. 2015). Poor institutions, weak governance and inadequate infrastructure – and uncertainty about taxation regimes – are typically much bigger disincentives to investment than corporate tax levels.

It is unlikely that lowering the tax rate can compensate for a bad investment climate. In surveys of investors conducted in seven African countries between 2009 and 2012, an average of 84% of respondents said that the availability of tax exemptions had not affected their investment decisions.[25] Before giving tax exemptions, governments should focus on improving the investment climate by tackling such issues as excessive regulation and red tape (e.g. for registering a business, or for construction permits); the quality of roads, ports, electricity, telecoms and other infrastructure; and the predictability of the tax and legal systems. If taxes were not waived and the revenue were used to help dissolve these obvious obstacles to investment, almost everyone might benefit.

We do not have fully reliable information on the prevalence and cost of tax exemptions in Africa. This is partly because of some technical disagreements about how they should be measured, but mainly because few governments maintain or publish much information on the subject. The incidence of exemptions seems to be increasing (Abramovsky et al. 2014; Keen and Mansour 2009: 18–20), with most estimates suggesting that they result in large revenue losses. The OECD recently assembled data relating to six countries in Africa that suggested that the value of tax exemptions on average amounted to 33% of taxes actually collected (OECD 2013).

Researchers have repeatedly concluded that the societal costs of tax exemptions are high and that the benefits, in terms of additional investment, are low. The frequency and persistence of exemptions are not due principally to ignorance about their effects, but because they are so beneficial to politicians.[26] Significantly reducing exemptions would generate large new tax revenues. But how can the politics of the process be turned around? It will be very difficult, but here are two possibilities:

- It would be useful if African countries were to draw up and then sign a set of principles about the grant of tax exemptions. That compact should both provide guidelines for when and how exemptions should be granted, and commit governments to make public the details of every exemption granted and the economic justification.

- More governments could produce regular tax expenditure reports (estimates of the cost in lost revenues of the tax exemptions that they grant). Few governments in Africa produce any reports of this nature, and even fewer use them as a basis for reforming the exemptions regime. Mauritius and Senegal are among the exceptions. In particular, the 2006 tax expenditure reform in Mauritius is considered a major success, resulting in a tax system that is simpler, less costly to administer and comply with, less arbitrary, and with fewer opportunities for political abuse in granting exemptions. Tax expenditures declined from almost 3.3% of GDP to around 1.3% in a few years.[27] Foreign investment continued to grow fast.

Publicity and transparency are not always very powerful weapons. They are, however, probably essential if the abuse of tax exemptions, as practised in so many Africa countries, is to be curbed.

Corruption

Tax collectors are well placed to extract bribes from taxpayers – and in turn offer taxpayers a 'reduced assessment', so that the real loser is the public treasury. The control of corruption has been a major theme in tax administration throughout recorded history. Corruption is likely when tax collectors meet taxpayers face to face and even more likely when those collectors are responsible for assessing the amount of taxes due as well as collecting the money. As we mentioned above, this is the typical situation in customs, but it also happens at a local level in Africa (Chapter 7). In a slightly different way, VAT creates opportunities for large-scale bribery over refunds: revenue staff can delay responding to refund claims until they are adequately incentivised (see above). As Fjeldstad and Heggstad (2011) discovered in Mozambique, Tanzania and Zambia, aggressive tax enforcement, apparently designed to elicit bribes, is perceived to be a major problem by many formal sector businesses. In practice, this kind of bribe seeking is almost indistinguishable from what, when aiming to reach revenue collection targets, tax collectors call 'hunting in the zoo': focusing on known, registered taxpayers rather than making the effort to identify and then tax unregistered businesses.

Corruption in tax collection is a global rather than a distinctively African issue, although there is certainly plenty of it in Africa. But how much? And where? We cannot answer those questions definitively, but recent research gives us some good clues.

- Between 2011 and 2013 Afrobarometer, a reliable survey organisation, asked questions about taxation to over 46,000 people in 29 countries of sub-Saharan Africa. Some 35% of respondents believed that 'most' or 'all' tax officials were corrupt; 39% thought that 'some' were; 17% did not know; and only 10% said that 'none' were corrupt (Aiko and Logan 2014).[28] The exact question is important, however: 'How many of the following people do you think are involved in corruption, or haven't you heard enough about them to say: tax officials, like Ministry of Finance officials or local government tax collectors?' In other words, these perceptions of high levels of corruption may not relate principally to the staff of central tax administrations, but more to the domain of local tax collection, where we know that harmful collection practices are widespread (Chapter 7).
- In 2013, Transparency International surveyed large samples of people in 17 countries in sub-Saharan Africa about their actual experiences of paying bribes to public servants in the previous year. People were asked whether they had paid a bribe when they had contact with the staff of various categories of public service organisations. The average results of those 17 countries are summarised in Table 6.1. Tax collectors do not seem to be particularly corrupt: the reported incidence of bribe payments

to tax collectors is close to the average for all eight types of services included in the survey. And, because these responses again refer to local- as well as to national-level tax collection, we can infer that the figures very likely overstate the incidence of corruption in national-level tax collection.

Table 6.1 Frequency of bribe payments by users of public services in 17 countries in sub-Saharan Africa, 2013

Type of public service	Proportion of respondents who, when they had contact with the service over the previous year, paid a bribe
Medical and health services	29%
Utilities	29%
Education services	33%
Land services	33%
Tax revenue	36%
Registry and permit services	38%
Judiciary	45%
Police	61%

The survey was conducted in Cameroon, Democratic Republic of Congo, Ethiopia, Ghana, Kenya, Liberia, Madagascar, Mozambique, Nigeria, Rwanda, Senegal, Sierra Leone, South Africa, South Sudan, Tanzania, Uganda and Zimbabwe.

Source: Transparency International (2013).

• The evidence from a different kind of survey reinforces the suspicion that the incidents of corruption reported in relation to taxation occur disproportionately at subnational level. Dr Merima Ali (in a personal communication) has analysed the results of the Enterprise Survey conducted by the World Bank in 17 African countries between 2014 and 2016. Firm managers were asked whether they were invited to pay bribes when visited by tax inspectors. On average, only 14% of managers said yes. That suggests a lower incidence of bribery than perceived or experienced by citizens generally (see above). Because the question was framed in terms of 'visits from tax inspectors', we can assume that the answers did not capture relationships between firms and customs staff, which are more likely to involve corruption.

- The results of the same survey revealed wide variation between countries: from almost 40% of 'yes' answers in the Democratic Republic of Congo to around 5% in Burundi and Tanzania. And there was a strong statistical pattern: the poorer the country, the higher the frequency of 'yes' answers.

We can conclude that: corruption remains a significant problem in national tax administration in Africa; it is appreciably larger in customs than in internal revenue collection; VAT refunds are a major trigger; the frequency of corruption is probably especially high at subnational level, while the very large individual sums ('grand corruption') are appropriated at the national level; and to some extent corruption is a product of poverty.

The underuse of IT

Tax administration revolves around gathering, collating and analysing data. Information technology makes possible enormous improvements in efficiency and effectiveness (Bird and Zolt 2008). This is not principally because IT enables pre-existing processes to be performed at lower cost; rather, it is that it enables processes that were previously challenging or effectively impossible. They include the following:

- Collating all information about a single individual or corporate taxpayer, uniquely identified by a tax identification number (TIN). This might include, for example, information collected separately by units dealing with import duties, PIT, corporate income tax, excise taxes or VAT.
- Collecting 'third party information' to help cross-check the validity of tax returns filed by individuals or companies. This

might include information from utility companies on the consumption of electricity or water; from the motor vehicle licensing authority on motor vehicle ownership; from banks and other financial institutions on ownership of liquid assets; and from the property registration authority on property ownership.

- Using this information to undertake statistical analysis that will improve operational effectiveness. For example, analysis of past behaviour makes possible estimates of the probability that particular taxpayers or types of taxpayers (e.g. restaurant owners or bus operators) will be more or less compliant. Those probabilities in turn allow for the more strategic use of audit and other administrative resources to encourage compliance, by focusing them where they are most needed. Equally, digitised data on interest payments made by local affiliates of transnational corporations to related companies abroad makes it possible to determine whether this channel is being used for tax avoidance (Chapter 3).

These kinds of uses of administrative tax information are possible only if the information is routinely entered into master databases that are accessible to and used by all units within a tax administration. Fragmentation of IT systems greatly reduces the chances of this happening, and diminishes the value of the digitised information that is available. We have no detailed studies of the ways in which African tax administrations employ IT. There is, however, considerable evidence of fragmentation and underuse, some anecdotal and some solid (see Box 6.3). There are several possible reasons for this:

- unwillingness or inability to control corruption;
- a fear that more effective IT systems would reveal too much about non-compliance by taxpayers who are currently 'protected' from taxation through their absence from tax administration records;

Box 6.3 Diverse IT systems

We know of an African revenue authority – admittedly among the poorest performers on the continent – that uses four IT systems to manage taxpayer information. System A is supposed to be the only means of generating TINs and recording tax payments. System A was originally introduced to replace system B. However, the migration from B to A was never completed after it was realised that A cannot perform some functions. Each is currently used to manage a large number of taxpayers. A is used mainly for personal and corporate income tax, and for withholding tax. The two systems are not interfaced, and they are managed by different departments. The information on them often conflicts. System C was introduced to replace system D, which was used to record VAT transactions. Although the revenue authority no longer recognises system D, some stations still use it and the 'Large Taxpayer Office' uses it as a backup. Because the four IT systems are not interfaced, some work is duplicated. The information on any one taxpayer is dispersed: registration details might be on one system, VAT payments on another, and income tax payments on a third. Staff with authorisation to use one system need to obtain permission from another department to access another system. TINs are supposed to be issued only through system A. However, some taxpayers have more than one TIN – which enables them to avoid some tax. Some are issued temporary TINs that are not recorded on any system.

- the desire of different sections of the revenue administration to maintain control over their own sources of information and their 'own' taxpayers; and
- an excessive dependence on complex, costly software, purchased from abroad, that is inappropriate to the local context and needs.

Whatever the exact mix of reasons, underuse of IT reduces both operational effectiveness and the scope for more transparency in tax administration.

Conclusions

In comparative international perspective, African national tax systems perform relatively well. This may come as a surprise to many readers, and especially to those who have learned to have low expectations of public sector performance in Africa. But the perceptions that really matter are those of African taxpayers. They are far less sanguine, and are likely to refer to corruption, inefficiency, harassment, unfairness, and the lack of any tangible return on their money. All taxpayers complain to some extent, but Africans are justified in doing so. There is a great deal of scope to improve tax policy and tax administration. And, leaving aside the critical issue of the politics, there is also considerable scope for African governments to raise additional revenues. The best ways of doing that vary from country to country, but some of the more evident 'tax gaps' appear almost throughout the continent (Moore and Prichard 2017). They include: a widespread failure to tax either the personal incomes of wealthy people or their property owner- ship; the gross under-taxation of mining; unusually low rates of excise taxes on tobacco and alcohol; very 'leaky' VAT systems; and insufficient use of various kinds of gross turnover or excise taxes to compensate for the ease with which transnational companies can avoid local corporate income taxes by shifting profits overseas (Durst 2015b: 18). As we explained in Chapters 3, 4 and 5, the ability of transnational companies to shift accounting profits to overseas jurisdictions and tax havens is a real constraint on domestic revenue mobilisation. But it is not the only constraint, and not always the most important one. African governments should certainly be more assertive in challenging multinational companies for activities such as transfer mispricing. The evidence suggests that this is likely to generate significant additional revenue (Moore and Prichard 2017). But they can also raise more revenue closer to home. One does not preclude the other. Indeed, progress is likely to be self-reinforcing: greater capacity to collect taxes at home will increase the ability to tax cross-border transactions, and vice versa.

Chapter 7

SMALL TAXES AND LARGE BURDENS: INFORMAL AND SUBNATIONAL REVENUES

Who pays taxes in Africa?

It is common to hear people say that a majority of Africans 'do not pay taxes'. This is true to the extent that only a small share of the population of most African countries – typically only a few per cent of the adult population – pay formal personal income tax. They are dominantly male. However, that does not mean that ordinary African men and women fail to bear their fair share of the overall tax burden. On the contrary, they often pay more of their income in taxes than do their more privileged fellow citizens. How so?

- First, as we note in the previous chapter, ordinary Africans are not alone in paying no personal income tax: large numbers of wealthy people fail to comply.
- Second, most people 'pay' – in the sense that ultimately they help bear the burden of – VAT, customs duties and excise taxes on tobacco, liquor and fuel. Those taxes collectively account for more than half the revenues collected by central governments in Africa.
- Third, and most importantly, individuals and small businesses often directly 'pay' a wide range of what we term *small taxes*. That is the subject of this chapter.

What are small taxes? Their common characteristics are: they are widely paid by ordinary people; they are either small or invisible in official statistics on revenue collections; their existence and significance are generally underappreciated; and they constitute the dominant taxpaying experience of African women in particular. We could loosely divide small taxes into three main subcategories:

- *Formal subnational taxes and charges paid by ordinary citizens*: revenues collected officially by various subnational levels of governments.
- *Formal taxes and payments on small and micro-businesses*, often levied by both subnational governments and central governments.
- *Informal taxes*, comprising both: (1) *illicit formal taxes* – payments collected by official tax collectors, and other state officials, but which are either outside the law (bribes) or, more frequently, are collected under the guise of formality but are not remitted to government budgets (i.e. embezzlement); and (2) revenues collected by a wide range of non-state agents and organisations.

These, however, are formal, analytic categories, which may not correspond at all closely to the perceptions of the people involved. The revenue-paying landscape in which most Africans live is sometimes quite ambiguous, particularly in low-income urban and more remote areas. People may hand over their cash without: (1) knowing whether the person taking it is legally authorized to collect it; (2) the basis on which the sums are calculated; or (3) how much will remain in the pocket of the collector. In Sierra Leone, traditional chiefs, who also collect informal taxes, play a major role in collecting formal local taxes on behalf of local councils in rural areas (Jibao et al. 2017: 24). Similarly, in Senegal the local offices of national tax agencies employ informal procedures and informal staff (Blundo 2006; Juul 2006). Even apparently 'voluntary' contributions may in fact involve mandatory payments to unelected local authorities, forced labour, and payments to vigilante groups or criminal gangs for protection. Contributions to community development associations to fill gaps in government service provision are particularly large in some contexts (Olken and Singhal 2011). From a formal legal perspective, and in local parlance, many of these payments are not 'taxes', but rather *levies, rates, user charges, fees for services, fines* and more or less compulsory payments to community development projects. But to the payer they all look similar. They are exactions by those in power that are, at least nominally, intended to contribute to the funding of government or public goods and services. The term 'small taxes' is a useful label for these diverse payments, but it is not a statement about their material impact on the taxpayer. These 'small' taxes may be more of a financial burden to most taxpayers than are the more familiar and better-documented national taxes – and they may play a major role in determining the distribution of tax burdens across different groups, including by gender.

The headline story of this chapter is that there is a meaningful distinction to be made for Africa between, at the extremes, two different tax worlds. The tax world to which we have referred in previous chapters is populated mainly by: central revenue authorities; relatively well paid public servants; a small number of taxes that collectively raise a great deal of revenue; relatively clear laws; some scope for formal appeal against assessments; banks; the relative predictability of tax obligations; and occasional tax policy debate. That world is important to governments and to formal sector companies, but it barely impinges visibly or directly on the daily life of the majority of Africans. Their tax world is likely to be characterised by a diversity of tax collectors; numerous small taxes; cash payments; few receipts; revenue systems that sometimes achieve nothing except the transfer of income to the collectors and their bosses; and the relative absence of processes of appeal or debate about 'tax policy'.

This distinction is not an absolute dichotomy. Much tax activity lies somewhere between the two poles. Some local small taxes –

particularly property taxes and business licences – are collected formally and predictably. The collection of some national taxes, particularly at customs posts, involves substantial informal negotiation and corruption. In larger countries such as the Democratic Republic of Congo, Ethiopia, Nigeria and Sudan, significant revenues are collected at intermediate (state or provincial) levels using relatively informal practices. In Nigeria, the collection of state-level taxes is sometimes undertaken by private contractors with close connections to leading political figures. But the distinction between national and small taxes is essential if we are to counter the heavy bias in most literature and discussion towards the former. The distinction usefully contrasts the experiences of those (larger, urban) taxpayers who have a voice and those (ordinary, rural) taxpayers who have little or no voice. It also draws attention to a potentially important difference in policy emphasis. Whereas national revenue reform has generally focused on increasing overall collection levels, when it comes to small taxes – and particularly to those other than property taxes – the most important tasks may lie in simplification, reducing informality, increasing equity and reducing aggregate burdens on those with the lowest incomes.

We begin this chapter with an account of the weakness of the more formal small taxes – that is, the largest subnational (or 'local') taxes and taxes on small businesses. We then discuss the prevalence of *nuisance taxes* and *informal taxes*. Finally, we explore options for reform of small taxes, drawing on evidence of progress in some areas.

Subnational and small business taxation

There is considerable diversity of systems of local taxation across Africa, including significant differences between (generally more centralised) Francophone countries, and (generally more decentralised) Anglophone countries. In principle and in law, in most countries local governments are expected to obtain most of the revenues that they collect from a few main sources. Notably, these include: taxes on land and property; taxes on small businesses, often in the form of business operating licences; charges on sellers operating in local (physical) markets; and user charges for other local services such as garbage collection and water supply. In practice, these revenues are generally inadequate and are collected inconsistently and inefficiently. The immediate outcomes include underfinanced local governments and dysfunctional, fragmented systems of local revenue raising. This state of affairs means that local governments are unable adequately to finance the provision of local services and public goods. More broadly, it limits the scope for building more effective relationships between the local governments and their citizens. Without substantial local revenue collection, the ties between local governments and citizens are likely to be weak, as are the incentives for local governments to be responsive to their citizens' needs.

Partly because local government revenue systems in Africa are so diverse, fragmented and informal, reliable information on how much money they collect and how they spend it is rarely available. Brun, Chambas and Fjeldstad assembled data for nine countries, of which eight were Francophone. In those cases, the total revenues raised by subnational governments ('own revenues') amounted to between 1.3% and 7% of total government revenues (Brun et al. 2011: 10). In many cases, especially outside the major urban centres, local revenues may amount to no more than $1 to $2 per head of the population. The tiny size of local budgets is both a cause and a reflection of the scarcity of effective, authoritative subnational governments.

The clearest reflection of the weakness of local revenue raising lies in property taxes, which are widely regarded as the best available instrument for funding local governments, because they are generally progressive, economically efficient, and potentially closely linked to local services. Despite their promise, property taxes are woefully underused across the continent. Recent IMF data suggests that, for most low-income African countries, property tax collections amount to less than 0.1% of GDP (IMF 2016a). The weakness of property taxation reflects the fact that in many places the majority of properties are not on tax rolls at all; those that are registered are often severely undervalued; tax rates are low; and collection procedures are weak. As discussed in greater detail below, this is attributable to a combination of historical legacies, institutional dysfunction, capacity challenges and, perhaps above all, political disinterest and resistance. As a result, property taxes offer perhaps the single greatest opportunity for strengthening local revenue systems – but they also pose plenty of political and institutional obstacles.

Alongside property taxes, another major actual or potential sources of revenue for local governments are taxes on small and micro businesses. The standard mechanism for mobilising revenues from businesses has been business licensing. Although the original intent was regulatory, local business licensing has increasingly become simply a revenue source. Typically, business licences generate between 5% and 30% of local government own revenues in urban councils. In many countries, however, the system has been quite unsatisfactory and often quite inequitable, and it has imposed high costs on business while generating relatively little money. In many African countries, obtaining a business licence involves multiple visits to various offices, sometimes over several days, with associated travel costs. Failure to provide the correct licence receipts to tax inspectors may result in closure of the premises. Consequently, the system is often riddled with rent seeking and corruption – while generating little revenue (Brun et al. 2011).

The most sophisticated small business taxes come in the form of business licences and other types of fees levied on local businesses in proportion to their operations and size. However, these same firms are frequently also taxed by national tax administrations, often through what are generically called 'presumptive taxes':

that is, taxes on presumed rather than measured profit. If levied on the basis of (measured) total business turnover, presumptive taxes require taxpayers to keep simpler accounts than do profit or income taxes. Accounts are not needed at all if presumptive taxes are based on physical proxies for business turnover, such as the size of retail premises, or the number of employees. There is a distinction in principle between a business licence (typically collected by local government) and a tax on business profits (typically collected by national government). However, those entrepreneurs obliged to pay multiple taxes, and who possibly suffer from competition for payments between local and national tax authorities, are unlikely to be impressed by or interested in such issues of principle. In Uganda, a common complaint from small and medium-sized enterprises has been that 'they do not know what to pay, where or to whom'.

Small businesses trading in physical market areas often face similar problems. They are relatively easy targets for frequent collections by multiple tax collectors – ranging from formal market dues to fees for market cleaning or toilets. Consequently, they often appear to bear a disproportionate share of the local tax burden. There may also be significant inequities among them: the relatively poor, migrants and ethnic minorities, those from neighbouring communities, those lacking personal connections and those who are not members of more powerful business associations are more likely to be targeted for formal and informal payments (Meagher 2016). One consequence is that, in much of West Africa in particular, where women play a leading role in market trading, there is a gender dimension to tax inequity (Prichard and van den Boogaard 2017). Research in Uganda shows that, while the majority of small, informal non-farm enterprises are poor enough to be exempted from the national business taxes (i.e. the small business tax and VAT), they end up paying a large share of their profits to local authorities, with the poorest paying the highest share. This is true of traders located both inside and outside formal market areas (Pimhidzai and Fox 2011).

In addition to property and business taxes, some local governments raise significant revenues from other sources, including user fees for services such as water and electricity, and various court fees and fines. Some local governments, particularly in Francophone Africa, continue to rely on small head (or poll) taxes (Brun et al. 2011: 7). Revenues from local mineral resource extraction are significant in some places, including Tanzania. With few exceptions, such as some of the larger cities in South Africa, the administrative apparatus of local revenue collection has remained relatively limited and rudimentary. There is little sign of the modernisation enjoyed by most central revenue administrations (Chapter 6). Local governments often rely on informal or more formal private contractors to undertake assessments and collections. IT is not widely or well used in local tax collection. Most procedures are still done manually, leaving a great deal of scope for face-to-face interactions between tax collectors and taxpayers. And the links between central and local revenue systems have generally remained weak, or perverse.

Nuisance taxes

One core dysfunctional feature of local revenue systems is *nuisance taxes*. These are taxes that are formally payable in small amounts on a very wide range of activities or assets. While presented as necessary revenue-raising tools, at best they generate inequity in the burden of taxation across different groups, undermine the transparency and accountability of tax systems, and create large economic distortions. At worst, they may serve principally to provide livelihoods for the collectors – and sometimes their superiors – either formally, where the revenues collected are adequate only to cover collection costs, or informally, where revenues enter the pockets of collectors rather than local government budgets. Nuisance taxes are widespread in Africa, especially at the local level:

- In the Democratic Republic of Congo, local government laws provide for more than 400 different taxes, fees and charges, including: special taxes on the production of particular goods; taxes on the movement of goods across provincial (or sometimes local) borders; taxes on the ownership of livestock; taxes on population movement; high fees for a huge array of government documents and obligatory permits; levies on marriages, births, deaths and other major events; and specific charges related to household economic activities. These taxes are not consistently or uniformly collected. If that were done, people would face an impossibly large tax burden. The tax code does not determine the tax burden, but rather provides public officials with a large armoury of potential levers that they can use to squeeze revenue from taxpayers. If one lever does not work, another may be used (Paler et al. 2017).

- Sudan is divided into 17 states and 133 districts. The state and district administrations levy a wide range of different taxes, licences, charges and fees. There are huge differences between localities. District authorities in North Kordofan state collect revenues from more than 50 main sources. In Bara district, more than 300 different categories of businesses are listed for licensing, each facing different licence rates depending on the type and size of business, location, social impact, and so on. In addition, a wide variety of fees are charged for official forms and permits. In some states, stamp duty is imposed on about 500 public documents, including invoices, receipts and title deeds. It is charged at various rates, some fixed and some *ad valorem*. Formally, stamp duty and similar charges are required for purposes of regulation. In practice, they are principally sources of income for the collectors. The distinction between *duties, licenses, charges, fees* and *taxes* is often unclear. A number of these levies are officially termed *charges*, but in reality they are taxes, since no service is rendered directly and exclusively to the payer (Fjeldstad 2016).

Local taxation is not always as exploitative and coercive as the examples above suggest. To some extent, the character of sub-national taxation and the extent and character of informal taxation reflect the nature of central state authority. If states exercise authority in a relatively stable and institutionalised fashion, and are able to 'broadcast' that authority over their more remote and rural populations, then local taxes are more likely to be more formal and regularised, and these nuisance taxes may be relatively rare. This seems broadly to be the case in much of Southern and Eastern Africa, in Ghana and in much of Ethiopia. The governments of Tanzania and Uganda have made considerable efforts to regularise local taxation, abolish some 'nuisance taxes', and establish more effective mechanisms for transferring central funds to local governments (Fjeldstad 2003; Fjeldstad and Therkildsen 2008). However, the fact remains that a great deal of local taxation in Africa, from a societal perspective, is dysfunctional and heavily coercive (Fjeldstad 2001; Fjeldstad and Semboja 2001; Fjeldstad and Therkildsen 2008).

Informal taxes

The prevalence of nuisance taxes is, in turn, closely related to the broader prevalence of *informal taxation* – a term that seems first to have been used in relation to Africa by the economist Rémy Prud'homme (1992). He was writing about the Democratic Republic of Congo (then called Zaire, and earlier simply the Congo). The Congo has never been ruled by an effective central political authority and has suffered recurrent and sometimes acute internal conflict since independence in 1960. Congolese public servants have routinely functioned as unofficial tax collectors simply to collect their salaries (ibid.: 4). Prud'homme distinguished six categories of informal taxation: *pinch* (misappropriation of money by authorised tax collectors), *extortion, requisition, contributions, gifts* and *donations* (to schools). He did not collect any statistics from either the collectors or their victims. His estimate that informal tax collections amounted to about 85% of total tax collections was based on anecdotal evidence and some simple arithmetic. However, contemporary evidence, summarised below, suggests that he may have been broadly right.

It is only recently that we have any reliable, survey-based evidence on the incidence of informal taxes in Africa – and that too is very limited. In 2013, 1,129 households located in 86 primary sampling units in three districts of Sierra Leone that had previously been affected by conflict were interviewed in detail about all the 'taxes', broadly defined, that they paid in the previous year, to either state or non-state actors (Jibao et al. 2017). The resulting estimates are conservative, in that they exclude: (1) levies paid in the form of labour rather than in cash or in kind; and (2) taxes paid by household members other than economically active household heads. The more significant findings are as follows:

- The average household paid 10% of income in taxes – though this excludes most payments related to accessing education, water or electricity, which were not covered by the survey.
- Of these payments, about 65% were reportedly paid to state authorities (including legally mandated payments to chiefs) and about 35% to non-state actors. While respondents viewed the vast majority of payments to local government officials as 'formal', in practice the levels of these payments were far larger than official government revenues, suggesting that much of what is collected is, in fact, informal – in that it either is used 'off budget' or simply enters the pockets of tax collectors.
- In its totality, the tax system was regressive. The 20% of households with the highest per capita incomes paid 7% of their incomes in tax, while the poorest 20% of households paid 16%. While the formal state taxes and user fees were slightly regressive, the informal and illegal levies were more so, often taking the form of flat-rate charges.[1]

- Nevertheless, attitudes to the informal taxes paid to chiefs and non-state actors were more positive than attitudes to payments to the state. Respondents felt that they obtained a better deal and a better return on these informal payments than on the money they handed over either to the remote central government or to their formal local government.[2] This mirrors findings from a smaller survey in Nigeria (Meagher 2016).

In 2015, a larger survey, managed by some of the same people, was conducted in the Kinshasa, North Kivu and Kasai Oriental provinces of the Democratic Republic of Congo (Paler et al. 2017). Approximately 2,400 households were surveyed, while a complementary smartphone reporting system made it possible to check the one-off survey results over a longer period of time. The main conclusions are listed below:

- On average, tax payments amounted to about 16% of total household expenditures. Earlier studies may have underestimated this value because respondents often forget to report smaller informal payments while responding to surveys. Those payments were captured by the smartphone reporting system.
- The overall tax burden was regressive, with poorer people paying a higher percentage of their income. User fees for essential services accounted for about a third of total tax payments.
- The researchers estimated that at least 70% – and quite likely 80% to 90% – of all tax payments, formal and informal, fail to reach the state, in the sense that they did not appear anywhere in official budgets. This is broadly in line with Prud'homme's 1992 estimate of 85% (see above).

Meanwhile, parallel research has focused more specifically on the emergence of such systems of informal taxation in rebel governed areas of the Democratic Republic of Congo, where taxation by armed groups is part extraction, part contribution to public goods, and part the construction of ties of mutual accountability between citizens and armed groups (Hoffmann et al. 2016).

There is a great deal of scope both to collect more information on informal taxes and to debate their significance. For example, is it appropriate to label as 'taxes' user fees for services such as education, health or water? There is no clear answer to this in principle. To the extent that Africans have some market-like choice among competitive providers of these services, then we might conclude that, while they reflect a kind of 'state failure', their substantial expenditures on these items are not equivalent to tax payments. However, it is clear that these payments form part of what it costs for citizens to access basic services that are often associated with (and claimed to be provided by) the state, and public authority is often used to extract revenue from users. Even if one were to prefer a term other than 'taxes', it is clear that these payments form a critical and overlooked part of local economic realities and are central to understanding local fiscal systems and local forms of political authority.

The sources of dysfunctional local taxation

These various deficiencies in local tax systems generally are not new. They have their roots in the colonial era and reflect enduring problems of establishing stable, effective and consensual political authority. Most colonial governments relied heavily on 'poll taxes' and taxes on imports, while formal structures of subnational revenue raising were very limited. Over time, taxes on property and small businesses were introduced into local government, drawing on models from Europe. All these various revenue sources have proven problematic. 'Poll taxes' were viewed as a legacy of oppressive colonial rule, and in any case were relatively arbitrary and locally unpopular (Fjeldstad and Therkildsen 2008; Kelsall 2000). Taxes on the local production of goods, while attractive as revenue sources, can impose heavy economic costs on producers and distort economies. They, too, have often been scaled back. Systems for valuing and taxing property have been overly complex, difficult to implement and prone to abuse, while small businesses and market traders came to be subject to the proliferating and sometime incoherent range of licences, fees and taxes described above.

The weakness of local taxation has been a reflection of – and has reinforced – the limited 'reach' of the formal state apparatus in many places. During the colonial period, the power that flowed through formal institutions was concentrated at the 'centre', while various more or less informal intermediaries held power locally. This pattern was frequently reproduced after independence (Young 1994). In countries that have experienced civil war, these trends have been further reinforced: local governments are poorly equipped to raise revenue through formal processes, but they may have the power to raise revenue informally. More recently, partly because they have been the prime beneficiaries of external support to strengthen tax systems, the revenue-collecting agencies of central government have had an advantage in exploiting opportunities to tap new sources of revenue. For example, while the business licensing system has generally languished, alternative means of taxing smaller business from capital cities, notably VAT, have expanded. In some countries, national tax administrations are beginning to collect property taxes – the classic revenue source for subnational governments. The result is that, in the face of tacit competition from better-resourced central tax administrations, many local governments have access to few good 'tax handles'. Given their reliance on fiscal transfers from central government and weak external oversight of their fiscal operations, they face weak incentives to collect revenue effectively.

There are then three broad reasons to reform small taxes – that is, subnational, small business and informal taxation:

- Many small taxes are damaging to the welfare of poor people. They are collected coercively, and are often regressive in their impact.

- Local governments are typically both under-resourced and, in some cases, financed through the exercise of coercion. This does not bode well for the prospects of democratic, accountable and effective local government.
- Small businesses are often overburdened with multiple, arbitrary, distorting and regressive taxes, while more generally small taxes fall too heavily on productive activities, where they are likely to be a disincentive to economic growth. If local taxes were shifted towards the ownership or occupation of real estate, especially in urban areas, the outcome would be more equitable and more efficient. Taxes on real estate generally have few negative effects on incentives to work and invest (see below).

Critically, the reform of small taxes should not be read simply as a call to expand revenue collection. As should be clear by now, where informal burdens are already heavy, particularly on the poor, the core challenge may lie in simplification, reducing the burdens on poorer people, making systems more progressive, and bringing informal payments to state agents into state accounts and budgets.

Reforming small taxes

The challenges to effective reform of small taxes are substantial. There are wide variations, both among and within countries, in the urgency of various problems and in the opportunities to address them. Further, we have rather few analytic cases studies of effective reform. The literature on small taxes is much better at identifying the problems, and in signalling what in general should be done, than at telling us how it could be done in the face of the inevitable political obstacles. The remainder of this chapter is not a reform manifesto, but highlights those issues on which likely reformers – whether from central or local governments, the tax professions, the electorate or civil society – might best concentrate their efforts.

Abolishing nuisance taxes

The huge range of nuisance taxes found at local levels raise relatively little revenue while multiplying burdens on low-income taxpayers, expanding the scope for corruption, increasing confusion, and undermining the potential for constructive bargaining between taxpayers and the state. It would be useful if civil society organisations were to draw up lists of the worst nuisance taxes and then campaign for their abolition. They would likely start with levies such as bicycle taxes, bicycle registration fees, pushcart fees, cattle trekking fees or, as in Hargeisa, Somaliland, separate local levies on camels and camel hooves. The evidence suggests that eliminating these nuisance taxes would have little impact on local revenues, and potentially significant benefits in reducing informality and attendant abuses and economic costs. In North Kivu province, in the Democratic Republic of Congo, for example, local governments in principle have the right to collect more than 400 categories of payments. But more than 90% of those categories raise either no revenue at all or less than $50,000 in total. Meanwhile, almost 70% of all revenue comes from only ten categories. This is an extreme case, but even cursory examinations of local government finances elsewhere quickly reveal lists of taxes that generate very little revenue but create potentially significant costs, and may best be eliminated.

Taxing small firms more effectively and equitably[3]

Concerns are sometimes raised in Africa about the apparent under-taxation of small businesses in the informal sector. As we explain above, these concerns appear overstated. Many small firms may pay as much, or more, than some larger firms, relative to their size, once one accounts for the ability of larger firms to use their accounting practices to reduce their effective tax liabilities, and the wide range of smaller licences, fees, levies and informal taxes that smaller firms confront.[4] In addition, there is evidence that compliance costs – the hassle and expense of actually paying taxes – are often higher for smaller firms (Coolidge 2012).

There is a compelling case for making small business taxation more efficient and equitable – and thus more likely to drive broad improvements in growth and governance. A degree of standardisation would be a good start. In a study of small and medium-sized enterprises in Zambia, Misch et al. found that the effective tax burden varied substantially. Enterprises faced a range of different taxes, fees and licences, and the types of taxes to which firms were subject differed not only between sectors but also between firms within the same sector. Even among market traders in the same municipality, the type of fees and levies paid sometimes varied substantially (2011).

Several African countries, including Kenya, Tanzania, Uganda and the Democratic Republic of Congo, have reformed or are in the process of reforming their local business licence systems, to make them simpler, more transparent, and more effective.[5] The main objectives are to enable local authorities to collect significantly more revenues, and to reduce the compliance burden on the businesses. In the late 1990s, Kenya pioneered a more customer-oriented single business permit system, which has since become a model for other countries in the region. Businesses are required to have only one business permit for each business location regardless of the range of activities carried out there – hence the term 'single business permit'. Local authorities are required to establish 'one-stop shops' where permits will be issued immediately on payment of the appropriate fee. The tariff structure is progressive, with smaller businesses paying less than larger ones. The system provides a standard tariff structure for all local authorities, but allows individual local governments discretion over the actual tariff rates. There are also improvements in administration, including a simplified single business permit registration form. The time required to obtain business permits has been reduced substantially. This has cut business compliance costs, but not necessarily the total costs to business, since the rates have been raised. Although there have been implementation challenges, the experience has been fairly positive:

more revenue for local authorities; reduced compliance costs for business; and fewer opportunities for rent seeking and corruption (Devas and Kelly 2001).

The larger question for many governments, however, is how much emphasis to place on taxing smaller firms. Critics point out that the administrative cost of collecting taxes from small businesses may be almost equal to the actual revenue collected. These taxes may thus represent an additional burden on already poor individuals, with significant scope for additional harassment and extraction, but with minimal revenue accruing to the state. For proponents, taxing small firms – even at quite a nominal level – may have broader benefits: bringing growing firms into the tax net; encouraging compliance by larger firms; supporting formalisation and potential growth benefits; and spurring organisation and political engagement by smaller firms because they have to pay taxes. There is some evidence to support this latter perspective, but the realisation of these benefits depends on whether the expansion of small business taxation is accompanied by increased legal security, reduced costs, better access to markets, equitable application, and the scope for engagement with government. In practice, these broader benefits are realised infrequently, and a focus on these complementary measures is likely to be essential to generating such benefits – as well as to encouraging compliance among these small firms. In virtually all circumstances, higher taxes on small firms are likely to reduce the rate of firm creation, and are therefore likely to reduce economic growth. New entrepreneurs typically find taxpaying more costly and problematic than established businesses do.

It is equally important to deal with the question of how responsibility for taxing small firms should be allocated between central and local tax agencies. At present, small firms often face overlapping demands from multiple tax collectors. And while the revenue generated from taxing small firms may be small from the perspective of national governments, that same revenue could be significant if transferred to subnational governments (Joshi et al. 2014).

Making more use of property taxes

There are a number of methods of taxing property. One of the more common is to levy a tax when ownership changes through either sale or inheritance. Another is the taxation of rental income, although this is formally a tax on income rather than on property itself. Some jurisdictions levy taxes on the construction of new properties. We focus here on the most widespread and promising means of taxing property: recurrent (normally annual) taxes on (some measure of) the value of real estate (land and buildings). These are typically termed 'property taxes'. In most of the world – although not everywhere in Africa – property taxes are collected and owned by local government. In the Francophone countries of West Africa, the property tax generally is designed and administered by the central government, with some form of revenue-sharing arrangement with local governments (Monkam 2011). Some Anglophone countries, including Rwanda, Tanzania and the Gambia, have recently explored similar models. Elsewhere, collection is undertaken locally, but the valuation of properties remains under the control of central valuations offices.

On balance, the evidence suggests that recurrent property taxes are best collected by local governments, or through cooperative arrangements with central governments in which local governments maintain the lead role. Over the medium term, this appears to hold the greatest potential to raise sustainable revenue while achieving broader governance benefits. Property taxes provide a stable income source for local governments. Unlike taxes on incomes or sales, the base for property taxes is immobile. Property taxes also have the most potential for encouraging greater local self-reliance. Because they are highly visible to taxpayers, and in principle linked to improved local services, property taxes have the capacity to act as a foundation for bargaining between taxpayers and local governments over revenue and public spending (Chapter 8). In the same spirit, because property taxes require the collection of accurate data on local assets and systematic record keeping and organisation, they can spur broader improvements in local administration (Chapter 8). And local governments have the greatest incentives to collect property taxes well – and fairly – because they are potentially such a large source of local revenues.

Not only are property taxes an especially appropriate source of funding for local governments, they are also, as economists agree, one of the best kinds of taxes for governments to collect. First, a property tax generally makes a tax system more progressive, because it is usually wealthier people who own more property. Second, because it is a tax on wealth, rather than on productive activities, property tax does not undermine the incentives to work or create wealth. In fact, many economists argue that property and other recurrent wealth taxes encourage a more productive use of wealth and property (Norregaard 2013; McCluskey et al. 2013; Kelly 2013; Bahl et al. 2008; Bird and Slack 2006).

The potential yield from property taxes is increasing steadily in Africa, as is the need to realise that potential. Populations, especially urban populations, are increasing faster in sub-Saharan Africa than in any other world region (World Bank 2016e). This creates huge challenges for urban governance and service delivery, and a sound revenue system is an essential precondition for handling these challenges. At the same time, the values of land and property – above all *urban* land and property – are growing fast. Investors are increasingly drawn towards high-value property development, which promise much better returns and lighter taxation than other investment options (Zinnbauer 2017). Five African property markets are ranked today among the top ten most dynamic emerging markets for real estate and property investments (Jones Lang LaSalle 2015). For example, property prices in the centre of Addis Ababa are beginning to rival those in cities such as New York and Geneva (Goodfellow 2015). A wealth of impressionistic and anecdotal evidence suggests that, while a few mega-rich people in Africa use offshore devices of various kinds to shelter their wealth, the vast majority of modestly or significantly wealthy people do not bother. They simply accumulate real estate, secure in the knowledge that it will be little taxed, either recurrently or at the points of purchase and sale (Chapter 6). Effective urban real estate[6] taxes would not only promote economic efficiency and provide subnational governments with revenue sources that they currently lack (Goodfellow 2017; Fjeldstad et al. 2017); they would also make tax systems less regressive and unfair.[7]

One would therefore like to see in Africa vibrant systems of recurrent property taxation principally managed by and serving to fund subnational governments – from the administrations of metropolitan cities down to smaller towns. Why, then, is property tax not more heavily exploited in Africa?[8] Bell and Bowman (2006) list some of the more immediate and visible reasons:

- with the exceptions of Botswana, Namibia and South Africa, property markets are not well developed;
- property registers and valuation rolls are often outdated or not in place;
- administrative capacity and equipment are often limited; and
- the tax base is generally narrowed by extensive legal exemptions.

This, in turn, is frequently a reflection of the deep political resistance to strong property taxation, as well as inherited (and dysfunctional) colonial legacies in the way in which property tax administration is set up. There are also challenges arising from the ambiguity of land rights in many African cities. Without clear land rights, it is hard to assign clear responsibility for paying property taxes (Goodfellow 2015; Goodfellow and Owen 2018). In smaller towns, where communal landholding is more common and property markets almost non-existent, property tax administrators need to be sensitive to the possibility of a weak correspondence at household level between asset holdings and income. Households that seem to have more assets may have little capacity to pay.

There is likely always to be some disagreement between those observers who are impressed by the formidable administrative and legal obstacles to establishing effective property systems and those who argue that these problems could be solved if politicians wanted to solve them. There is, however, no doubt that the political resistance to property taxes is strong, in Africa as elsewhere. Real estate is a primary means of accumulating wealth in much of Africa. Effective property taxes impact directly on wealthy people, and people with considerable property wealth usually have considerable political power. As argued by Burgess and Stern (1993: 802) more than two decades ago, low utilisation of property and land taxation 'reflects the success of the resistance of the rich and powerful to measures which harm their interests'.

Nevertheless, many efforts have been made to reform property taxes in Africa. Franzsen and Youngman (2009) counted a dozen reforms at national level in Anglophone Africa between 1997 and 2009. Recent research in Ghana, Sierra Leone and Tanzania (Jibao and Prichard 2016; Franzsen and McCluskey 2017) suggests that significant, and relatively rapid, improvements in property tax collection are possible even in relatively low-capacity environments. The most inspiring success story comes from Lagos State in Nigeria. On the surface it presented an unlikely site for tax reform: Nigeria's governments have shown little interest in building a stronger tax system – or even in maintaining the one in place – since they began to enjoy oil wealth in the early 1970s. In addition, widespread corruption and uncertain land rights posed practical barriers to reform. However, successive Lagos State governors made expanding revenue a priority as part of a push to reduce fiscal reliance on the central government (ruled by a different political party) and to remake Lagos as a modern metropolis. Despite significant hurdles, and an enormously complex setting, major gains have been achieved, above all in collecting income tax but also in introducing an automated system for property tax administration and a simple, predictable arrangement for property valuation. Tax compliance has increased greatly, as have income and property tax revenues (Cheeseman and de Gramont 2017; Goodfellow and Owen 2018). While each case of successful reform is different, some useful general lessons emerge.

First, property tax can be represented as a highly complex activity that requires high-level expertise, especially in identifying and valuing properties. Existing valuation systems, which sometimes have their origins in colonial rule, can be excessively intricate and demanding. But valuation and other aspects of property tax can be simplified to match local capacities. There is growing evidence that simplified valuation methods, based on measurable and observable physical features of properties (including locations), can be effective, low cost and implemented by locally trained staff lacking experience or high-level education. By building capacity for local valuation, bottlenecks are eliminated, authority is given to the actors most interested in success, costs are reduced and sustainability is increased.

Second, advances in IT mean that the processes of property identification, valuation, billing and tax collection can be computerised to varying degrees, especially in urban areas, but also in small and remote towns – though the latter is relatively rare to date. Technology is not, of course, a solution on its own, but it can be an invaluable tool. For example, geographic information system tools can be used to help identify properties, IT systems can implement formulas to translate observable features of properties into valuations and automate billing, and IT may increasingly offer improved options for making payments (Lall et al. 2017). It can also, particularly in more sophisticated urban areas, be progressively used to link basic revenue administration functions, including database maintenance, billing and enforcement, with other revenue sources such as business permits, property registers, house rents, land rents and user charges for water and electricity. Yet, in practice, technological solutions appear to fail at least as often as they succeed. Research suggests that success is more likely when:

- the technology is kept simple, so that it can be used effectively, and without errors, by local staff, to do what is essential;
- costs are kept low by relying on simple, low-cost solutions – be they open source international options, or locally developed systems – that avoid the high fees typically charged by international firms;[9] and
- the technology is brought close to users. Relatively low-skilled staff are very capable of managing a computerised system, but only if it is designed with their needs in mind, if they are given hands-on training, and if local support is available when needed (Prichard 2015).

Third, new or enhanced property tax payments need to be linked to public spending and citizen benefits, both in citizens' minds and in reality. Because the primary barriers to improved property taxes are political, successful reform is likely to depend on building popular support for new taxation – which is consistently difficult where trust in political authorities is low. The clearest route to building such trust and support lies in drawing clear and visible connections between expanded revenue and specific public spending – even if the targets of that public spending are initially modest. At one extreme, governments in very low-trust environments may find it useful to earmark revenue for specific activities in order to create a clear benchmark for building public trust. In any case, this is likely to demand more than simply making budget information publicly available. It also requires explicit outreach activities, including public meetings, radio shows, and visible support from influential local figures (Jibao and Prichard 2015; 2016).

Fourth, there is a range of tactics that are likely to help reformers overcome the inevitable political resistance to reform:

- If a property tax system is being established from scratch, focus on building a local organisation for implementing and administering it. The staff can become a very important supportive constituency.

- Make the processes of reform and property valuation transparent, including by educating taxpayers on the rationale, procedures, obligations and responsibilities related to property tax.
- Explain and communicate continually to the public and to the people affected.
- Ensure that local elites are seen to pay their fair share of reformed property taxes.
- Be selective and opportunistic in supporting local leaders who are motivated to implement sustainable reform.
- Do not seek perfection. Focus first on constructing a workable system that generates additional revenue and is broadly seen as fair. Once 'money is on the table', policymakers and taxpayers may be more likely to focus their attention on ironing out problems and achieving further gains.

The gender dimensions of small and informal taxes

There has been growing interest in the gender dimensions of taxation in Africa. The ways in which the issue has been articulated to date sometimes mirror too closely the experiences of high-income countries (Joshi 2017). There, the personal income tax (PIT) regime has been a major concern. For example, if women's PIT liabilities are in one way or another amalgamated with those of their marriage partners, women can be disadvantaged. But concerns about potential biases in PIT regimes have very little traction in most of Africa, where few people pay PIT and those who do mainly pay it on their employment incomes through PAYE (Chapter 6). It is possible that a gender audit of the taxes collected by many African revenue authorities would conclude that they embody a bias against men, because men are the main consumers of the alcohol and tobacco on which most African governments levy excise taxes – although, of course, this spending on alcohol and tobacco may come at the expense of their families.

Understanding the links between gender and tax in Africa requires greater attention to local contexts, rather than simply importing debates and concerns from elsewhere. On the basis of evidence that remains largely fragmentary and anecdotal, we believe that biases against women in African tax systems are likely to be most pronounced at the level of tax administration rather than tax policy – and for that reason possibly hard to change. There are, however, signs of progress at the level of central government tax administrations. Although their staff are still dominantly male, new recruits include more women (African Tax Administration Forum 2017: 143–5). The only information we have on the implications of this for organisational performance comes from an ongoing study conducted on and by the Uganda Revenue Authority (URA). Women account for a higher proportion of staff in the URA – almost 40% – than in any other tax administration in Africa.[10] The URA has also been led by female commissioners-general since 2004. Initial results from the URA research indicate that women employees on average receive higher scores in their annual performance evaluations and leave their jobs less frequently than males. More research is needed, but these findings are at least consistent with the belief that the presence of a critical minimum number of women in an organisation can boost organisational performance. But will a more balanced gender ratio in tax collection organisations help with what we suspect to be the more important issue about gender and tax in Africa: disadvantages suffered by women taxpayers, above all in the 'small taxes' domain?

The evidence on this is fragmentary and often anecdotal, and the conclusions so far have been mixed. There have been – and to some extent remain – some biases against men. The poll tax and the successor local taxes that are still collected in some localities were and are levied almost exclusively on men. In East Africa it was male defaulters who were treated badly, experiencing imprisonment and forced labour under harsh conditions (Fjeldstad and Therkildsen 2008). Conversely, we know that a disproportionate burden of local taxes often falls on market traders. Insofar as women are over-represented among traders, which is true on much of the continent, this would constitute an implicit bias against women – although it is less clear whether female traders are generally exploited more than male traders. We know that very large amounts of money are extracted illegally from traders who cross Africa's national borders (Amin and Hoppe 2013; Bilangna and Djeuwo 2013; Cantens 2012b; Cuvelier and Mumbunda 2013; Titeca 2009; Titeca and Kimanuka 2012). But do women traders fare worse than men? Titeca and Kimanuka explored this question in the Great Lakes region. Their respondents reported that women and men were (mis)treated alike, and suggested that women were actually better at negotiating with their tormentors. Men found the humiliation harder to bear (2012: 34–6). From similar research on Sierra Leone's borders with Guinea and Liberia, Jibao et al. found evidence that women were *less* likely to have goods confiscated, but, in relation to tax – as in other spheres of life – they were more likely to experience physical or sexual harassment (2017). The recent study of informal taxation in the Democratic Republic of Congo revealed that female-headed households paid more in formal and informal taxes, broadly defined, than male-headed households. But this was primarily because they paid more in informal user fees for services such as health and education. It is unclear whether this indicates heavier extraction from women, or their greater consumption of public services – although the latter would suggest the added costs to women of systems in which the financing of public goods is heavily informal and private (Paler et al. 2017).

In the same vein, we conclude with the results of a recent study on the taxation of market traders in Dar es Salaam.[11] The researchers found that, while men and women paid the same taxes and fees to trade in markets, a major cost of doing business was the charge to use toilets, and this was a much heavier burden for women traders, especially pregnant women, than for men. From a narrow perspective, we could conclude that there is no gender bias in taxation in this case. But we are interested in taxes not for their own sake, but because of the public services they might fund, and their broader societal impacts and implications. In the Dar es Salaam markets we see a failure to provide a basic and inescapable public service at a reasonable cost, resulting in heavier informal payments by women. Whether this failure stems from problems in public revenue collection or revenue use, women are disadvantaged. It is impossible usefully to debate the gender dimensions of taxation without straying beyond the narrowly defined boundaries of tax collection. Instead, it seems necessary to us to consider the broader provision and funding of public services, and how the costs of accessing them differ by gender. Debates will be contentious. But that is to be welcomed; it should help generate the research that is needed. Until that research tells us otherwise, we assume that there are likely to be net biases against women in revenue systems in Africa, broadly defined; that those biases often take the form of verbal, physical or sexual harassment; that they may not always be very evident to the external observer or to someone adopting an accountant's perspective on taxation; and that, in most cases, they are embedded in the informality of tax collection in the 'small taxes' domains.

Conclusions

There is evidence that reforms to small taxes can produce positive results. Repeated citizen surveys in Tanzania indicate that people have become more positive about local taxation (Fjeldstad et al. 2009). This was due partly to improvements in service delivery, particularly in education, health, and law and order, but also partly the result of reforms that led to less oppressive local revenue collection and the abolition of some nuisance taxes. Further, the reforms led to more citizen engagement around taxes. There was, for instance, an increasing demand for information on revenues collected and how the revenues were spent. In Sierra Leone, property tax collection increased several fold over a five-year period after the implementation of a simple reform programme – and in some locations this was matched by improved local services and significant popular support for reform (Jibao and Prichard 2016.)

A great deal of reform is needed. We suggest that four issues should be considered for priority action:

- curbing nuisance taxes – although this will inevitably generate opposition from the people who collect them and those who benefit indirectly from collection;
- using property taxes more extensively;
- taxing small firms more fairly, consistently and efficiently; and
- reducing the incidence of informal taxes – while recognising that they are very diverse in character and implication, and that some represent useful ways of funding public goods and services in situations where formal state agencies are unable to provide them.

The best approaches to deal with these issues are likely to vary, because the problems are diverse, as are the contexts in which they appear. Further, there is considerable interdependence among both the problems and the solutions. For example, one reason why subnational governments depend so much on nuisance taxes and informal taxes is that they lack alternative revenue sources. The best way to abolish nuisance taxes might be first to develop alternatives – a local property tax base or more consistent and predictable fiscal transfers from central to local government – before attempting prohibition. Solutions need to be sought through local experience and experimentation. We can, however, be sure that success in reforming small taxes will in large part depend on the broader institutional and fiscal environment.

One aspect of this broader reform story surrounds the willingness of central authorities to provide support. If we take into account only formal taxes, Africa tends to be a continent of fiscally centralised countries: central governments account for a very high proportion of both revenue collection and spending. External involvement in revenue issues has tended to exacerbate this imbalance, with aid donors and providers of technical assistance such as the IMF focusing on improving central revenue systems. The small scale and informality of many subnational revenue systems in Africa make it difficult for international organisations to engage effectively.[12] It is not clear whether, in many African countries, there is a strong will or drive to change this situation at the level of central government agencies. But without central support – in the form of technical capacity, wider opportunities for local governments to tax more 'juicy' revenue sources, and a combination of local autonomy with some central regulatory oversight – local tax reform will be very difficult.

Control over property taxes is becoming an increasingly important issue in the fiscal relationships between central and local governments. It is a sign of the growing interest in property taxes that in recent years national revenue authorities in Ethiopia, Rwanda and Tanzania have taken over collection from subnational governments, to varying degrees. This option is being discussed in other countries. In the short term, central revenue authorities are able to deploy digital technologies and perhaps reduce the degree to which local elites are able to evade property taxes. On the other hand, they may have higher operating costs and weak incentives to collect property taxes in poorer and less urban localities, they may lack local knowledge and sensitivity, and they are badly placed to connect property tax compliance with improved local services. At a minimum, careful attention needs to be paid to the implications of changing the relationship between central and local tax collection. Is this just another step in the process of central authorities taking for themselves the more 'juicy' revenue sources that subnational governments should be developing? And may this weaken local governments, and the broader bonds between citizens and their governments?

Finally, the structure of systems of intergovernmental transfers is likely to shape incentives to reform. Worldwide, it is very common to find that: subnational governments are very dependent on transfers from central government (or some other higher level); the formulae for allocating transfers between individual subnational jurisdictions are complex and poorly understood; and actual transfers are unpredictable and shaped by partisan political considerations. This is broadly the situation in Africa. These transfers are certain to remain critical to local financing for the foreseeable future, and strengthening them is thus important to broader reform. In part, this means ensuring that they should be adequate and predictable, which is frequently not the case (Jibao 2009; Fjeldstad et al. 2010).[13] It also means paying attention to how they shape incentives for local tax collection. Where transfers are too small, or unpredictable, they can weaken local institutions and increase inequality. But where transfers are large, and completely unconnected to the performance of local government, local politicians have little incentive to build local revenue capacity. Linking transfers to revenue-raising performance is thus attractive in the abstract, but it raises challenges around how to assess local tax effort while avoiding the risk of incentivising highly coercive local extraction designed solely to access expanded transfers (Fjeldstad 2001). Finding a reasonable balance in supporting, encouraging and incentivising local tax reform will remain a very challenging task.

Chapter 8

DOES TAXATION LEAD TO IMPROVED GOVERNANCE?[1]

Much of this book has focused on a simple question: how can governments build stronger and more equitable tax systems? Raising more revenue is not inherently a good thing. It is desirable only if governments translate additional public revenue into valuable goods and services that improve public welfare. Often, this does not happen. Historically, many governments have extracted revenue from citizens while offering little in return. Opinion surveys suggest that many Africans perceive that this is what is happening today. They see taxation as important to national development, and express a willingness to pay more taxes if they receive services in return. But when asked whether they currently think that their government uses revenue effectively, the majorities in most countries say 'no' (Aiko and Logan 2014). This raises an important question: if we contribute to strengthening African tax systems, might we simply help unaccountable governments extract even more money from citizens and businesses, while offering little in return?

Proponents of higher levels of taxation in Africa need a compelling argument that new tax revenue will indeed be translated into public benefits. Even corrupt and unaccountable governments benefiting from higher revenues might use some of them for good public purposes. But there is a wider argument about why higher taxes may benefit citizens in the long term: over time, increased tax collection may generate pressure for governments to strengthen state institutions and become more accountable to taxpayers. Put differently, when governments are forced to rely more for their incomes on taxes from their own citizens – as opposed to natural resource revenues or foreign aid – there may be more popular demands for governments to use that revenue effectively, and incentives for governments to be responsive to those demands. In fact, the expansion of taxation may lead to improvements in the performance of governments in three ways:

- It can create incentives for governments to promote economic growth, as a way of expanding the tax base.
- It can spur improvements in the quality of public administration more generally, to facilitate tax collection.
- It can be a catalyst for mobilising and empowering citizens to demand greater reciprocity and accountability from governments, while encouraging governments to be responsive in order to encourage tax compliance.

Increased taxation may provide the spark for improving the quality of government and for building a 'fiscal social contract' between taxpayers and governments.

We have evidence that these types of positive connections have actually occurred in Africa. In Ghana in 1995, for example, the weakly democratic government attempted to introduce a new VAT, only to face unprecedented national protests, which forced it to withdraw the tax. This show of popular opposition not only pushed the government to hold more open elections the subsequent year, but also saw it earmark subsequent increases in the tax for popular social programmes (Prichard 2009; 2015). In a similar fashion, the introduction of a new property tax regime by Bo City Council in Sierra Leone in 2008 led the council to emphasise the connections between taxation and increases in spending on popular items – thus ensuring that taxpayers would reap benefits from their extra contributions (Jibao and Prichard 2015). More recently there is evidence that the extension of the same property tax reform to smaller towns in Sierra Leone has been accompanied by improvements in service provision, and expanded political knowledge among taxpayers (Prichard et al. forthcoming).

However, the idea that taxation contributes to state building and government accountability is also potentially misleading. While the possibility of a positive link is very attractive, the reality is far from simple. In Ghana, the earmarking of revenues for health and education was not in itself a guarantee that those revenues would be used as promised, or used productively. The success that has been enjoyed has depended on the creation of monitoring institutions, and continuous oversight by civil society. Similarly, the 2008 tax reforms in Bo City Council, Sierra Leone, now seem to be under threat. Concerns that public money is being misused are being voiced. These examples highlight the need to consistently monitor and reinforce fiscal contracts linking taxation to effective services. They also point to the risk that a naive belief in the potential for taxes to stimulate broader governance benefits can lead to an uncritical embrace of increased taxation as a goal in itself. Increases in taxes have sometimes led to more widespread governance improvements, but in other cases they have done little except hurt the livelihoods of the poor and increase inequality. During the colonial period, the expansion of taxation by colonial powers was associated with the strengthening of control and coercion – and, in some cases, significant violence – rather than improved governance (Gardner 2012). More recently, research has stressed the difficulties encountered by so-called informal sector businesses – and particularly those led by more marginalised groups – in mobilising collectively to demand reciprocity for their tax payments (Meagher 2016; Prichard and van den Boogaard 2017).

The bottom line from recent research is that the emergence of positive connections between taxation and the quality of governance is critically dependent on *how* tax is collected and on the political and institutional context. Potential benefits do not emerge automatically but are rooted in power and political relationships – and, more specifically, in the ability of taxpayers, and their allies, to successfully demand fairer rules, stronger institutions and greater reciprocity from governments. The most interesting question is thus not *whether* taxes can lead to improved governance, but *what kinds* of bargains are likely in different contexts, *how* these positive outcomes may be encouraged, and *how* coercive or destructive outcomes can be avoided. Supporters of increased taxation need also to focus on fairness, equity, transparency and popular engagement around tax collection.

Linking taxation to improved governance

The idea that taxation may drive state building and improved governance was once controversial but has quickly come to be widely accepted. In some contexts it has almost reached the status of conventional wisdom. It is assumed either that governments that are dependent only on taxes for revenue are likely to be more accountable to taxpayers, or that tax increases will generate more accountability and a stronger social contract. These claims frequently lack supporting evidence and a plausible explanation of how and why taxes have beneficial effects. It thus seems useful to sketch the tax–governance arguments more precisely.

Prominent sociologists were arguing more than a century ago that the way in which governments raised their revenue was critical to understanding the ways in which they governed (Moore 2004). Classic accounts of the emergence of modern European states have long emphasised the ways in which the need to expand tax collection contributed to building improved public administration and greater accountability to taxpayers. Perhaps most famously, the idea is captured in the American revolutionary slogan 'No taxation without representation' – or, more precisely, by its implied inverse: 'No representation without taxation.'[2] However, it is only comparatively recently that taxation has begun to figure prominently in discussions of politics and development in Africa and other low-income regions.

There are three distinct ways in which the need for states to tax – instead of relying on revenues from 'captive' sources such as oil or foreign aid – may drive improved governance. We label them *common interest* processes, *state apparatus* processes, and *accountability and responsiveness* processes (Prichard 2010: 13), and we address each in turn.

Common interest processes are based on the idea that where governments are dependent on taxes, and therefore on the prosperity of taxpayers, they will have stronger incentives to promote economic growth. This possibility, which in some ways is the most intuitively appealing, has been studied the least. All else being equal, where a government needs tax revenue, it will have a stronger interest in encouraging the prosperity of taxpayers. The wealthier taxpayers become, the larger the potential tax revenue (see, for example, Bates 2008).

State apparatus processes are founded on the proposition that dependence on taxes, especially direct taxes, requires states to develop a complex bureaucratic apparatus for tax collection, which may in turn become the leading edge of far-reaching improvements in public administration. Collecting taxes is complex and requires new organisational systems, collaboration among government agencies, and the effective socialisation and disciplining of staff. The push to strengthen taxation might thus also encourage extensive improvements in public administration – including in important areas such as justice, land rights and public service delivery. This argument is rooted in historical experience in Europe, where the need to strengthen tax administration prompted improvements in a range of other areas of public administration. What might these state apparatus processes look like in contemporary developing countries? Recent writing suggests three possibilities (Brautigam 2008; Chaudhry 1997; Prichard and Leonard 2010; Prichard 2010):

- *Demonstration effects*: Investments in modernising tax agencies can set new standards for other parts of the public service with respect to issues such as meritocratic recruitment, opportunities for career advancement, performance measurement, or IT and data sharing.
- *Spillover effects*: A state wishing to tax more will be forced to invest in building a strong tax agency, but also in strengthening parallel agencies, including ministries of finance, business registration, land registration, property valuation, the police and the judiciary.
- *Information-sharing effects*: Data gathered by tax agencies can be used to help other state agencies, for example to improve economic policymaking, target public services more effectively, or enforce the law (Gavin et al. 2013; Pieterse et al. 2016).

Finally, most attention has been paid to the possibility that taxation may stimulate *accountability and responsiveness processes*: the experience of taxation leads taxpayers to demand reciprocity from government, while governments have incentives to respond to those demands in exchange for tax compliance. On the one hand, a government seeking to raise more tax revenue will face greater pressure to make concessions to taxpayers, in order to overcome potential resistance and increase compliance. On the other hand, the more taxes citizens are required to pay, the more likely they are to assert ownership over those revenues and demand something in return – and the more political leverage they will enjoy in making those demands, owing to the possibility that they will resist or evade current or future taxes. Put more simply, the need for governments to raise more taxes may increase the relative power of taxpayers in seeking reciprocity from governments – a process of implicit or explicit negotiation often referred to as 'tax bargaining' (Moore 2008).

The term 'tax bargaining' may evoke an image of taxpayers and government engaged in open, direct negotiation about what taxes should be paid, and what government might concede in return. This kind of thing sometimes occurs. However, bargaining processes are more likely to be what social scientists sometimes term 'strategic interaction': they are implicit and indirect, and possibly long term and conflictual. Taxpayers and governments behave according to how they believe the other party might react, and they adjust their behaviour in the light of experience. Improved outcomes may emerge only after periods of protracted conflict, with continuous resistance by taxpayers eventually giving way to positive reform. That reform might not be openly discussed or agreed, but simply emerge from the processes of interaction and the search for less conflictual ways of meeting joint objectives (Moore 2007; Tilly 1992: 98–9). The unifying logic of these processes of 'tax bargaining' lies in the claim that pressure for responsive and accountable governance is increased by virtue of governments needing to raise revenues from their own citizens.

Research has identified various specific dimensions of tax bargaining: *direct tax bargaining, tax resistance and changes in government*, and *expanded political capabilities of taxpayers* (Prichard 2015):

- *Direct tax bargaining* occurs when governments make relatively explicit concessions to taxpayers. Concessions may be made pre-emptively, prior to attempting to introduce new taxes, or later in response to popular protests or resistance to taxation. These concessions may range from new or improved public services through to the strengthening of institutions of representation and accountability. Useful examples come from Ghana. As noted above, protests against the introduction of VAT in 1995 put pressure on the government to become more transparent and democratic in the lead-up to subsequent elections. In later years, the government twice earmarked increases in the VAT rate to specific public services – a Ghana Education Trust Fund, and a National Health Insurance Scheme. In both cases the element of reciprocity was clear: the government would dedicate some of its additional revenues to popular public services in exchange for public acceptance of new taxes.

State–citizen interactions about taxation are rarely as consensual or as subject to explicit debate as in the Ghana case. More often, governments introduce and (attempt to) collect new or higher taxes without significant consultations with or concessions to the public or potential taxpayers. Over the short or medium term, these processes may involve significant extraction and coercion. However, a full understanding of the links between taxation, responsiveness and accountability demands an exploration of the potential political consequences of these more protracted conflicts.

• One possibility is a process of *tax resistance and changes in government*. In many cases in Africa and elsewhere, taxpayers have actively resisted attempts to increase taxes, especially attempts made by unpopular governments, either through protest or tax avoidance and evasion. In the short term, this leads to conflict and reduced revenue. But over the long term, this type of tax resistance can make it difficult for (unpopular) governments to raise revenue and thus it can increase the pressure for changes in government and/or new concessions to taxpayers. In the lead-up to the Kenyan general elections of 2002, the increasingly unpopular Moi government found that tax collection levels were plummeting. While this partly reflected the weak performance of the national economy, senior government officials were sure that the revenue decline reflected an implicit opposition strategy to reduce state income. Ultimately, the Moi government lost power, and the new government pursued significant reform – including clearer links between taxes and expenditure. A similar pattern played out around the 2000 elections in Ghana. This pattern appears to be replicated more generally, as cross-country analysis indicates that revenue often declines most rapidly in advance of elections where incumbent governments are particularly unpopular (Prichard 2018). Indeed, recent research suggests that increasing resistance to taxation – and expanding anti-tax protests – played a role in hastening the end of colonial rule in some countries (Gardner 2012).

- An alternative possibility is that tax increases may help to *expand the political capabilities of taxpayers* through the formation and mobilisation of civil society groups. The failure of governments to respond positively to the political mobilisation of citizens around tax issues might provoke the creation or mobilisation of new civil society actors, and thus strengthen the ability of citizens to demand responsiveness from governments over the long term. In Ghana, for example, the 1995 anti-tax protests mentioned earlier not only contributed to immediate improvements in transparency and democracy, but also saw the creation of a powerful advocacy network, the Committee for Joint Action, which remained a regular feature of popular demands for improved services and greater democracy in the two succeeding decades. Elsewhere, in many cases agitation around new or unpopular taxation appears to have helped strengthen business associations, both large and small. They in turn have sought to engage government over a wider range of political issues (Prichard 2015; Meagher 2016).

The bottom line is that 'tax bargaining' may sometimes be obvious, and may be reflected in mutually beneficial exchanges between government and taxpayers. But it is more often a part of the messier, and more conflictual, reality of politics. Tax systems often remain relatively extractive and coercive. The promise made by proponents of expanded taxation is that, over time, taxation can also act as an additional stimulus to public mobilisation, and can be an extra lever through which taxpayers may gain power in seeking improved outcomes. But does this promise hold true in practice?

Does taxation lead to improved governance in practice?

Researchers, policymakers and practitioners are now regularly presented with compelling but very general stories about the ways in which expanded taxation may improve governance. It is only recently that research has begun to break these broad arguments into more specific claims that can be tested by research and applied in practice.

Taxation and economic growth

There is relatively little research evidence on the (potential) links between tax and the incentives for governments to promote economic growth. Some researchers have argued that the need for revenue was an important driver of economic growth in parts of South East Asia in recent decades (Doner et al. 2005). Perhaps the most intriguing evidence has come from China. Some scholars argue that, when national tax policy changes made local governments more reliant on their own tax revenue, they responded by making more efforts to accelerate local economic growth (Jin et al. 2005). Further, governments of some oil-producing countries have adopted policies to promote growth of the non-oil economy in part in response to the need to replace declining oil revenues (Callen et al. 2014).

Yet while tax needs can and have created incentives to promote economic growth, nuance is needed. Governments are often short-sighted. While encouraging economic growth may be a long-term route to increased revenue, they may often nonetheless adopt more narrow, or destructive, short-term strategies of revenue maximisation. Gehlbach (2008), for example, has argued that the former Soviet states, which were in need of revenue, favoured large manufacturing firms that paid the most taxes. This was a useful short-term strategy for revenue raising, but not necessarily a route to long-term revenue growth. Recent research has suggested that, in China, many local governments have resorted to leasing out land to raise revenue – again, a short-term approach (Ong 2014). In much of Africa during the decades immediately after independence, agricultural exports were heavily taxed (Chapter 2). This raised revenue in the short term but undermined the agricultural sector (McMillan 2001). And, of course, stimulating economic growth is far from straightforward, even where governments are interested in doing so. The message is that, while the need for revenue may create extra incentives for promoting growth, the outcomes will depend on the incentives that are created for various actors in specific political and economic contexts. By extension, sharp declines in access to non-tax revenue have the potential to promote new commitments to economic modernisation – as currently seems to be happening in Saudi Arabia – but may equally result in fiscal crises and wider development challenges.

Taxation and state building

There is no doubt that the push to strengthen tax systems has sometimes spurred state building. In Rwanda, the revenue authority has been a leader in outreach to the private sector to support policymaking (Moore 2014). In Uganda, the tax agency has sought to spark greater cooperation and information sharing between central and local governments. More recently, the Uganda Revenue Authority (URA) has introduced a public sector office to monitor and collect revenue initially collected by other state agencies or local governments, most notably through withholding taxes (Goodfellow and Owen forthcoming). The need for improved accounting around these revenues appears to have begun to act as an important check against corruption in public contracting across government. In South Africa, the South African Revenue Service (SARS) has been a pioneer in using tax data to investigate a wide range of questions of public interest, and has shared that data throughout government in order to better design and target government policy (Gavin et al. 2013; Pieterse et al. 2016). In Sierra Leone, expansion of the property tax also led to the creation of the first detailed GIS maps of the localities concerned. These maps were then used for more general planning purposes. Elsewhere, the introduction of property taxation has contributed to regularising land titles (Saka 2017).

Yet we also know that such positive spillovers are far from guaranteed. Spillover effects, demonstration effects and information-sharing effects appear more likely where tax agencies are more closely linked to other branches of government. This proximity is what can allow reforms in the tax administration to generate pressure for development and learning elsewhere in the public sector, and that can allow information to be productively shared across government. By contrast, if there is little trust or cooperation between revenue agencies and the rest of government, opportunities for information sharing are likely to be squandered. Likewise, where revenue agencies have their own very distinct procedures for hiring, performance management and the like – or where there is little trust or engagement with other parts of government – best practices are unlikely to spill over.

Unfortunately, the current situation in much of Africa is not very conducive to the creation of stronger links between tax administrations and other public agencies. Recent trends have been almost contrary to this. The creation of semi-autonomous revenue authorities, described in Chapter 6, explicitly aimed to increase the independence of revenue authorities from the rest of the civil service, in order to increase flexibility, reduce corruption and minimise political interference. These motives are widely supported, and in many countries revenue authorities have enjoyed significant successes. But in at least some cases this has also increased the distance between revenue authorities and the rest of government: there is very little information sharing, recruitment often works differently, and pay scales and human resource management practices are distinct. Within other parts of government, there is often resentment of the 'privileges' enjoyed by revenue authority staff. In order to make connections between taxation and state building a reality, there is likely to be a need to think more explicitly about how interactions and cooperation between semi-autonomous revenue authorities and other branches of the state may be encouraged (Prichard 2016b).

Taxation, responsiveness and accountability

Within the literature linking taxation to governance, most attention has been paid to the possibility that taxation generates the kind of political mobilisation that in turn makes government more responsive to taxpayers and, more especially, more accountable to them. Our conclusions on this are similar to those about taxation and state building. There is increasingly compelling evidence that taxation can and has been a stimulus to improvements in responsiveness and accountability in Africa and elsewhere. This evidence is from diverse sources: cross-country econometric studies showing that states where governments are more reliant on taxes are more democratic (e.g. Prichard et al. 2014; Wiens et al. 2014; Andersen and Ross 2014); national cases studies tracking the ways in which conflicts over taxation have prompted improvements in governance (Prichard 2015); the discovery that, within countries, subnational governments that are more reliant on raising their own revenues through taxation have better service delivery (Gadenne 2017; Martinez 2015); surveys showing that taxes are associated with stronger demands on government (McGuirk 2013), and that taxpayers are more willing to pay taxes when they receive desired benefits in return (Flores-Macías 2014; 2016); and experimental evidence that, when individuals need to pay for public services through taxes, they are also more likely to demand accountability from governments (Paler 2013; Martin 2016).

Yet, while there is evidence that tax can induce improved accountability, this outcome is far from guaranteed. Taxation is, at its root, a coercive activity through which governments appropriate resources from citizens. As Ross (2004) explains:

> many people dislike paying taxes, and some will cause trouble when governments raise them. But democracy is only one

possible outcome of these conflicts. Historically, people have
borne crushingly high tax rates with few rebellions; when they
do revolt, they have often been met with intensified repression,
not democratic concessions.

It would be wrong to assume that expanded taxation will be automatically translated into greater pressure for more effective use
of public resources. The fact that taxation contributed to the
expansion of accountability in parts of early modern Europe is
no guarantee of similar processes in the very different context of
today's lower-income countries. Even in Europe, taxation contributed to accountability in only some contexts, while in other places
sometimes violent coercion persisted over decades, and even centuries. And these processes were often led by the elite, with new rights
granted to larger taxpayers – but few benefits for the lower-income
majority. Indeed, in some cases the 'tax bargain' that took shape
saw only moderate taxation of elites, while imposing a heavy
extractive burden on smaller taxpayers (Prichard 2015). The realities of taxation in much of contemporary Africa – particularly at the
subnational level – frequently appear more conducive to extended
periods of coercion rather than to the construction of stronger
social contracts. In some areas at least, the formal tax burdens
borne by small firms – often through an array of small levies and
fees – are larger than those borne by larger firms. Many taxpayers
express a belief that they get little in return for their tax payments,
and have little influence over government priorities. And, critically,
existing evidence suggests that relatively marginalised groups –
migrants, ethnic minorities, women, the poor – frequently bear the
heaviest relative tax burdens but have the most limited capacity to
push for reciprocity.

With this in mind, recent research has begun to shift its focus.
Acknowledging clear evidence that taxation can promote improved
governance, it has sought to understand what makes positive
bargaining over taxation more likely in specific contexts. The

evidence remains incomplete, but five factors seem to be particularly important (Prichard 2015):

1. *The level of revenue pressure facing governments*: A government facing more acute revenue pressure is more likely to be willing to compromise with taxpayers in order to secure new taxes or greater tax compliance.

2. *The potential for tax resistance*: Some taxes are more vulnerable to resistance or avoidance by taxpayers – owing to the nature of the tax, or the political strength of taxpayers. People or firms paying those taxes are likely to enjoy greater leverage in pushing for concessions from governments. For example, resistance to taxation by unpopular governments in Kenya, described above, centred particularly on income taxes, which are comparatively difficult to collect.

3. *The potential for collective action*: A key means by which taxpayers may win reciprocity from governments is through collective mobilisation, and this is more likely where there is political space for it and where there are existing organisations to support it. For example, more repressive governments may make tax bargaining less likely, while the relative absence of organisations representing taxpayers in Africa likely undermines the potential for bargaining. Research on small informal businesses in Nigeria has highlighted the very different capacities for collective action among different groups of small firms and segments of the population (Meagher 2016). Similarly, the strength and unity of business associations have shaped the ability of business groups to make reciprocal demands on governments.

4. *The nature of political institutions for bargaining*: The potential for bargaining depends in part on the existence of forums for

taxpayers to organise and make demands for reciprocity: parliaments, transparent budget consultations, business–government forums and the like. Where these forums exist, it is more likely that taxpayers will be able to press for explicit benefits in return for taxes. Where they don't, tax 'bargaining' is more likely to happen implicitly, through continuous conflict between extractive governments and unhappy taxpayers.

5. *The political salience of taxation*: Taxation is more likely to prompt bargaining and expanded accountability when taxpayers are aware of the taxes that they pay, and consider them politically important. Taxes such as VAT, trade taxes, or even withholding taxes on income are often hidden from view of those paying them. Measures that increase awareness of taxes, and the potential for popular engagement, may thus play an important role.

Importantly, the conditions described above are not strongly present in many low-income contexts – while they may be particularly elusive for the lower-income majority of taxpayers. When governments face acute revenue pressure, they often have recourse to borrowing and support from aid donors to reduce the need to compromise with taxpayers. While income and other direct taxes offer greater scope for tax resistance, they are among the most ineffectively enforced taxes at the national level across much of the continent, while the impacts of the other major national taxes – VAT and customs – are often obscure to taxpayers. Direct taxes are more widespread, and more salient, at the subnational level, but research has highlighted significant barriers to collective action in these contexts. Meanwhile, despite the rhetorical commitment of many governments to greater tax transparency, actual institutional spaces for engagement between tax authorities and taxpayers remain limited – and sometimes are shrinking, including through increased restrictions on civil society. This does not mean that tax bargaining is not possible in challenging contexts. Prichard (2015), for example, has documented important forms of implicit bargaining around the expansion of taxation in Ethiopia despite a sharp lack of political freedoms and few civil society organisations. But there is little doubt that scepticism about automatic outcomes – and proactive efforts to encourage positive outcomes – is essential if taxation is to be translated into public benefits.

Finally, it is important to note that the content of any 'tax bargain' may vary sharply across countries – and some 'bargains' might be more desirable than others from the perspective of different groups. This is unsurprising, given research that has highlighted the very different social contracts that have underpinned political power in different African countries (Nugent 2010). The cases noted earlier from Ghana have involved relatively broad-based tax bargains that have delivered improvements in valued public services. They have, however, been notable also for the important intermediary role of the dominant political parties in shaping outcomes. By sharp contrast, traditional chiefs have loomed large in processes of tax bargaining in Sierra Leone, where they have acted as gatekeepers to the expansion of property taxes and, at least to some extent, have negotiated with formal government actors on behalf of taxpayers. This has made the distribution of gains highly dependent on the characteristics of individual chiefs. Moore (2015) has argued that, in Rwanda, tax bargaining has appeared to be led by the elite and businesses, at the risk of excluding more popular voices. Other research has noted that, in some cases, tax bargains struck between trade associations and governments have benefited association leaders more than rank-and-file members (Joshi and Ayee 2008). These divergent outcomes reflect the particular political histories of individual countries. Understanding the ways in which taxation may contribute to shaping state building and accountability demands an openness to the variety of these processes.

What are the implications for public policy?

Because strong tax–governance links are far from guaranteed, there is an urgent need for a shift in the policy discussion towards a focus on *how* such positive outcomes can be fostered, *where* constructive connections are likely, and *what* this means for the design and targeting of tax reform efforts. Without such a discussion, increased taxation risks being presented as an unambiguous development good, devoid of risks, rather than as an element in a wider strategy. Such a debate should make it clear that, in some contexts, the most urgent reform challenge may not be to increase revenue collection, but to transform the character of existing revenue collection and strengthen the ability of taxpayers to demand reciprocity.

This tension is illustrated by debates surrounding the UN Sustainable Development Goals (SDGs), and a debate about whether the SDGs should establish a minimum target for tax collection by governments (as a percentage of GDP). The argument in favour of the target is clear: governments of low-income countries urgently need expanded public revenues to fund public services, and the expansion of domestic taxation has the potential to stimulate general improvements in governance, grounded in local processes of bargaining between taxpayers and governments. Yet, the proposed minimum tax collection target was eventually abandoned, for two main reasons. First, it was too simplistic. It became increasingly clear to those involved that it is not enough to call for more taxation, unless that call is accompanied by a push for fairer, more transparent and more inclusive tax systems. A simple tax collection target would have failed to capture key elements of *how* tax is collected. Second, it simply *felt* wrong. Presenting greater tax collection as a goal in and of itself confuses means and ends. Taxation is merely a means to the eventual goal of a more effective public sector, and more effective public services. A push for increased taxation only makes sense if combined with concrete strategies to link taxation to these wider goals.

What, then, might a more holistic tax reform agenda look like? Previous chapters have highlighted key elements: greater fairness, more transparency, and an emphasis on public engagement. In this chapter we try to answer a more specific question. What could be key elements of a governance-focused tax reform agenda – by which we mean an agenda that aims explicitly to strengthen the links between increased taxation and more or better economic growth, state building, government responsiveness and accountability? While research is far from providing all the answers, it has begun to allow us to map the main components of such an agenda.

Linking taxation and economic growth

Arguments linking the reliance of governments on taxes to economic growth are general and even a bit fuzzy. Their policy implications are not very precise. Most obviously, they suggest that, where states rely more on broad taxation – and less on alternative sources of revenue, notably natural resource wealth – economic growth will likely be faster over the long term. This might imply that, in resource-rich states, taxation of the non-resource sector would motivate governments to support its long-term growth. There is no evidence, however, to support that proposition. We cannot assume that heavier taxes will lead to faster economic growth in the long term, via the motivating effects they have on public policy. Heavier taxation may simply dampen investment.

At the level of subnational government, in countries where subnational governments have few revenue sources, we can more convincingly argue a particular policy line. If subnational governments had control over a larger range of revenue sources, and were more reliant on revenue they raised themselves, they would have stronger incentives to promote local economic growth. Local responsibility for presumptive taxes on small businesses, as discussed in Chapter 7, might be very appropriate. Making fiscal transfers from central government dependent on local revenue-raising efforts – so that success in raising local revenue is rewarded by larger transfers – is another widely advocated option. While this is attractive in principle, it can be practically and politically difficult to implement (Bird and Smart 2002). Estimating revenue effort requires knowledge of the local tax potential, which is frequently not available. The policy may risk exacerbating inequality among localities. Similarly, decentralising tax responsibilities is often complex in practice. The most important national taxes – income taxes, customs duties and VAT – are not very amenable to decentralisation, owing to the mobility of individuals, corporations and goods. Small business taxes and property taxes remain the most promising local revenue sources, but are rarely enough to fund a large proportion of local government spending outside large cities. Ultimately, efforts to increase the revenue pressure on local governments need to get the incentives right, by giving governments enough revenue tools to fund local needs, but not so many that incentives to collect taxes – and promote local economic growth – are eliminated.

Linking taxation and state building

The evidence discussed so far suggests four reform strategies that could help strengthen connections between taxation and state building:

1. *Build strong links between tax agencies and related branches of government.* The potential state-building benefits of taxation flow in part through spillovers, where a push to strengthen taxation creates pressure to reform other public agencies on which the tax administration relies for enforcement purposes. These may include the judiciary, ministries of finance, business registration bodies, and agencies involved with land registration and transactions. Unsurprisingly, spillover effects of this kind appear more likely when there are clear links between such agencies through efforts to collaborate and share data.

2. *Emphasise bureaucratic reforms in tax administration that could be replicated elsewhere in government.* Just as spillover effects are more likely when there are close ties across government agencies, there is greater potential for demonstration effects where aspects of tax administration reform are potentially replicable and can provide a model for improvements elsewhere. There are two dimensions to the task of realising this potential. First, and most simply, where there are strong links between tax agencies and other branches of government, innovations such as meritocratic hiring, computerisation or performance monitoring are more likely to be adopted elsewhere. Second, some types of reform strategies are inherently more universal in their potential to spread across government, while others are more idiosyncratic. For example, dramatic increases in pay for revenue officials may not offer a model for other agencies constrained by civil service pay scales. By contrast, the intro-duction of improved performance monitoring, customer service and recruitment practices may be more generally replicable.

3. *Focus on effective data gathering, and on sharing data across government.* Among the most important ways for tax agencies to strengthen public sector performance is through the collec-tion and sharing of high-quality data. The standard bearer in Africa is SARS, which has increasingly become a key source of detailed data used for economic and social planning in the country (Gavin et al. 2013; Pieterse et al. 2016). Most revenue authorities neither collect nor compile and analyse the rich data that is available to them. Nor do they share it more widely within government. This appears to reflect a general lack of connection between government agencies, a lack of trust, and a desire for secrecy and the power that can come from control over data. New investments in this area, coupled with a political commit-ment to greater data sharing and transparency, could have large and immediate governance benefits.

4. *Focus on strengthening links between central and local administrations.* Closer links between central and local tax agencies could have similarly beneficial effects, with central tax agencies becoming catalysts for improvements at the local level. As discussed in Chapter 7, the absence of such cooperation is among the most important barriers to more effective local taxation in much of Africa. As a result, even modest efforts to strengthen these links not only could improve policy and administrative coordination, but could also be a critical tool in strengthening capacity, IT systems and oversight at the local level.

Existing institutional arrangements reduce the likelihood of these kinds of spillovers. During the period of their creation, SARAs were intentionally distanced from other branches of government. The dynamics of patronage politics can discourage data sharing and cooperation across agencies. Overlapping tax responsibilities have often led to conflict rather than cooperation between national and subnational revenue agencies. Yet in at least some countries there are signs that these barriers are being eroded. Uganda is an interesting case. Over the past three years, data sharing across government has expanded substantially. This was initially motivated by efforts to identify tax avoidance and evasion, both by HNWIs and by firms with contracts to provide goods and services to government. There are already signs of the emergence of wider benefits: cooperation between the URA and local councils has enhanced capacity for local revenue mobilisation; pressure from the URA has led to improvements in the ways in which other government agencies account for and manage the contracts they have with external providers; and best practices from the URA are being shared across government. Those changes in turn stand to underpin further improvements in the performance of the URA through better tracking of government contracts and contractors, improved data on property ownership and values, and more abundant information on the economic activities of HNWIs. The same potential for virtuous circles of improved cooperation among government agencies exists in other countries.

Linking taxation, responsiveness and accountability

The most detailed existing research in this area has focused on how to encourage tax bargaining and thus translate the expansion of taxation into stronger public services and increased accountability. In many contexts the most important reform challenge may lie not in expanding revenue, but in achieving these wider changes that can contribute to greater public benefits from taxation. This may be particularly true where existing systems of formal and informal taxation impose large burdens on taxpayers but offer few reciprocal benefits. Four sets of policies appear potentially most relevant – although these ideas require more thorough testing (Prichard 2016b):

1. *Enhance the political salience of taxation – including by strengthening direct taxes.* When taxpayers are more aware of the taxes that they pay, they are more likely to be able to resist taxes levied by unaccountable governments, and to demand reciprocity. Yet they are often unaware. The most direct way to strengthen the political salience of taxes is likely to be to increase direct taxation – including through income taxes, property taxes, and presumptive taxes on smaller businesses – as these are often more visible to taxpayers. However, there is mounting evidence that indirect taxes such as VAT can also stimulate political engagement – as was the case in Ghana, noted above – through efforts to raises awareness by civil society, the media and other groups.

2. *Focus on horizontal equity in tax enforcement.* A central obstacle to realising the potential for tax bargaining comes from the difficulty taxpayers face in engaging in collective action. Where taxpayers are divided, they struggle to make effective demands on governments. In practice, they frequently are divided.

Where enforcement of taxes is uneven, taxpayers – and politically powerful taxpayers in particular – are more likely to seek benefits and exemptions for themselves rather than working with other taxpayers to demand reciprocity. By contrast, where there is more consistent tax enforcement, taxpayers will have weaker incentives to seek narrow benefits, and stronger incentives to work collectively to ensure fairness, responsiveness and accountability. As a result, selective tax exemptions, tax avoidance by elites or the use of international channels for tax evasion by wealthy taxpayers not only are economically damaging but also undermine the potential for tax bargaining. Likewise, the potential for tax bargaining by small business associations may be undermined where internal divisions and hierarchies of power incentivise powerful individuals and groups to seek exemptions from taxation, rather than working collectively to secure more general benefits. For these reasons, tax bargaining may be more challenging – and taxation more contentious – in communities characterised by sharp ethnic or political differences that are reflected in uneven tax enforcement (Meagher 2016).

3. *Expand transparency around taxation and budgeting – including, possibly, tax earmarking.* Transparency has been widely cited as a strategy to empower citizens. While transparency alone is not a guarantee of accountability, there is substantial evidence that it can help. This is true of taxation. Better informed taxpayers seem better able, and more likely, to demand reciprocity from governments for the taxes that they pay. The reasons are various: transparency may increase the political salience of taxation; it may highlight ineffectiveness in the use of tax revenue; it may empower taxpayers to make more precise demands for reciprocity; and, critically, in the best cases it can build trust, allowing taxpayers to see any benefits delivered in exchange for their tax payments. While transparency can take many forms, its most extreme form is earmarking, which entails tying revenue

from a tax to specific areas of spending. While this may reduce fiscal flexibility, in contexts in which there is little trust between taxpayers and governments it may be a useful strategy for rebuilding trust, and for facilitating bargaining over taxation.

4. *Directly support popular engagement, including the creation of inclusive institutional spaces for tax bargaining.* While measures to expand political salience, equity and transparency can encourage demands for reciprocity by taxpayers, there is also scope to directly encourage popular engagement with tax issues – something that is currently all too rare. One option is to create specific forums – such as participatory budgeting or more general budget consultations – in which taxpayers can directly ask questions of, and voice concerns to, the government. It is essential that these efforts include a broad base of taxpayers, so that tax bargaining is not dominated by larger taxpayers. There is evidence that participatory budgeting processes can also encourage tax compliance (Beuermann and Amelina 2014; Torgler 2005). A more modest approach observed in several countries in recent years has been regular call-in radio programmes with members of government, which offer a space for questions and complaints about taxation and the budget. Because callers can be anonymous and the costs of participation are low, radio programmes can enable a wide range of views and voices to be heard. Another policy option is support to the media, civil society and business associations, all of which can be catalysts for engagement and collective action by taxpayers. Perhaps most interesting have been efforts by NGOs in many countries to link engagement with tax issues to wider advocacy campaigns pushing for transparency, improved public services and greater accountability. Several such campaigns begin with a simple message to their members: as taxpayers you help pay for government, and you have a corresponding right to demand both information and reciprocity. Tax issues have thus served

as a framework for mobilisation of public attention and engagement in activities such as public expenditure tracking. While the effects of these initiatives have not been rigorously studied, anecdotal evidence points towards some success in prompting popular engagement with government (Prichard 2015: 222–3).[3]

While these policy suggestions are ambitious, they are not in tension with more technical approaches to tax reform. Keen (2012) has argued that, while a governance-focused tax agenda may look somewhat different to a more classically technical reform agenda, many of the components – be they stronger income tax enforcement, greater transparency, or requiring more small firms to pay very simple taxes – have long formed part of the standard advice from the IMF. A governance-focused tax reform agenda would thus primarily mark a change in emphasis towards the 'softer' elements of tax reform. It would involve: some shift away from a narrow focus on revenue collection, in favour of more emphasis on process, equity, transparency and space for popular engagement; greater openness to tax earmarking – to be used selectively, and in limited ways – where there is a clear need to strengthen trust between taxpayers and governments; more emphasis on direct taxes; and greater concern about tax exemptions – both formal and informal – that may undermine constructive tax bargaining.

The most important message is perhaps the greater stress on expanding popular engagement with tax issues. For many tax professionals and governments, it has long been (unspoken) conventional wisdom that the best route to successful tax reform is to do it quietly, thus minimising potential resistance. A senior policymaker during the period of rapid tax reform in Kenya has been quoted as arguing that 'the more you involve people in reform the less likely you are to achieve your goals. The less transparent you are the more likely you are to succeed' (Prichard 2015: 154). Aid donors have often appeared to reinforce this tendency, whether intentionally or not. Relatively standard tax reforms have been implemented across

Africa over the past three decades, often with donor support and accompanied by donor conditionality, and strikingly little public engagement (Chapter 6). While this has sometimes proved effective in advancing reform quickly, the dangers of this approach are increasingly clear. Most obviously, where policy and administrative reform have shallow political roots, they may be agreed on paper but not implemented in practice. More relevant to the discussion here, a closed and secretive approach to tax reform is likely to undermine the potential for taxation to stimulate fiscal social contracts.

Barriers to building stronger tax–governance links

While there is mounting evidence that taxation can be an impetus for improved governance, efforts to realise the potential connections are likely to encounter three particular challenges. First, although these types of reforms are desirable from a common interest perspective, they may be staunchly opposed by many governments. Second, where greater accountability is driven by bargaining over taxation, there is significant risk of these processes being captured by small groups of powerful taxpayers. Third, these processes are most needed in comparatively autocratic and unaccountable environments, but it is in precisely those areas that tax bargaining may be most difficult to achieve. We address each issue briefly in turn.

1. Although there is a strong public interest argument for making taxation more equitable, transparent and inclusive – and for seeking to spark stronger fiscal contracts – many governments are not interested in expanded accountability. Indeed, many would likely prefer tax reform strategies designed precisely to *minimise* the potential for tax bargaining, along with minimising information sharing and transparency. Where, then, might support for reform come from? The most basic answer is common to almost any public sector reform: reform is likely to follow the emergence of windows of opportunity, for example

with the appointment of supportive senior officials (Crook 2010). A second potential answer lies in the role of aid donors. International donors have historically wielded a powerful influence over tax reform, both directly and through the creation of epistemic communities of tax professionals (Fjeldstad and Moore 2008b; Sanchez 2006). If these donors were to shift their emphasis towards a more governance-focused reform agenda, it is not hard to imagine some shift in outcomes as well. There has, at least rhetorically, been recent movement in that direction. Finally, perhaps the most important potential allies are tax administrators themselves. Whereas governments may resist greater accountability, many (though certainly not all) tax collectors are interested in improvements in the way in which public revenue is spent: this is likely to make their jobs as tax collectors easier. At least publicly, it has become increasingly common to hear senior tax administrators refer to their broader role as state builders. For example, in a speech made in 2009 at the launch of the African Tax Administration Forum, the Commissioner-General of the URA, Allen Kagina, argued that: 'We should elevate ourselves from being just tax collectors and tax administrators to being state builders.' The second pillar of the mission of the African Tax Administration Forum is to 'advance the role of taxation in African governance and state building'. It argues in its mission statement that 'better tax administration will ... increase accountability of the state to its citizens' (African Tax Administration Forum n.d.).

2. Tax bargaining may be dominated by a narrow group of large taxpayers and fail to deliver more inclusive outcomes. A key premise of arguments linking taxation to expanded accountability is that those who pay for government will be able to shape its activities. A simple message follows: larger taxpayers may gain the greatest political power because they are most important to government finances.[4] There is plenty of evidence of

this kind of dynamic across Africa. Large taxpayers frequently receive precise, individualised benefits, be it through access to government contracts, special government investments, or targeted tax benefits. Broader-based tax bargaining is thus likely to depend on identifying strategies to engage and empower a wider range of taxpayers, rather than only a small elite. In principle, this is entirely possible: taxation can be a spark for public mobilisation even among smaller taxpayers, while opposition to new taxation by smaller taxpayers can undermine government tax collection more widely. However, the ability of these smaller taxpayers to mobilise collectively to make demands on government is often constrained by limited access to information, vulnerability, weak political voice, and significant internal differences. In these contexts, it is likely to be particularly important to work proactively to strengthen the prospects for tax bargaining: increasing the political salience of taxation; identifying links between revenue and expenditure; creating institutions to facilitate engagement by these groups; and supporting civil society actors who can support such engagement. In many cases it may be important to pursue these goals as a precursor to increasing taxation, given the coerciveness of existing tax systems and the risks of reinforcing them. Incorporating smaller taxpayers into fiscal contracts may present the single greatest barrier to realising the potential positive links between taxation and improved governance.

3. A final question is whether taxation can be an effective spur to improvements in governance in areas of particularly weak or autocratic rule. These are the contexts in which the promise of a tax–governance relationship is most appealing, as an entry point to indigenous processes of bargaining and state building. Yet the research summarised in this chapter raises an obvious concern: strong links between taxation, state building and accountability are least likely – or at least most complex – where

there is autocracy and weak governance. Where tax systems are fragmented and incoherent and there is little cooperation between government agencies, the prospects for taxation to stimulate improvements in state building and accountability are the least promising. In the Democratic Republic of Congo, decentralisation reforms adopted in 2008 opened space for expanded provincial and local-level taxation and enjoyed significant support from donors, based in part on the promise of building stronger fiscal links between citizens and subnational governments. At least in the short term, these potential gains appear to have remained illusory. Available evidence suggests that decentralisation allowed for the proliferation of local taxes and the expansion of extraction from lower-income taxpayers, but that this extraction has been relatively arbitrary, scarcely any of that revenue has reached the government budget, and there has been little – if any – popular engagement around tax issues. This case illustrates the risks posed by tax reforms that increase the potential for extraction without significant attention to strategies for linking revenue raising to wider benefits. Where there are harsh controls on political freedom, limited transparency and weak civil society, it is particularly difficult for taxpayers to mobilise collectively to demand reciprocity from governments. Worryingly, many of the civil society organisations across Africa that are engaged with governments around tax issues have reported declining political space for popular mobilisation. None of this should be taken as suggesting that gains are not possible in these contexts. We have examples of meaningful tax bargaining in post-conflict settings (e.g. Jibao and Prichard 2015). But it again highlights the importance of placing tax governance ahead of a simple focus on revenue expansion.

Conclusions

At the beginning of this book we argued that taxation was important because it is among the most fundamental tasks of any government, and lies at the heart of the relationship between citizens and governments. For these reasons, the promise of tax reform lies not only in increased revenue collection, but in sparking more encompassing processes of state building and tax bargaining. Indeed, it is the promise of such larger governance gains that is central to the recent emergence of taxation as a leading issue on the global development agenda. Yet it is important to recall that the development field has long been prone to fads, and those fads can lead to the oversimplification of more complex ideas. Taxation is no different. There is a powerful case to be made that taxation can be central to strategies for strengthening services, the state, responsiveness and accountability. But such positive outcomes require more than wishful thinking. They require clear strategies to design tax reform to encourage wider gains, and consistent efforts to empower taxpayers and reformers to make these possibilities a reality.

Increased taxation has increasingly been identified, implicitly, as a development objective in its own right, rather than a means to an end. In practice, there has been limited attention to the types of measures that might promote a more effective use of tax revenue and strengthen ties between revenue, state building and accountability. And there is a range of reasons to worry that such tax–governance linkages may be particularly elusive in relation to lower-income taxpayers and in areas of particularly weak and autocratic governance. Real progress is needed in building a wider tax agenda.

There has been a corresponding temptation in some quarters to argue that efforts to expand taxation are misguided, particularly in areas of weak governance. Certainly, this may be true in some contexts. Yet, on balance, we suspect that a well-conceived policy for strengthening tax systems is likely to remain an important part of development strategies. While the problem of ensuring effective governance of taxation is likely to be especially challenging in areas of weak governance and among more marginalised taxpayers, this is not unique to taxation: any approach to strengthening development outcomes will face greater hurdles in these situations. But we do have case studies that show taxation fostering useful bargaining and compromise even in such settings. Conversely, the alternative strategy of disengagement from tax reform, at least as it affects low-income groups, would represent a major abrogation of responsibility. In areas of weak governance, poor people often face heavy burdens of informal taxation, making payments that fund no public goods and no social purpose (Chapter 7). In such contexts, carefully conceived reforms aimed explicitly at simplification, regularising formal taxation and improving prospects for reciprocity and state building, may avoid increasing aggregate burdens on the majority of taxpayers while offering a potential entry point for improved governance outcomes. What is critical is that a narrow focus on revenue raising be complemented by careful attention to strategies for strengthening the public benefits of expanded public revenue.

Chapter 9

THE WAY FORWARD

The re-discovery of taxation in Africa

Until recently, taxation in Africa typically has been viewed as a narrow technical field, marginal to more important discussions about governance, development and economic growth. The recent resurgence of interest can be viewed as a *re*-discovery of the centrality of taxation. Why a *re*-discovery? Because taxation figured prominently in debates about society and development in the colonial and early independence periods.

As described in Chapter 2, the origins of contemporary African tax systems lie in the political economy of colonialism. Taxation lay near the centre of the colonial enterprise, and the relationship between Africans and colonial states. Internal taxes, dominated by poll taxes and taxes on the production of cash crops, were levied mainly on Africans. They were designed not only to raise revenue, but also to help transform economies – by coercing African labour into the cash economy, especially into the labour force working on European-owned farms and mines. These taxes were, unsurprisingly, a focus of early resistance to colonial power, ranging from the 1898 Hut Tax War in Sierra Leone to the creation of taxpayers' associations in Kenya in the 1930s.

Immediately after independence, African governments expanded the scope of taxation, both directly and indirectly, to extract from agricultural and mining exporters the economic surpluses that they believed should be channelled into industrialisation. Those policies in part reflected the political dominance of small urban populations over the rural majority, in situations where democracy was weak or entirely absent. The policies were also motivated by beliefs about the most effective route to 'development' – beliefs often shared by influential voices from within former colonial powers. Newly independent African governments followed most other governments in the world in adopting aggressively progressive income tax regimes – at least on paper, and nominally to redistribute income to poorer people. In sum, it was widely accepted that taxation should appropriate resources from agriculture and from high-income earners and channel them, through governments, into industrialisation.

This orthodoxy was overturned in the 1980s and 1990s, in large part through the influence of the IMF and World Bank. Typically justified by a broad emphasis on markets and competition rather than public action, and a narrative about the need for 'structural adjustment' of national economies, international organisations and aid donors supported reforms involving the near elimination of taxes on commodity exports, reductions in the nominal rates of income and other taxes, and the much wider use of consumption taxes, above all through the introduction of the new VAT. While the attitudes of African political elites to these reforms were ambiguous, they ultimately, and often grudgingly, went along with them. In agreeing to abolish most taxes on agricultural commodity exports, political elites may have been motivated in part by incentives to become more responsive to the interests of rural voters: contested elections were becoming more common. But voters were rarely directly consulted in any way. Reforms were debated and agreed within small networks of national politicians, technical experts and aid donor staff.

Over the past two decades, the development strategies and economic policies of African governments have changed only incrementally, with the broad market orientation remaining. There have, however, been significant, if complex, changes in the political processes underlying economic policy choices. Aid donors generally have lost influence. African political elites are increasingly asser-tive in seeking to shape their own development pathways. Although often still weak, organised civil society exercises more voice. Devel-opment challenges have come to be understood in more complex terms. In contrast to the simple prescriptions of structural adjust-ment, there is more emphasis on linking the local, national and international dimensions of development, and on confronting both its technical and its political roots.

These trends raise two questions about future tax reform. First, can leaders chart an African-owned pathway towards stronger tax systems? Second, to what extent will debates about tax issues on the continent move beyond narrow circles of experts, to reflect broader popular concerns? The answers to these questions are likely to be pivotal for future developments.

The pace of reform

As discussed in the preceding chapters, we think we know a great deal about taxation in Africa: both the ways in which the effec-tiveness of taxation and tax agencies have improved, and the more obvious weaknesses of existing systems. The latter include highly ineffective income and property taxes; uneven taxation of corpo-rations as a result of an imperfect international system for taxing transborder transactions and extensive formal and informal tax exemptions; the under-taxation of the extractives sector, espe-cially mining; continued challenges around administration, data sharing and corruption; weak systems of local taxation; and, perhaps most importantly, continued challenges in ensuring that increased revenue is translated into more effective and accountable governance.

While these challenges are significant, this book has also sought to highlight important areas of progress and opportu-nity. Committed African governments almost certainly have both the knowledge and the capacity to significantly improve the level, equity, transparency and reciprocity of revenue collection. These are not easy tasks, but significant progress is possible where governments make these goals a political priority. The main obstacle lies in the fact that governments generally have only a lukewarm interest in tax reform. They would like to increase revenues, but not at the cost of confronting powerful vested interests. Their concerns about the dire state of local taxation are not sufficient to motivate them to take the steps needed to eliminate coercive, counterproductive collection practices. They have made some improvements in transparency and engagement with taxpayers to make taxpaying easier, but they make no consistent commitment to a more reciprocal relationship with them. At the same time, attempts to reform international taxation have also encountered barriers grounded in the realities of political power: while there has been some attention paid to the concerns of lower-income countries, the reforms that have been agreed at the global level only weakly reflect their priorities.

A locally owned tax reform agenda

If it is to be implemented effectively, a tax reform agenda for Africa needs to be locally 'owned': that is, designed in Africa, for Africans, in line with African conditions. It needs to transcend the disadvantages of the colonial inheritance and a history of over-reliance on external advice.

Africa's colonial and immediate postcolonial inheritance has shaped tax systems in important, and often perverse, ways. Some elements of that inheritance have already declined sharply in importance, including the heavy reliance on taxing agricultural exports nationally, and on relatively arbitrary poll taxes locally. Other legacies persist. In the realm of property taxation, most countries continue to rely on excessively complex valuation regimes inherited from colonial rule, with Francophone countries in particular adopting highly centralised property tax systems that seem poorly suited to African realities. More broadly, the weakness of local taxation can be traced back in part to the dysfunctional structures of colonial governance (Chapter 7). In similar fashion, many national revenue systems continue to bear the costs of tax treaties signed during, or soon after, the colonial period, and in some cases these entrenched significant tax benefits for the former colonial powers (Hearson and Kangave 2016), while they have long relied almost exclusively on complex approaches to international taxation modelled on European experience.

The external advice and influence that have shaped tax reform in the post-independence period have been a mixed blessing. Much international advice has undoubtedly been well placed and helpful in supporting the modernisation of African tax systems (Chapter 6). However, the influence of external actors on tax systems has perhaps been stronger in Africa than in any other part of the world, potentially limiting local ownership and local innovation. Even as revenue administrations in parts of Africa have become more competent and sophisticated, tax policy units in ministries of finance have frequently remained understaffed and heavily reliant on external policy guidance. The lack of local ownership would seem to be reflected in a characteristic feature of African tax reforms in recent decades: the disjuncture between formal policy and practical action. Despite formal policy changes, the political commitment – to strengthen revenue administrations, to ensure that high earners file income tax returns and declare real earnings, and to make effective use of property taxes – typically has been absent.

This is not to argue that taxation systems would be better in the absence of international support and involvement. The message is more forward looking. Most African governments are now principally dependent on taxes for their incomes and have experience of tax reform. Their tax collectors are increasingly well trained and educated, and provide a growing proportion of expatriate technical assistance for tax reform within the region. There is increasing scope for African leaders to craft and implement their own tax reform agendas, and to find locally appropriate solutions and locally effective ways of bypassing the political barriers to action. External support can be very valuable to complement local political commitment, but it can rarely either generate or substitute for that local commitment.

There are some reasons for optimism. In recent years, African leaders have become more assertive in seeking to shape their own tax future. The African Tax Administration Forum (ATAF) was created in 2009 as forum to link African tax administrators across the continent and to serve as a platform for sharing experience – including, potentially, the development of best practices for African conditions. African leaders have become more vocal in engaging with international tax rules. This has been reflected, for example, in the High Level Panel on Illicit Financial Flows from Africa led by Thabo Mbeki (UNECA 2015), and ATAF's drafting of an African model tax treaty.

Meanwhile, discussions around tax policy options potentially better suited to African contexts seem to be expanding. These include alternative approaches to curbing international tax abuses (Durst 2015a; 2016a; Hearson and Kangave 2016; Oguttu 2016; 2017); simplified models for taxing the natural resource sector (Clausing and Durst 2015; Durst 2016b); renewed interest in withholding and alternative minimum taxes to improve enforcement of income taxes (Durst 2015a); innovative thinking about the use of mobile technology to simplify the collection of small taxes (Orlale 2016);[1] and emerging discussion of the implications of informal taxation for African tax systems (van den Boogaard and Prichard 2016; Prichard 2016a). In all of these areas, discussions remain nascent and outcomes uncertain. But the development of indigenous policy discussion and options appears to be an important step towards greater local ownership of outcomes.

But where is political support for more thoroughgoing reform likely to be found?

Popular engagement, and a new politics of taxation

The challenges facing African tax systems stretch well beyond a simple need for greater revenue. At least as important are efforts to improve fairness, equity, reciprocity and accountability. These are, however, more politically challenging goals. Most governments welcome greater revenue. Fewer are willing to take the politically difficult steps of challenging powerful vested interests to achieve fairness and equity, or to deliver reciprocity and accountability.

In some respects, these political barriers to better tax systems are predictable. In Africa, as elsewhere, powerful interests are able to shape tax systems to reflect their interests, at the levels of both policy and implementation. From another perspective, the weak commitment to tax reform may seem quite surprising. For the vast majority of citizens, more effective taxation of the relatively rich would generate obvious benefits and few costs. A political commitment to collecting more money from income taxes, curbing tax exemptions and expanding property taxation could drive major increases in revenue and, potentially, corresponding improvements in services.

The near absence of substantial tax reforms indicates the power of vested interests and the infrequency of popular organisation and popular mobilisation around tax issues. This in turn suggests one potential road to more significant reform: the empowerment of a wider range of voices in tax debates, to motivate and support political leaders willing to drive progress. Excepting sporadic local-ised reactions against coercive local taxation, significant popular engagement in tax debates has been rare in Africa in recent decades. This, however, has begun to change.

The process behind a recent VAT reform in Tanzania offers a vivid illustration of one kind of intensified public engagement in tax matters. VAT was introduced in Tanzania in 1998 with a great deal of support from the IMF. There are many ways of designing such a tax. VAT does not come as 'one size fits all'. In part because it allowed for few exemptions and the zero-rating of only a limited range of products, Tanzania's 1997 VAT Act was widely perceived as a model for other developing countries. However, domestic political forces gradually eroded its exemplary features. Successive legislative amendments created more exemptions and increased the number of goods and services that were zero-rated. Some of these amendments were framed as incentives for investors, while others reflected private deals between individual business owners and ministers. The minister of finance was empowered to authorise exemptions without seeking approval from the legislature. As a result, VAT administration became more complex, opportunities for abuse and avoidance multiplied, and VAT collections decreased sharply. Reform was needed. In 2013, the IMF organised a mission on the topic and engaged a consultant. The government established a technical reform team composed of staff from the Ministry of Finance, the Tanzania Revenue Authority and the Office of the Attorney General. The team produced a new VAT bill that allowed only a few exemptions and zero-ratings (mostly on food, agricultural implements and other necessities) and removed the discretionary power of the minister of finance to grant and modify tax exemptions. Any future changes in existing exemptions would have to be approved by parliament, and new exemptions could be created or modified only through legislation.

The new bill was tabled at the National Assembly in May 2014, along with an explanation of the reasons for reform. In contrast to 1997, the private sector quickly mobilised to oppose it, with individual businesspeople pushing for their own special interests. More strikingly, the lobbying of parliament and the Ministry of Finance was coordinated by business associations, especially the Tanzania Private Sector Foundation. They employed the services of tax consultants from the big global accounting and professional services firms and a former deputy commissioner-general of the Tanzania Revenue Authority. The lobbyists argued that the abolition of exemptions would make the country unattractive for investors and leave Tanzanian companies uncompetitive in domestic and regional markets. They were successful. The VAT Act that the president signed in December 2014 reintroduced many exemptions that had been abolished in the draft bill, and restored to the minister of finance some discretionary power to grant further exemptions. A member of the VAT technical team in the Ministry of Finance described the new act as 'completely diluted'.

In some ways this is yet another example of powerful interests securing special treatment. However, the political process was very different from that around the introduction of VAT two decades earlier. This time, the decision was not made quietly behind closed doors, but through a highly public and contested process. This exemplifies the increasingly active participation of business associations in tax policy debates across the continent. In order for this new trend to yield broad public benefits, the question now is whether this greater business activism will be matched by more general engagement by ordinary African taxpayers in creating a new politics of taxation.

There are tentative signs that such broader mobilisation is beginning to occur – and a correspondingly strong case for supporting it. Perhaps the sector that has the deepest history of advocacy engagement is extractives, where local activist groups have long protested against the inadequate taxation of mining in particular. The level of interest of civil society organisations in the taxation of extractives has risen over time, partly because of increasing external stimulus and support from international tax justice campaigners and from rule- or norm-creating organisations such as the Extractive Industries Transparency Initiative (the EITI, founded in 2003). In Sierra Leone, local advocacy groups pressured governments over minerals contracts that involved large tax exemptions for international investors, leading to their renegotiation (Jibao and Prichard 2010). In Zambia, activists challenged what they viewed as overly generous minerals legislation, leading the government to significantly raise tax rates – and sparking a long and continuing debate over the revenue raised from mining enterprises (Manley 2015). Similar processes have taken root across the continent.

Earlier in the book we mentioned somewhat more surprising civil society protests about international tax evasion and avoidance by MNCs and wealthy individuals. International tax issues are highly complex. They are not obviously prime material for popular political engagement; one might expect them to remain the preserve of experts. Yet, over the past decade, civil society engagement has expanded steadily. Although closely linked to international NGOs working on the same issues, advocacy in Africa has been driven by the emergence of a growing group of African activists, journalists and academics deeply versed in international tax issues. The effects have been tangible, with significant national and international attention being paid to firms accused of engaging in aggressive tax avoidance strategies in Africa and to wealthy Africans accused of holding significant wealth overseas (see, for example, the reporting of Africans exposed in Swiss Leaks (Spooner 2015), African Panama Papers investigations (ANCIR 2017), and Paradise Papers stories (AllAfrica 2017; Fitzgibbon 2017)). The Tax Justice Network-Africa (TJN-A) has brought increasing attention to tax treaties that undermine national interests, including taking the government of Kenya to court over a treaty with Mauritius (TJN-A 2015; Hearson 2015). This focus on international taxation has been mirrored by growing civil society interest in the granting of unjustified tax exemptions. Civil society organisations, for example, have completed studies on the fiscal costs of tax exemptions across a range of African countries and regions, including Sierra Leone, Nigeria and East and West Africa (Budget Advocacy Network 2014; ActionAid 2016a; TJN-A and ActionAid International 2015; 2016). They have also campaigned for greater transparency around tax exemptions (see, for example, Tax Justice Alliance Uganda 2017; Zambia Tax Platform 2016; Oxfam and TJN-A 2016).

Another regular target of civil society mobilisation has been VAT, which activists have presented as regressive and damaging to the interests of poorer people. In technical terms, these critiques of VAT are open to question (Chapter 6). While VAT is not a progressive tax, it does not appear to be obviously regressive in practice. And it is potentially such an effective way of raising additional revenue that, were that revenue spent in the right ways, VAT could have an overall progressive effect. Yet, even if complaints about the allegedly regressive effects of VAT are misguided or unproven, the process of open debate and criticism itself may be important. Where publics are increasingly engaged in tax debates, governments are forced to justify their policies, and to demonstrate the contribution of VAT to national development. In Ghana, for example, protests against the introduction of VAT put pressure on the government to earmark some VAT revenues for spending on popular health and education programmes (Chapters 6 and 8; Prichard 2009).

Recently, some activist civil society groups in Africa have begun to consider pivoting away from their focus on international tax and VAT towards campaigns on a simpler message: ensuring that wealthy Africans pay their taxes. This would move the emphasis of campaign work to income taxes and property taxes, and to the political heart of the tax challenge in Africa: the inability or unwillingness of tax authorities to seriously confront tax evasion and avoidance by (sometimes readily identifiable) elites. One of the attractions of campaigning about tax in these terms is that it offers a simple and uncontroversial message about equality under the law, which research suggests has been a particularly effective way of mobilising popular action elsewhere in the world (Fairfield 2013).

Finally – and perhaps of greatest interest – more public engagement with tax issues could nurture an alliance between tax administrations and civil society tax activists. Tax advocacy has traditionally taken the form of what we might call 'negative campaigning': highlighting the failures of revenue administrations as part of broader narratives of injustice. However, there are also signs of more 'positive campaigning': making a constructive case for more effective taxation, fewer tax exemptions (which tax administrators dislike because they are obstacles to the achievement of revenue collection targets), and greater transparency around public spending, in order to help build stronger 'fiscal contracts' and a larger constituency for tax reform.

An example of this more positive campaigning comes from civil society groups that have argued in favour of stronger links between tax and public spending. In Kenya, the National Taxpayers' Association brought together a coalition of groups that originally worked primarily on budget monitoring. Over time, tax issues have begun to figure more prominently on their agenda. They focus on the message that taxes are essential for national development, but they need to be collected from *all* taxpayers, including the elites; and on the potential for mobilising citizens *as taxpayers* to make demands about how *their* money is used. Similar advocacy efforts in Zambia supported by the international NGO ActionAid contributed to a significant expansion of taxpayer efforts to seek new information about how tax revenues were used within local communities – thus generating incentives for improvement.

Many of the approaches outlined here remain very much in their infancy. The politics of taxation are still driven largely by comparatively narrow and powerful interest groups. And the barriers to broader popular engagement remain substantial. The issues can appear distant and complex. Limited trust in governments and tax authorities undermines the potential for 'positive campaigning'. And in at least some cases, governments have begun to limit the political space available to these groups as part of wider efforts to curb the influence of international NGOs in particular. But the outlines of a new dynamic can be seen in the efforts of civil society groups to create a more inclusive politics of taxation, and in the possibility that political leaders may see that there are both votes and revenue to be obtained by promoting more equitable and responsive tax systems.

BIBLIOGRAPHY

Aarsnes, F. and Lundstøl, O. (2013) *The Case for Windfall Taxes: a guide to optimal resource taxation*. Oslo: Publish What You Pay Norway.

Abbas, S. and Klemm, A. (2013) 'A partial race to the bottom: corporate tax developments in emerging and developing economies', *International Tax and Public Finance* 20 (4): 596–617.

Aberbach, J. D. and Christensen, T. (2007) 'The challenges of modernizing tax administration: putting customers first in coercive public organisations', *Public Policy and Administration* 22 (2): 155–82.

Abraham, A. (1974) 'Bai Bureh, the British, and the Hut Tax War', *International Journal of African Historical Studies* 7 (1): 99–106.

Abramovsky, L., Klemm, A. and Phillips, D. (2014) 'Corporate tax in developing countries: current trends and design issues', *Fiscal Studies* 35 (4): 559–88.

ActionAid (2012) *Calling Time: why SABMiller should stop dodging taxes in Africa*. London: ActionAid UK. Available at: https://www.actionaid.org.uk/sites/default/files/doc_lib/calling_time_on_tax_avoidance.pdf (accessed 27 November 2017).

ActionAid (2013) *Sweet nothings: the human cost of a British sugar giant avoiding taxes in southern Africa*. Chard: ActionAid UK. Available at: http://www.actionaid.org/sites/files/actionaid/sweet_nothings.pdf (accessed 20 January 2018).

ActionAid (2015) *Levelling Up: ensuring a fairer share of corporate tax for developing countries*. London: ActionAid UK. Available at: https://www.actionaid.org.uk/sites/default/files/publications/levelling_up_final.pdf (accessed 20 January 2018).

ActionAid (2016a) *Leaking Revenue: how a big tax break to European gas companies has cost Nigeria billions*. London: ActionAid UK. Available at: https://www.actionaid.org.uk/sites/default/files/publications/leakingrevenue.pdf (accessed 22 January 2018).

ActionAid (2016b) *Mistreated: the tax treaties that are depriving the world's poorest countries of vital revenue*. Johannesburg: ActionAid International. Available at: http://www.actionaid.org/publications/mistreated-tax-treaties-are-depriving-worlds-poorest-countries-vital-revenue (accessed 25 March 2017).

Africa Progress Panel (2013) *Africa Progress Report 2013. Equity in extractives: stewarding Africa's natural resources for all*. Geneva: Africa Progress Panel.

Available at: http://www.africaprogresspanel.org/publications/policy-papers/africa-progress-report-2013/ (accessed 25 March 2017).

African Tax Administration Forum (n.d.) 'About the ATAF: overview'. Available at: https://www.ataftax.org/en/about/overview (accessed 21 April 2017).

African Tax Administration Forum (2017) *African Tax Outlook 2017: second edition*. Pretoria: African Tax Administration Forum. Available at: https://www.ataftax.org/en/news-library/library (accessed 20 November 2017).

Ahlerup, P., Baskaran, T. and Bigsten, A. (2015) 'Tax innovations and public revenues in sub-Saharan Africa', *Journal of Development Studies* 51 (6): 689–706.

Ahmad, A. (2017) *Jihad & Co.: black markets and Islamist power*. New York NY: Oxford University Press.

Aiko, R. and Logan, C. (2014) 'Africa's willing taxpayers thwarted by opaque tax systems, corruption'. Afrobarometer Policy Paper 7. Available at: http://afrobarometer.org/sites/default/files/publications/Briefing%20paper/ab_r5_policypaperno7.pdf (accessed 16 March 2017).

Ali, M., Fjeldstad, O. H. and Sjursen, I. H. (2014) 'To pay or not to pay? Citizens' attitudes toward taxation in Kenya, Tanzania, Uganda, and South Africa', *World Development* 64: 828–42.

AllAfrica (2017) 'African power players named in Paradise Papers'. Available at: http://allafrica.com/view/group/main/main/id/00056640.html (accessed 22 January 2018).

Alvaredo, F., Atkinson, A. B., Saez, E and Piketty, T. (2012) 'The world top incomes database: South Africa'. Available at: http://wid.world/country/south-africa/ (accessed 19 March 2017).

Amegashie, A. (2011) *Ghana's Regime of Exemptions from Taxes and Duties: guidelines for reform*. Guelph, Canada: Department of Economics, University of Guelph.

Amin, M. and Hoppe, M. (2013) 'Where informal procedures are quasi-formal: cross-border trade between West and Central Africa'. Africa Trade Policy Notes 78406. Washington DC: World Bank. Available at: http://documents.worldbank.org/curated/en/463501468193501223/Where-informal-procedures-are-quasi-formal-cross-border-trade-between-West-and-Central-Africa (accessed 10 April 2017).

ANCIR (2017) 'The Panama Papers'. Available at: https://panamapapers.investigativecenters.org/ (accessed 22 January 2018).

Andersen, J. J. and Ross, M. L. (2014) 'The big oil change: a closer look at the Haber-Menaldo analysis', *Comparative Political Studies* 47 (7): 993–1021.

Bahl, R. W., Martinez-Vazquez, J. and Youngman, J. M. (2008) 'The property tax in practice' in R. W. Bahl, J. Martinez-Vazquez and J. M. Youngman (eds), *Making the Property Tax Work: experiences in developing and transitional countries*. Cambridge MA: Lincoln Institute of Land Policy.

Barma, N., Kaiser, K., Le, T. M. and Viñuela, L. (2012) *Rents to Riches? The political economy of natural resource-led development*. Washington DC: World Bank.

Barry, F. (2015) 'Capital flight, safe havens and secrecy jurisdictions' in I. Ajayi and L. Ndikuman (eds), *Capital Flight from Africa*. Oxford: Oxford University Press.

Bates, R. (1977) *Markets and States in Tropical Africa: the political basis of agricultural policies*. Berkeley CA: University of California Press.

Bates, R. H. (2008) *When Things Fell Apart: state failure in late-century Africa*. New York NY: Cambridge University Press.

Baunsgaard, T. and Keen, M. (2009) 'Tax revenue and (or?) trade liberalization', *Journal of Public Economics* 94 (9–10): 563–77.

Bayart, J.-F. (1993) *The State in Africa: the politics of the belly*. London: Longman.

Bayart, J.-F., Ellis, S. and Hibou, B. (1999) *The Criminalization of the State in Africa*. Oxford: International African Institute in association with James Currey.

Bell, M. E. and Bowman, J. H. (2006) *Implementing a Local Property Tax Where There Is No Real Estate Market: the case of commonly owned land in rural South Africa*. Cambridge MA: Lincoln Institute of Land Policy.

BEPS Monitoring Group (2016) 'Presentation to the Enlarged Framework on BEPS of the OECD Committee on Fiscal Affairs'. Paper presented at the meeting of the Enlarged Framework of the Organisation for Economic Co-operation and Development (OECD) Committee on Fiscal Affairs, Kyoto, Japan, 29 June. Available at: https://bepsmonitoringgroup.files.wordpress.com/2016/07/presentation-to-cfa-if-june-2016.pdf (accessed 20 January 2018).

Best, M. C., Brockmeyer, A., Kleven, H. J., Spinnewijn, J. and Waseem, M. (2015) 'Production versus revenue efficiency with limited tax capacity: theory and evidence from Pakistan', *Journal of Political Economy* 123 (6): 1311–55.

Beuermann, D. W. and Amelina, M. (2014) 'Does participatory budgeting improve decentralised public service delivery?' IDB Working Paper 547. Washington DC: Inter-American Development Bank.

Bezemer, D. and Headey, D. (2008) 'Agriculture, development, and urban bias', *World Development* 36 (8): 1342–64.

Bilangna, S. and Djeuwo, M. (2013) 'The figures culture in Cameroon customs' in T. Cantens, R. Ireland and G. Raballand (eds), *Reform by Numbers: measurement applied to customs and tax administrations in developing countries*. Washington DC: World Bank.

Bird, M. (2015) 'Africa's millionaire explosion: the 16 countries where the ultra-wealthy are booming', *Business Insider*, 7 August. Available at: http://uk.businessinsider.com/new-world-wealth-african-millionaires-2015-8 (accessed 19 March 2017).

Bird, R. M. and Slack, E. (2006) 'Taxing land and property in emerging economies: raising revenue … and more?' in G. K. Ingram and Y.-H. Hong (eds), *Land Policies and their Outcomes*. Cambridge MA: Lincoln Institute of Land Policy.

Bird, R. M. and Smart, M. (2002) 'Intergovernmental fiscal transfers: international lessons for developing countries', *World Development* 30 (6): 899–912.

Bird, R. M. and Zolt, E. M. (2003) 'Introduction to tax policy design and development'. Draft prepared for a course on 'Practical Issues of Tax Policy in Developing Countries'. Washington DC: World Bank. Available at: http://www.gsdrc.org/document-library/introduction-to-tax-policy-design-and-development/ (accessed 8 April 2017).

Bird, R. M. and Zolt, E. M. (2005) 'Redistribution via taxation: the limited role of the personal income tax in developing countries', *UCLA Law Review* 52 (6): 1627–95.

Bird, R. M. and Zolt, E. M. (2008) 'Technology and taxation in developing countries: from hand to mouse', *National Tax Journal* 61 (4): 791–821.

Blundo, G. (2006) 'Dealing with the local state: the informal privatization of street-level bureaucracies in Senegal', *Development and Change* 37 (4): 799–819.

Bolnick, B. (2004) *Effectiveness and Economic Impact of Tax Incentives in the SADC Region*. USAID Technical Report. Arlington VA: Nathan–MSI Group for USAID/RCSA SADC Tax Subcommittee, SADC Trade, Industry, Finance and Investment Directorate. Available at: http://pdf.usaid.gov/pdf_docs/Pnacy929.pdf (accessed 14 April 2017).

Bradbury, M. (2008) *Becoming Somaliland*. London: Progressio.

Brautigam, D. (2008) 'Taxation and state-building in developing countries' in D. Brautigam, O.-H. Fjeldstad and M. Moore (eds), *Taxation and State-building in Developing Countries: capacity and consent*. Cambridge: Cambridge University Press.

Brun, J.-F., Chambas, G. and Fjeldstad, O.-H. (2011) 'Local government taxation in Africa'. Paper presented at International Centre for Tax and Development (ICTD) Annual Conference, Brighton, 23 June. Available at: https://www.cmi.no/publications/4077-local-government-taxation-in-africa (accessed 22 April 2017).

Budget Advocacy Network (2014) *Losing Out: Sierra Leone's massive revenue losses from tax incentives*. Freetown: Budget Advocacy Network. Available at: http://curtisresearch.org/wp-content/uploads/Losing-Out.-Final-report.-April-2014.pdf (accessed 22 January 2018).

Burgess, R. and Stern, N. (1993) 'Taxation and development', *Journal of Economic Literature* 31 (2): 762–830.

Callen, T., Cherif, R., Hasanov, F., Amgad, H. and Khandelwal, P. (2014) 'Economic diversification in the GCC: past, present, and future'. IMF Staff Discussion Notes 14/12. Washington DC: International Monetary Fund (IMF). Available at: https://www.imf.org/en/Publications/Staff-Discussion-Notes/Issues/2016/12/31/Economic-Diversification-in-the-GCC-Past-Present-and-Future-42531 (accessed 17 November 2017).

Cantens, T. (2012a) 'Is it possible to reform a customs administration? The role of the customs elite on the reform process in Cameroon' in A. H. Amsden, A. DiCaprio and J. A. Robinson (eds), *The Role of Elites in Economic Development*. Oxford: Oxford University Press.

Cantens, T. (2012b) 'Other people's money and goods: the relationship between customs officers and users in some countries of sub-Saharan Africa' in T. Cantens, R. Ireland and G. Raballand (eds), *Reform by Numbers: measurement applied to customs and tax administrations in developing countries*. Washington DC: World Bank.

Cantens, T. and Rabelland, G. (2017) 'Cross-border trade, insecurity and the role of customs: some lessons from six field studies in (post)-conflict regions'. ICTD Working Paper. Brighton: International Centre for Tax and Development (ICTD), Institute of Development Studies.

Cantens, T., Ireland, R. and Raballand, G. (eds) (2013) *Reform by Numbers: measurement applied to customs and tax administrations in developing countries*. Washington DC: World Bank.

Cantens, T., Kaminski, J., Raballand, G. and Tchapa, T. (2014) 'Customs, brokers, and informal sectors: a Cameroon case study'. Policy Research Working Paper 6788. Washington DC: World Bank. Available at: http://documents. worldbank.org/curated/en/954731468236664030/Customs-brokers-and-informal-sectors-a-Cameroon-case-study (accessed 14 April 2017).

Carter, A. (2013) *International Tax Dialogue: key issues and debates in VAT, SME taxation and the tax treatment of the financial sector*. International Tax Dialogue. Available at: www.itdweb.org (accessed 10 April 2017).

CEQ Institute (Commitment to Equality) (2017) 'CEQ data centre on fiscal redistribution'. Available at: http://www.commitmentoequity.org/ (accessed 14 April 2017).

Chabal, P. and Daloz, J.-P. (1999) *Africa Works: disorder as political instrument*. Oxford and Bloomington IN: James Currey and Indiana University Press.

Chakravarty, A., Ghosh, S. and Kuo, E. (2015) 'Location specific advantages', *Global Transfer Pricing*, November. Available at: https://www2.deloitte.com/ content/dam/Deloitte/us/Documents/Tax/us-tax-beps-changes-transfer-pricing-location-specific-advantages.pdf (accessed 16 January 2018).

Chaudhry, K. A. (1997) *The Price of Wealth: economies and institutions in the Middle East*. Ithaca NY: Cornell University Press.

Cheeseman, N. and de Gramont, D. (2017) 'Managing a mega-city: learning the lessons from Lagos', *Oxford Review of Economic Policy* 33 (3): 457–77.

Chitembo, A. (2009) 'Fiscal decentralisation: a comparative perspective'. Paper presented to traditional leaders sitting on the Zambian National Constitutional Conference (NCC), Andrews Motel, Lusaka, 8 June.

Christensen, J., Kapoor, S. and Murphy, R. (2007) *Closing the Floodgates: collecting tax to pay for development*. London: Tax Justice Network.

Christians, A. (2007) 'Hard law and soft law in international taxation', *Wisconsin International Law Journal* 25 (2): 325–34. Available at: https://ssrn.com/abstract=988782 (accessed 14 December 2017).

Chuhan-Pole, P. (2015) 'Drop in global commodity prices, electricity bottlenecks, and security risks slow Africa's economic growth', *Africa's Pulse*, October. Washington DC: World Bank. Available at: https://openknowledge.worldbank.org/bitstream/handle/10986/22722/9781464807381.pdf (accessed 24 November 2017).

Clausing, K. A. and Durst, M. C. (2015) 'A price-based royalty tax?' ICTD Working Paper 41. Brighton: International Centre for Tax and Development (ICTD), Institute of Development Studies.

Cobham, A. and Jansky, P. (2015) 'Measuring misalignment: the location of US multinationals' economic activity versus the location of their profits'. ICTD Working Paper 42. Brighton: International Centre for Tax and Development (ICTD), Institute of Development Studies.

Cobham, A. and Jansky, P. (2017) 'Global distribution of revenue loss from tax avoidance: re-estimation and country results'. WIDER Working Paper 2017/55. Helsinki: United Nations University World Institute for Development Economics Research (WIDER). Available at: https://www.wider.unu.edu/sites/default/files/wp2017-55.pdf (accessed 14 December 2017).

Collier, P. (2010) *The Plundered Planet: how to reconcile prosperity with nature.* London: Allen Lane.

Coolidge, J. (2012) 'Findings of tax compliance cost surveys in developing countries', *eJournal of Tax Research* 10 (2): 250.

Credit Suisse (2017) *Global Wealth Report 2017.* Zurich: Credit Suisse. Available at: https://www.credit-suisse.com/corporate/en/research/research-institute/global-wealth-report.html (accessed 14 December 2017).

Crivelli, E., Keen, M. and de Mooij, R. (2015) 'Base erosion, profit-shifting and developing countries'. IMF Working Paper 15/118. Washington DC: International Monetary Fund (IMF). Available at: https://www.imf.org/external/pubs/ft/wp/2015/wp15118.pdf (accessed 11 April 2017).

Crook, R. C. (2010) 'Rethinking civil service reform in Africa: "islands of effectiveness" and organisational commitment', *Commonwealth and Comparative Politics* 48 (4): 479–504.

Cuvelier, J. and Mumbunda, P. M. (2013) 'Réforme douanière néolibérale, fragilité etatique et pluralisme normatif. Le cas du guichet unique à Kasumbalesa', *Politique Africaine* 1 (129): 93–112.

Daniel, P., Keen, M. and McPherson, C. P. (eds) (2010) *The Taxation of Petroleum and Minerals: principles, problems and practice.* London and New York NY: Routledge and International Monetary Fund.

Das, S. (2014) 'Vedanta KCM's Anil Agarwal, March 2014, Bangalore, India'. Available at: https://www.youtube.com/watch?v=98yKosnwb-Y (accessed 25 March 2017).

de Gramont, D. (2015) 'Governing Lagos: unlocking the politics of reform'. Washington DC: Carnegie Endowment for International Peace. Available at: http://carnegieendowment.org/2015/01/12/governing-lagos-unlocking-politics-of-reform-pub-57671 (accessed 30 November 2017).

de Mooij, R. A. and Ederveen, S. (2003) 'Taxation and foreign direct investment: a synthesis of empirical research', *International Tax and Public Finance* 10 (6): 673–93.

Devas, N. and Kelly, R. (2001) 'Regulation or revenues? An analysis of local business licences, with a case study of the single business permit reform in Kenya', *Public Administration and Development* 21 (5): 381–91.

Dogbevi, E. K. (2016) 'How Ghana started but failed to remain a tax haven', *Ghana Business News*, 12 April. Available at: https://www.ghanabusinessnews.com/2016/04/12/how-ghana-started-but-failed-to-remain-a-tax-haven/ (accessed 27 November 2017).

Dom, R. (2017) 'Semi-autonomous revenue authorities in sub-Saharan Africa: silver bullet or white elephant'. CREDIT Research Paper 17/01. Nottingham: Centre for Research in Economic Development and International Trade (CREDIT), University of Nottingham. Available at: https://www.nottingham.ac.uk/credit/documents/papers/2017/17-01.pdf (accessed 10 April 2017).

Doner, R. F., Ritchie, B. K. and Slater, D. (2005) 'Systemic vulnerability and the origins of developmental states: Northeast and Southeast Asia in comparative perspective', *International Organization* 59 (2): 327–61.

Due, J. F. (1963) *Taxation and Economic Development in Tropical Africa*. Cambridge MA: MIT Press.

Durst, M. (2015a) 'Beyond BEPS: a tax policy agenda for developing countries'. ICTD Working Paper 18. Brighton: International Centre for Tax and Development (ICTD), Institute of Development Studies.

Durst, M. (2015b) 'The tax policy outlook for developing countries: reflections on international formulary apportionment'. ICTD Working Paper 32. Brighton: International Centre for Tax and Development (ICTD), Institute of Development Studies.

Durst, M. (2016a) 'Developing country revenue mobilisation: a proposal to modify the "transactional net margin" transfer pricing method'. ICTD Working Paper 44. Brighton: International Centre for Tax and Development (ICTD), Institute of Development Studies.

Durst, M. (2016b) 'Improving the performance of natural resource taxation in developing countries'. ICTD Working Paper 60. Brighton: International Centre for Tax and Development (ICTD), Institute of Development Studies.

Ebeke, C., Mansour, M. and Rota-Graziosi, G. (2016) 'The power to tax in sub-Saharan Africa: LTUs, VATs, and SARAs'. Working Paper – Development Policies 154. Clermont-Ferrand: Fondation pour les Études et Recherches sur le Développement International. Available at: https://halshs.archives-ouvertes.fr/halshs-01332049/ (accessed 10 April 2017).

EITI (2016a) 'The EITI standard'. Extractive Industries Transparency Initiative. Available at: https://eiti.org/document/standard (accessed 16 November 2017).

EITI (2016b) 'Summary data from EITI reports'. Extractive Industries Transparency Initiative. Available at: https://eiti.org/summary-data (accessed 16 November 2017).

Elsayyad, M. and Konrad, K. A. (2012) 'Fighting multiple tax havens', *Journal of International Economics* 86 (2): 295–305.

Eunomix Research (2017) *A Review of the UNCTAD Report on Trade Misinvoicing, with a Full Counterfactual on South African Exports.* Johannesburg: Eunomix Research. Available at: https://www.eunomix.com/cmsAdmin/uploads/eunomix-final-report-review-of-unctad-misinvoicing-report-5-june-2017-published-docx_001.pdf (accessed 14 December 2017).

Fairfield, T. (2013) 'Going where the money is: strategies for taxing economic elites in unequal democracies', *World Development* 47: 42–57.

FATF (2012) *International Standards on Combating Money Laundering and the Financing of Terrorism and Proliferation: FATF recommendations.* Paris: Financial Action Task Force (FATF). Available at: http://www.fatf-gafi.org/media/fatf/documents/recommendations/pdfs/FATF_Recommendations.pdf (accessed 27 March 2017).

Financial Transparency Coalition (2017) 'Unequal exchange: how poor countries are blindfolded in the global fight against banking secrecy'. Available at: https://financialtransparency.org/unequal-exchange/ (accessed 20 January 2018).

Findley, M. G., Nielson, D. and Sharman, J. C. (2014) *Global Shell Games: experiments in transnational relations, crime, and terrorism.* New York NY: Cambridge University Press.

Fitzgibbon, W. (2017) 'Tax haven Mauritius' rise comes at rest of Africa's expense', *International Consortium of Investigative Journalists*, 7 November. Available at: https://www.icij.org/investigations/paradise-papers/tax-haven-mauritius-africa/ (accessed 22 January 2018).

Fjeldstad, O.-H. (2001) 'Taxation, coercion and donors: local government tax enforcement in Tanzania', *Journal of Modern African Studies* 39 (2): 289–306.

Fjeldstad, O.-H. (2003) 'Fighting fiscal corruption: lessons from the Tanzania Revenue Authority', *Public Administration and Development* 23 (2): 165–75.

Fjeldstad, O.-H. (2006) 'Corruption in tax administration: lessons from institutional reforms in Uganda' in R.-A. Susan (ed.), *International Handbook on the Economics of Corruption.* Cheltenham: Edward Elgar.

Fjeldstad, O.-H. (2016) 'Revenue mobilization at sub-national levels in Sudan'. Sudan Report 2016:1. Bergen: Chr. Michelsen Institute. Available at: https://www.cmi.no/publications/5749-revenue-mobilization-at-sub-national-levels-in (accessed 22 April 2017).

Fjeldstad, O.-H. and Heggstad, K. K. (2011) 'Tax systems in Mozambique, Tanzania and Zambia: capacity and constraints'. CMI Report 2011:3. Bergen: Chr.

Michelsen Institute (CMI). Available at: https://www.cmi.no/publications/file/4045-taxation-mozambique-tanzania-zambia.pdf (accessed 14 April 2017).

Fjeldstad, O.-H. and Heggstad, K. K. (2014) 'Capital flight from Africa – with a little help from the banks' in A. da Rocha (ed.), *Fuga de Capitais e a Política de Desenvolvimento a Favor do Mais Pobres em Angola* [*Capital Flight and Pro-poor Development Policy in Angola*]. Luanda: CEIC/NCA.

Fjeldstad, O.-H. and Moore, M. (2008a) 'Revenue authorities and state capacity in Anglophone Africa'. CMI Working Paper 2008:1. Bergen: Chr. Michelsen Institute (CMI). Available at: https://www.cmi.no/publications/2952-revenue-authorities-and-state-capacity-in (accessed 10 April 2017).

Fjeldstad, O.-H. and Moore, M. (2008b) 'Tax reform and state-building in a globalised world' in D. Brautigam, O.-H. Fjeldstad and M. Moore (eds), *Taxation and State-building in Developing Countries: capacity and consent.* Cambridge: Cambridge University Press.

Fjeldstad, O.-H. and Semboja, J. (2001) 'Why people pay taxes: the case of the development levy in Tanzania', *World Development* 29 (12): 2059–74.

Fjeldstad, O.-H. and Therkildsen, O. (2008) 'Mass taxation and state–society relations in East Africa' in D. Brautigam, O.-H. Fjeldstad and M. Moore (eds), *Taxation and State-building in Developing Countries: capacity and consent.* Cambridge: Cambridge University Press.

Fjeldstad, O.-H., Ali, M. and Goodfellow, T. (2017) 'Taxing the urban boom: property taxation in Africa'. CMI Insight 1. Bergen: Chr. Michelsen Institute (CMI). Available at:—https://www.cmi.no/publications/6190-taxing-the-urban-boom-property-taxation-in-africa (accessed 23 April 2017).

Fjeldstad, O.-H., Katera, L. and Ngalewa, E. (2009) 'Maybe we should pay tax after all? Citizens' views on taxation in Tanzania'. REPOA Special Paper 29. Dar es Salaam: Research on Poverty Alleviation (REPOA). Available at: https://www.cmi.no/publications/3349-tax-compliance-tanzania (accessed 23 April 2017).

Fjeldstad, O.-H., Katera, L., Ngalewa, E. and Msami, J. (2010) 'Local government finances and financial management in Tanzania: empirical evidence of trends 2000–2007'. REPOA Special Paper 10. Dar es Salaam: Research on Poverty Alleviation (REPOA). Available at: https://www.cmi.no/publications/3841-local-government-finances-and-financial-management (accessed 23 April 2017).

Flores-Macías, G. A. (2014) 'Financing security through elite taxation: the case of Colombia's "democratic security taxes"', *Studies in Comparative International Development* 49 (4): 477–500.

Flores-Macías, G. A. (2016) 'Building support for taxation in developing countries: experimental evidence from Mexico'. ICTD Working Paper 51. Brighton: International Centre for Tax and Development (ICTD), Institute of Development Studies.

Forslund, D. (2012) 'Personal income taxation in South Africa and the struggle against poverty and inequality'. Paper presented at the Budget Justice seminar, Cape Town, February 2013. Available at: https://www.researchgate. net/publication/282972498_Nov_2012_Personal_income_taxation_in_ South_Africa_and_the_struggle_against_poverty_and_inequality (accessed 24 November 2017).

Forstater, M. (2015) 'Can stopping "tax dodging" by multinational enterprises close the gap in development finance?' CGD Policy Paper 69. Washington DC: Centre for Global Development (CGD). Available at: https://www.cgdev.org/ publication/can-stopping-tax-dodging-multinational-enterprises-close-gap-development-finance (accessed 26 April 2017).

Fossat, P. and Bua, M. (2013) 'Tax administration reform in the Francophone countries of sub-Saharan Africa'. IMF Working Paper 13/173. Washington DC: International Monetary Fund (IMF).

Frankema, E. (2010) 'Raising revenue in the British empire, 1870–1940: how "extractive" were colonial taxes?', *Journal of Global History* 5 (3): 447–77.

Frankema, E. (2011) 'Colonial taxation and government spending in British Africa, 1880–1940: maximizing revenue or minimizing effort?', *Explorations in Economic History* 48 (1): 136–49.

Franzsen, R. C. D. (2007) 'Property taxation in Anglophone Africa', *Land Lines*, April. Cambridge MA.: Lincoln Institute of Land Policy. Available at: http:// www.lincolninst.edu/publications/articles/property-taxation-anglophone-africa (accessed 23 April 2017).

Franzsen, R. C. D. and McCluskey, W. (eds) (2017) *Property Tax in Africa: status, challenges and prospects.* Cambridge MA: Lincoln Institute of Land Policy.

Franzsen, R. C. D. and Youngman, J. M. (2009) 'Mapping property taxes in Africa', *Land Lines*, July. Cambridge MA.: Lincoln Institute of Land Policy. Available at: https://www.lincolninst.edu/sites/default/files/pubfiles/mapping-property-taxes-in-africa-090703-full.pdf (accessed 23 April 2017).

Fuest, C., Hebous, S. and Riedel, N. (2011) 'International debt shifting and multinational firms in developing economies', *Economics Letters* 113 (2): 135–8.

Gadenne, L. (2017) 'Tax me, but spend wisely? Sources of public finance and government accountability', *American Economic Journal: Applied Economics* 9 (1): 274–314.

Gardner, L. A. (2012) *Taxing Colonial Africa: the political economy of British imperialism.* Oxford: Oxford University Press.

Gavin, E., Breytenbach, D., Carolissen, R. and Leolo, M. (2013) 'The roles of tax administration data in the production of official statistics in South Africa.' Paper presented at the 59th ISI World Statistics Congress, Hong Kong, 25–30 August. Available at: http://www.2013.isiproceedings.org/Files/STS021-P2-S.pdf (accessed 17 April 2017).

Gehlbach, S. (2008) *Representation through Taxation: revenue, politics, and development in post-communist states.* Cambridge: Cambridge University Press.

Ghazvinian, J. H. (2007) *Untapped: the scramble for Africa's oil.* Orlando FL: Harcourt.

Gillis, M. (1990) 'Micro- and macroeconomics of tax reform: Indonesia' in R. M. Bird and O. Oldman (eds), *Taxation in Developing Countries.* Baltimore MD: Johns Hopkins University Press.

Goode, R. (1993) 'Tax advice to developing countries: an historical survey', *World Development* 21 (1): 37–53.

Goodfellow, T. (2015) 'Taxing the urban boom: property taxation and land leasing in Kigali and Addis Ababa'. ICTD Working Paper 38. Brighton: International Centre for Tax and Development (ICTD), Institute of Development Studies.

Goodfellow, T. (2017) 'Taxing property in a neo-developmental state: the politics of urban land value capture in Rwanda and Ethiopia', *African Affairs* 116 (465): 549–72.

Goodfellow, T. and Owen, O. (2018) 'Taxation, property rights and the social contract in Lagos'. ICTD Working Paper 73. Brighton: International Centre for Tax and Development (ICTD), Institute of Development Studies.

Gray, L., Hansen, K., Recica-Kirkbride, P. and Mills, L. (2014) *Few and Far: the hard facts on stolen asset recovery.* Washington DC: World Bank.

Growth Lab (2016) 'Atlas of economic complexity'. Growth Lab, Centre for International Development, Harvard University. Available at: http://atlas.cid.harvard.edu/ (accessed 22 January 2018).

Guguyu, O. (2016) 'Kenya: treasury defends controversial Mauritius tax agreement', *The Nation*, 4 February. Available at: http://allafrica.com/stories/201602041381.html (accessed 27 November 2017).

Guldbrandsen, C. (2013) *Stealing Africa: why poverty?* (film). Available at: https://www.youtube.com/watch?v=WNYemuiAOfU (accessed 25 March 2017).

Harrison, G. and Krelove, R. (2005) 'VAT refunds: a review of country experience'. IMF Working Paper 05/218. Washington DC: International Monetary Fund (IMF). Available at: http://www.imf.org/en/Publications/WP/Issues/2016/12/31/VAT-Refunds-A-Review-of-Country-Experience-18646 (accessed 14 April 2017).

Hausman, D. and Zikhali, P. (2016) 'Raising tax revenue' in A. Alam, R. Mokate and K. A. Plangemann (eds), *Making It Happen: selected case studies of institutional reforms in South Africa.* Washington DC: World Bank.

Haysom, S. (2016) 'Sars, Krejcir and the destruction of state capacity', *Mail & Guardian*, 1 April. Available at: https://mg.co.za/article/2016-04-01-00-sars-krejcir-and-the-destruction-of-state-capacity/ (accessed 8 April 2017).

Hearson, M. (2013) 'Double tax treaties: a poisoned chalice for developing countries?' Paper presented at Strathmore Business School, Nairobi, 11 September. Available at: https://www.slideshare.net/martinhearson/double-tax-treaties-a-poisoned-chalice (accessed 24 November 2017).

Hearson, M. (2015) *Tax Treaties in Sub-Saharan Africa: a critical review.* Nairobi: Tax Justice Network-Africa. Available at: https://martinhearson.files.wordpress.com/2015/11/tjna_treaties.pdf (accessed 24 November 2017).

Hearson, M. (2016) 'Measuring tax treaty negotiation outcomes: the ActionAid tax treaties dataset'. ICTD Working Paper 47. Brighton: International Centre for Tax and Development (ICTD), Institute of Development Studies.

Hearson, M. and Kangave, J. (2016) 'A review of Uganda's tax treaties and recommendations for action'. ICTD Working Paper 50. Brighton: International Centre for Tax and Development (ICTD), Institute of Development Studies.

Henry, J. S. (2012) *The Price of Offshore Revisited: new estimates for missing global private wealth, income, inequality and lost taxes.* Chesham, UK: Tax Justice Network. Available at: http://taxjustice.nonprofitsoapbox.com/storage/documents/The_Price_of_Offshore_Revisited_-_22-07-2012.pdf (accessed 26 April 2017).

Herb, M. (2005) 'No representation without taxation? Rents, development, and democracy', *Comparative Politics* 37 (3): 297–316.

Hoffmann, K., Vlassenroot, K. and Marchais, G. (2016) 'Taxation, stateness and armed groups: public authority and resource extraction in Eastern Congo', *Development and Change* 47 (6): 1434–56.

ICIJ (2015) 'Swiss Leaks data'. International Consortium of Investigative Journalists (ICIJ). Available at: http://www.icij.org/project/swiss-leaks/explore-swiss-leaks-data (accessed 22 January 2018).

ICIJ (2017a) 'All our investigations'. International Consortium of Investigative Journalists (ICIJ). Available at: https://www.icij.org/investigations/ (accessed 18 December 2017).

ICIJ (2017b) 'Frequently asked questions: ICIJ offshore leaks database'. International Consortium of Investigative Journalists (ICIJ). Available at: https://offshoreleaks.icij.org/pages/about (accessed 18 December 2017).

ICRICT (2015) 'Declaration'. Independent Commission for the Reform of International Corporate Taxation (ICRICT). Available at: https://www.icrict.com/icrict-documentsthe-declaration (accessed 17 November 2017).

ICTD/UNU-WIDER (2017) 'Government revenue dataset'. Available at: https://www.wider.unu.edu/project/government-revenuedataset (accessed 22 January 2018).

IMF (2011) 'Revenue mobilization in developing countries'. Washington DC: International Monetary Fund (IMF). Available at: http://www.imf.org/external/pp/longres.aspx?id=4537 (accessed 6 March 2017).

IMF (2012) 'Fiscal regimes for extractive industries: design and implementation'. Washington DC: International Monetary Fund (IMF). Available at: http://www.imf.org/en/Publications/Policy-Papers/Issues/2016/12/31/Fiscal-Regimes-for-Extractive-Industries-Design-and-Implementation-PP4701 (accessed 25 March 2017).

IMF (2014) 'Spillovers in international corporate taxation'. Policy Paper. Washington DC: International Monetary Fund (IMF). Available at: https://www.imf.org/external/np/pp/eng/2014/050914.pdf (accessed 13 April 2017).

IMF (2015) 'Current challenges in revenue mobilization: improving tax compliance'. Washington DC: International Monetary Fund (IMF). Available at: http://www.imf.org/en/Publications/Policy-Papers/Issues/2016/12/31/Current-Challenges-in-Revenue-Mobilization-Improving-Tax-Compliance-PP4944 (accessed 8 May 2017).

IMF (2016a) 'IMF data: world revenue longitudinal data – at a glance'. Washington DC: International Monetary Fund (IMF). Available at: https://data.world/imf/world-revenue-longitudinal-dat (accessed 22 April 2017).

IMF (2016b) *United Republic of Tanzania: selected issues*. Country Report 16/254. Washington DC: International Monetary Fund (IMF). Available at: https://www.imf.org/external/pubs/ft/scr/2016/cr16254.pdf (accessed 1 December 2017).

IMF et al. (2015) *Options for Low Income Countries' Effective and Efficient Use of Tax Incentives for Investment: a report to the G-20 Development Working Group by the IMF, OECD, UN and World Bank*. Washington DC: International Monetary Fund (IMF), Organisation for Economic Co-operation and Development (OECD), United Nations (UN) and World Bank. Available at: http://www.oecd.org/tax/tax-global/options-for-low-income-countries-effective-and-efficient-use-of-tax-incentives-for-investment-call-for-input.pdf (accessed 14 April 2017).

Isbell, T. (2017) 'Tax compliance Africans affirm civic duty but lack trust in tax department'. Afrobarometer Policy Paper 43. Available at: http://afrobarometer.org/publications/pp43-tax-compliance-africans-affirm-civic-duty-lack-trust-tax-department (accessed 7 December 2017).

Jibao, S. (2009) 'Property taxation in Anglophone West Africa: regional overview'. Working Paper. Cambridge MA: Lincoln Institute of Land Policy.

Jibao, S. and Prichard, W. (2010) *Building a Fair, Transparent and Inclusive Tax System in Sierra Leone*. Freetown: Christian Aid Sierra Leone.

Jibao, S. and Prichard, W. (2015) 'The political economy of property tax in Africa: explaining reform outcomes in Sierra Leone', *African Affairs* 114 (456): 404–31.

Jibao, S. and Prichard, W. (2016) 'Rebuilding local government finances after conflict: lessons from a property tax reform programme in post-conflict Sierra Leone', *Journal of Development Studies* 52 (12): 1759–75.

Jibao, S., Prichard, W. and van den Boogaard, V. (2017) 'Informal taxation in post-conflict Sierra Leone: taxpayers' experiences and perceptions'. ICTD Working Paper 66. Brighton: International Centre for Tax and Development (ICTD), Institute of Development Studies.

Jin, H., Qian, Y. and Weingast, B. R. (2005) 'Regional decentralization and fiscal incentives: federalism, Chinese style', *Journal of Public Economics* 89 (9–10): 1719–42.

Jones Lang LaSalle (2015) *Emerging Beyond the Frontier: An Overview of Sub-Saharan Africa's Real Estate Capital Markets.* Johannesburg: Jones Lang LaSalle. Available at: https://www.jllrealviews.com/economy/10-african-cities-attracting-attention/ (accessed 23 April 2017).

Joshi, A. (2017) 'Tax and gender in developing countries: what are the issues?' ICTD Summary Brief 6. Brighton: International Centre for Tax and Development (ICTD), Institute of Development Studies.

Joshi, A. and Ayee, J. (2008) 'Associational taxation: a pathway into the informal sector' in D. Brautigam, O.-H. Fjeldstad and M. Moore (eds), *Taxation and State-building in Developing Countries: capacity and consent.* Cambridge: Cambridge University Press.

Joshi, A., Prichard, W. and Heady, C. (2014) 'Taxing the informal economy: the current state of knowledge and agendas for future research', *Journal of Development Studies* 50 (10): 1325–47.

Juul, K. (2006) 'Decentralization, local taxation and citizenship in Senegal', *Development and Change* 37 (4): 821–46.

Kafeero, E. (2008) 'Customs and trade facilitation in the East African Community (EAC)', *World Customs Journal* 2 (1): 63–71.

Kaldor, N. (1963) 'Will underdeveloped countries learn to tax?', *Foreign Affairs*, 1 January. Available at: https://www.foreignaffairs.com/articles/asia/1963-01-01/will-underdeveloped-countries-learn-tax (accessed 10 April 2017).

Kangave, J., Nakato, S., Waiswa, R. and Zzimbe, P. L. (2016) 'Boosting revenue collection through taxing high net worth individuals: the case of Uganda'. ICTD Working Paper 45. Brighton: International Centre for Tax and Development (ICTD), Institute of Development Studies.

Keefe, P. R. (2013) 'Buried secrets', *The New Yorker*, 8 July. Available at: http://www.newyorker.com/magazine/2013/07/08/buried-secrets (accessed 27 March 2017).

Keen, M. (2009) 'What do (and don't) we know about the value added tax? A review of Richard M. Bird and Pierre-Pascal Gendron's *The VAT in Developing and Transitional Countries*', *Journal of Economic Literature* 47 (1): 159–70.

Keen, M. (2012) 'Taxation and development – again'. IMF Working Paper 12/220. Washington DC: International Monetary Fund (IMF).

Keen, M. (2013) 'The anatomy of the VAT'. IMF Working Paper 13/111. Washington DC: International Monetary Fund (IMF).

Keen, M. (2017) 'False profits', *Finance and Development* 54 (3): 10–13. Available at: http://www.imf.org/external/pubs/ft/fandd/2017/09/keen.htm (accessed 24 November 2017).

Keen, M. and Mansour, M. (2009) 'Revenue mobilization in sub-Saharan Africa: challenges from globalization'. IMF Working Paper 09/157. Washington DC: International Monetary Fund (IMF). Available at: https://www.imf.org/external/pubs/ft/wp/2009/wp09157.pdf (accessed 14 April 2017).

Kelly, R. (2013) 'Property tax collection and enforcement' in W. J. McCluskey, G. C. Cornia and L. C. Walters (eds). *A Primer on Property Tax: administration and policy.* Hoboken NJ: Wiley-Blackwell.

Kelsall, T. (2000) 'Governance, local politics and districtization in Tanzania: the 1998 Arumeru Tax Revolt', *African Affairs* 99 (397): 533–51.

Kloeden, D. (2011) *Revenue Administration Reforms in Anglophone Africa Since the Early 1990's.* Washington DC: International Monetary Fund (IMF). Available at: https://www.imf.org/external/pubs/cat/longres.aspx?sk=25027.0 (accessed 8 April 2017).

Knight Frank Research (2017) *The Wealth Report.* London: Knight Frank Research. Available at: http://content.knightfrank.com/research/83/documents/en/the-wealth-report-2017-4482.pdf (accessed 14 December 2017).

Kraus, J. (2018) 'Guest post: global progress on beneficial ownership transparency', *Global Anticorruption Blog*, 16 January. Available at: https://globalanticorruptionblog.com/2018/01/16/guest-post-global-progress-on-beneficial-ownership-transparency/ (accessed 23 January 2018).

Kumar, C. (2014) *Africa Rising? Inequalities and the essential role of fair taxation.* London: Christian Aid and Tax Justice Network.

Lall, S. V., Henderson, J. V. and Venables, A. J. (2017) *Africa's Cities: opening doors to the world.* Washington DC: World Bank Group.

Laporte, B. and Quatrebarbes, C. de (2015) 'What do we know about mineral resource rent sharing in Africa?' ICTD Working Paper 39. Brighton: International Centre for Tax and Development (ICTD), Institute of Development Studies.

Lavallée, E., Razafindrakoto, M. and Roubaud, F. (2008) 'Corruption and trust in political institutions in sub-Saharan Africa'. Working Paper 102. Afrobarometer. Available at: http://afrobarometer.org/sites/default/files/publications/Working%20paper/AfropaperNo102.pdf (accessed 1 May 2017).

Leon, S. and Hirst, N. (2017) 'Two years on, we're still in the dark about the UK's 86,000 anonymously owned homes', *Global Witness*, 7 December. Available at: https://www.globalwitness.org/en-gb/blog/two-years-still-dark-about-86000-anonymously-owned-uk-homes/ (accessed 14 December 2017).

Levi, M. (1988) *Of Rule and Revenue.* Berkeley CA: University of California Press.

Lewis, A. (2013) 'A review of international business tax reform', *University of Miami International and Comparative Law Review* 21 (1): 141.

Li, J. (2012) 'The Great Fiscal Wall of China: tax treaties and their role in defining and defending China's tax base', *Comparative Research in Law and Political Economy* 44.

Lieberman, E. S. (2003) *Race and Regionalism in the Politics of Taxation in Brazil and South Africa*. New York NY and Cambridge: Cambridge University Press.

Lipton, M. (1977) *Why Poor People Stay Poor: urban bias in world development*. Cambridge MA: Harvard University Press.

Logan, C. (2009) 'Selected chiefs, elected councillors and hybrid democrats: popular perspectives on the co-existence of democracy and traditional authority', *Journal of Modern African Studies* 47 (1): 101–28.

Lundgren, C. J., Thomas, A. H. and York, R. C. (2013) 'Boom, bust, or prosperity? Managing sub-Saharan Africa's natural resource wealth'. Departmental Paper 13/11. Washington DC: International Monetary Fund. Available at: http://www.imf.org/external/pubs/cat/longres.aspx?sk=40476 (accessed 25 March 2017).

Lundstøl, O., Raballand, G. and Nyirongo, F. (2015) 'Low government revenue from the mining sector in Zambia and Tanzania: fiscal design, technical capacity or political will?' ICTD Working Paper 9. Brighton: International Centre for Tax and Development (ICTD), Institute of Development Studies.

Mailey, J. R. (2015) *The Anatomy of the Resource Curse: predatory investment in Africa's extractive industries*. ACSS Special Report. Washington DC: Africa Centre for Strategic Studies (ACSS). Available at: http://africacenter.org/wp-content/uploads/2015/12/Africa-Center-Special-Report-No.-3-EN.pdf (accessed 25 March 2017).

Manley, D. (2015) 'Caught in a trap: Zambia's mineral tax reforms'. ICTD Working Paper 5. Brighton: International Centre for Tax and Development (ICTD), Institute of Development Studies.

Mann, A. (2004) *Are Semi-autonomous Revenue Authorities the Answer to Tax Administration Problems in Developing Countries?: A practical guide*. Washington DC: Development Alternatives Inc.

Martin, L. (2016) 'Taxation, loss aversion, and accountability: theory and experimental evidence for taxation's effect on citizen behaviour'. Working Paper. New Haven CT: Innovations for Poverty Action. Available at: http://www.poverty-action.org/publication/taxation-loss-aversion-and-accountability-theory-and-experimental-evidence-taxation%E2%80%99s (accessed 17 April 2017).

Martínez, L. R. (2015) 'Sources of revenue and local government performance: evidence from Colombia'. Job Market Paper. London: London School of Economics and Political Science. Available at: http://economia.uc.cl/wp-content/uploads/2016/01/MARTINEZ-LUIS-PAPER.pdf (accessed 17 April 2017).

Mascagni, G. and Mengistu, A. (2017) *Effective Tax Rates and Size: the distribution of corporate tax burden in theory and in practice*. Brighton: International Centre for Tax and Development (ICTD), Institute of Development Studies.

McCluskey, W. J., Cornia, G. C. and Walters, L. C. (eds) (2013) *A Primer on Property Tax: administration and policy*. Hoboken NJ: Wiley-Blackwell.

McGuirk, E. F. (2013) 'The illusory leader: natural resources, taxation and accountability', *Public Choice* 154 (3–4): 285–313.

McMillan, M. (2001) 'Why kill the golden goose? A political-economy model of export taxation', *Review of Economics and Statistics* 83 (1): 170–84.

Meagher, K. (2016) 'Taxing times: taxation, divided societies and the informal economy in Northern Nigeria', *Journal of Development Studies* 54 (1): 1–17. Available at: http://dx.doi.org/10.1080/00220388.2016.1262026 (accessed 17 November 2017).

Michielse, G. (2016) 'BEPS and developing countries'. Paper presented at the Global Tax Policy Conference, Amsterdam.

Michira, M. (2014) 'Taxpayers could lose Sh600m in KRA tax if Karuturi deal is true', *The Standard*, 29 March. Available at: https://www.standardmedia.co.ke/business/article/2000108060/taxpayers-could-lose-sh600m-in-kra-tax-deal-with-karuturi (accessed 20 January 2018).

Misch, F., Koh, H.-J. and Paustian, N. (2011) 'SME taxation in Zambia'. Paper presented at the International Growth Centre Workshop, Lusaka, 16 November. Available at: https://www.theigc.org/wp-content/uploads/2014/08/Christopher-Mulenga-SME-Taxation-in-Zambia.pdf (accessed 27 March 2017).

Mkandawire, T. (2010) 'On tax efforts and colonial heritage in Africa', *Journal of Development Studies* 46 (10): 1647–69.

MNE Tax (2015) 'OECD transfer pricing consultation addresses special measures, related party contracts'. Available at: http://mnetax.com/7712-7712 (accessed 20 March 2017).

Monkam, N. F. (2011) 'Property tax administration in Francophone Africa: structures, challenges, and progress', *Public Finance and Management* 11 (1): 48–81.

Moore, M. (2004) 'Revenues, state formation, and the quality of governance in developing countries', *International Political Science Review* 25 (3): 297–319.

Moore, M. (2007) 'How does taxation affect the quality of governance?' IDS Working Paper 280. Brighton: Institute of Development Studies (IDS).

Moore, M. (2008) 'Between coercion and contract: competing narratives on taxation and governance' in D. Brautigam, O.-H. Fjeldstad and M. Moore (eds), *Taxation and State-building in Developing Countries: capacity and consent.* Cambridge: Cambridge University Press.

Moore, M. (2014) 'Revenue reform and statebuilding in Anglophone Africa'. ICTD Working Paper 10. Brighton: International Centre for Tax and Development (ICTD), Institute of Development Studies.

Moore, M. (2015) 'Tax and the governance dividend'. ICTD Working Paper 37. Brighton: International Centre for Tax and Development (ICTD), Institute of Development Studies.

Moore, M. and Prichard, W. (2017) 'How can governments of low-income countries collect more tax revenue?' ICTD Working Paper 70. Brighton: International Centre for Tax and Development (ICTD), Institute of Development Studies.

Muñoz, M. S. and Cho, S. S.-W. (2003) 'Social impact of a tax reform: the case of Ethiopia'. IMF Working Paper 03/232. Washington DC: International Monetary Fund.

Mwanyumba, R., Maranga, J. and Magare, M. (2017) *A Review of the Nairobi International Financial Centre: Nairobi International Financial Centre or Nairobi tax haven?* Vienna: Vienna Institute for International Dialogue and Cooperation.

Naseemullah, A. and Staniland, P. (2016) 'Indirect rule and varieties of governance', *Governance: An International Journal of Policy, Administration, and Institutions* 29 (1): 13–30.

Natural Resource Governance Institute (2014) *Natural Resource Charter: Second Edition.* New York NY: Natural Resource Governance Institute. Available at: http://resourcegovernance.org/approach/natural-resource-charter (accessed 27 March 2017).

Natural Resource Governance Institute (2015) *Resource Governance Index.* New York NY: Natural Resource Governance Institute. Available at: https://resourcegovernance.org/analysis-tools/publications/2017-resource-governance-index (accessed 27 March 2017).

New World Wealth (2017) *AfrAsia Bank Africa Wealth Report 2017.* Johannesburg: New World Wealth. Available at: https://d16akly8855cs7.cloudfront.net/wp-content/uploads/2017/03/30174202/Africa-wealth-report-20171.pdf (accessed 14 December 2017).

Ngugi, B. (2016) 'New bill seeks to make Nairobi financial hub', *Daily Nation*, 27 May. Available at: http://www.nation.co.ke/business/New-Bill-seeks-to-make-Nairobi-financial-hub/996-3221468-wscr1/index.html (accessed 25 March 2017).

Norregaard, M. J. (2013) 'Taxing immovable property revenue potential and implementation challenges'. IMF Working Paper 13/129. Washington DC: International Monetary Fund (IMF).

Novack, J. (2013) 'Ernst & Young pays $123 million, avoids tax shelter prosecution', *Forbes*, 1 March. Available at: http://www.forbes.com/sites/janetnovack/2013/03/01/ernst-young-pays-123-million-avoids-tax-shelter-prosecution/ (accessed 19 March 2017).

Nugent, P. (2010) 'States and social contracts in Africa.' *New Left Review* II (63): 35–68.

OECD (2013) *Analysis of Tax Expenditures in Ghana.* Paris: Organisation for Economic Co-operation and Development (OECD) Tax and Development Programme.

OECD (2015a) *Measuring and Monitoring BEPS, Action 11 – 2015 Final Report.* Paris: Organisation for Economic Co-operation and Development (OECD). Available at: http://www.oecd.org/ctp/measuring-and-monitoring-beps-action-11-2015-final-report-9789264241343-en.htm (accessed 14 December 2017).

OECD (2015b) *OECD/G20 Base Erosion and Profit Shifting Project: explanatory statement*. Paris: Organisation for Economic Co-operation and Development (OECD). Available at: http://www.oecd.org/ctp/beps-explanatory-statement-2015.pdf (accessed 27 November 2017).

OECD (2016) *Development Aid at a Glance: statistics by region. 2: Africa (2016 edition)*. Paris: Organisation for Economic Co-operation and Development (OECD). Available at: https://www.oecd.org/dac/stats/documentupload/2%20 Africa%20-%20Development%20Aid%20at%20a%20Glance%202016.pdf (accessed 24 November 2017).

OECD (2017). *Revenue Statistics in Africa 1990–2015*. Paris: Organisation for Economic Co-operation and Development (OECD). Available at: http://www. oecd.org/publications/revenue-statistics-in-africa-2017-9789264280854-en-fr.htm (accessed 30 November 2017)

Oguttu, A. W. (2016) 'Tax base erosion and profit shifting in Africa. Part 1: Africa's response to the OECD BEPS action plan'. ICTD Working Paper 54. Brighton: International Centre for Tax and Development (ICTD), Institute of Development Studies.

Oguttu, A. W. (2017) 'Tax base erosion and profit shifting in Africa. Part 2: A critique of some priority OECD actions from an African perspective'. ICTD Working Paper 64. Brighton: International Centre for Tax and Development (ICTD), Institute of Development Studies.

Olken, B. A. and Singhal, M. (2011) 'Informal taxation', *American Economic Journal: Applied Economics* 3 (4): 1–28.

Ong, L. H. (2014) 'State-led urbanization in China: skyscrapers, land revenue and "concentrated villages"', *China Quarterly* 217: 162–79.

Orlale, O. (2016) 'The use of geo-spatial mapping in identifying untapped and underutilised sources of revenue in properties and the informal sector'. Paper presented at the meeting of the African Tax Research Network, Seychelles.

Oxfam and TJN-A (2016) *Fair Tax Monitor: composite report 2016*. The Hague: Oxfam Novib and Tax Justice Network-Africa. Available at: https:// maketaxfair.net/assets/wbb-publications/1628/FTM%20Composite%20 Report%202016.pdf (accessed 20 January 2018).

Palan, R., Murphy, R. and Chavagneux, C. (2010) *Tax Havens: how globalization really works*. Ithaca NY: Cornell University Press.

Paler, L. (2013) 'Keeping the public purse: an experiment in windfalls, taxes, and the incentives to restrain government', *American Political Science Review* 107 (4): 706–25.

Paler, L., Prichard, W., Sanchez de la Sierra, R. and Samii, C. (2017) *Survey on Total Tax Burden in the DRC: final report*. Kinshasa: Department for International Development.

Picciotto, S. (2013) 'Is the international tax system fit for purpose, especially for developing countries?' ICTD Working Paper 13. Brighton: International Centre for Tax and Development (ICTD), Institute of Development Studies.

Picciotto, S. (2017) 'The current context and a little history' in S. Picciotto (ed.), *Taxing Multinational Enterprises as Unitary Firms*. Brighton: Institute of Development Studies.

Pieterse, D., Kreuser, F. and Gavin, E. (2016) *Introduction to the South African Revenue Service and National Treasury Firm-level Panel*. Helsinki: United Nations University World Institute for Development Economics Research. Available at: http://hdl.handle.net/10419/146262 (accessed 17 April 2017).

Pimhidzai, O. and Fox, L. (2011) 'Taking from the poor or local economic development: the dilemma of taxation of small informal enterprises in Uganda'. Paper prepared for the World Bank Africa Regional Project on Improving the Productivity and Reducing Risk of Household Enterprises. Washington DC: World Bank.

Platform for Collaboration on Tax (2017) *Discussion Draft: the taxation of offshore indirect transfers – a toolkit*. Paris: International Monetary Fund (IMF), Organisation for Economic Co-operation and Development (OECD), United Nations (UN) and World Bank Group (WBG). Available at: https://www.oecd.org/tax/discussion-draft-toolkit-taxation-of-offshore-indirect-transfers.pdf (accessed 9 April 2018).

Prats, A., Teague, K. and Stead, J. (2014) *FTSEcrecy: the culture of concealment throughout the FTSE*. London: Christian Aid. Available at: http://eurodad.org/files/pdf/1546212-ftsecrecy-the-culture-of-concealment-throughout-the-ftse.pdf (accessed 13 March 2017).

Prichard, W. (2009) 'The politics of taxation and implications for accountability in Ghana 1981–2008'. IDS Working Paper 330. Brighton: Institute of Development Studies (IDS).

Prichard, W. (2010) 'Taxation and state building: towards a governance-focused tax reform agenda'. IDS Working Paper 341. Brighton: Institute of Development Studies (IDS).

Prichard, W. (2015) *Taxation, Responsiveness and Accountability in Sub-Saharan Africa: the dynamics of tax bargaining*. Cambridge: Cambridge University Press.

Prichard, W. (2016a) 'Informal taxation and post-conflict statebuilding'. African Studies Association, Washington DC, 6 December.

Prichard, W. (2016b) 'What have we learned about taxation, statebuilding and accountability?' ICTD Summary Brief 4. Brighton: International Centre for Tax and Development (ICTD), Institute of Development Studies.

Prichard, W. (2018) 'Electoral competitiveness, tax bargaining and political incentives in developing countries: evidence from political budget cycles affecting taxation', *British Journal of Political Science* 48 (2): 427–57.

Prichard, W. and Leonard, D. K. (2010) 'Does reliance on tax revenue build state capacity in sub-Saharan Africa?', *International Review of Administrative Sciences* 76 (4): 653–75.

Prichard, W. and van den Boogaard, V. (2017) 'Norms, power, and the socially embedded realities of market taxation in Northern Ghana', *African Studies Review* 60 (1): 171–94.

Prichard, W., Salardi, P. and Segal, P. (2014) 'Taxation, non-tax revenue and democracy: new evidence using new cross-country data'. ICTD Working Paper 23. Brighton: International Centre for Tax and Development (ICTD), Institute of Development Studies.

Prichard, W., Jibao, S., van den Boogaard, V. and Orgeira, N. (forthcoming 2018) 'Subnational property tax reform and tax bargaining: a quasi-randomized evaluation from Sierra Leone'. ICTD Working Paper. Brighton: International Centre for Tax and Development (ICTD), Institute of Development Studies.

Prud'homme, R. (1992) 'Informal local taxation in developing countries', *Environment and Planning C: Government and Policy* 10 (1): 1–17.

Public Accounts Committee (2015) *Tax Avoidance: the role of large accountancy firms follow-up*. HC 860, 2014–15, EV 38. London: UK Parliament. Available at: https://www.parliament.uk/business/committees/committees-a-z/commons-select/public-accounts-committee/news/report-tax-avoidance-the-role-of-large-accountancy-firms-follow-up/ (accessed 19 March 2017).

Public Eye (2012) *Zambia: good copper, bad copper* (film). Available at: https://www.youtube.com/watch?v=uamzirLswjk (accessed 25 March 2017).

Readhead, A. (2016) *Preventing Tax Base Erosion in Africa: a regional study of transfer pricing challenges in the mining sector*. New York NY: National Resource Governance Institute. Available at: http://www.resourcegovernance.org/analysis-tools/publications/preventing-tax-base-erosion-africa-regional-study-transfer-pricing (accessed 25 March 2017).

Riaño, J. and Hodess, R. (2008) *2008 Bribe Payers Index*. Berlin: Transparency International. Available at: https://issuu.com/transparencyinternational/docs/2008_bpi_report_final_08_12-1/1 (accessed 1 May 2017).

Robinson, J., Acemoglu, D. and Johnson, S. (2003) 'An African success story: Botswana' in D. Rodrik (ed.), *In Search of Prosperity: analytic narratives on economic growth*. Princeton NJ: Princeton University Press.

Ross, M. L. (2004) 'Does taxation lead to representation?', *British Journal of Political Science* 34 (2): 229–49.

Ross, M. L. (2012) *The Oil Curse: how petroleum wealth shapes the development of nations*. Princeton NJ: Princeton University Press.

Ryle, G., Guevara, M. W., Hudson, M., Hager, N., Campbell, D. and Candea, S. (2013) 'Secrecy for sale: inside the global offshore money maze', Center for Public Integrity. Available at: https://www.publicintegrity.org/2013/04/03/12421/inside-global-offshore-money-maze (accessed 30 November 2017).

Rystad Energy (2015) 'Rystad Energy on CNN Money'. Available at: https://www.rystadenergy.com/NewsEvents/PressReleases/rystad-energy-on-cnn-money (accessed 27 March 2017).

Saka, H. (2017) 'Why tax administrations should consider a public sector office: the case of the Uganda Revenue Authority'. Paper presented at the International Centre for Tax and Development (ICTD) Annual Conference, Entebbe, Uganda. Available at: https://www.slideshare.net/ICTDTax/the-public-sector-as-a-taxpayer-segment-why-it-is-relevant/1 (accessed 9 April 2018).

Sanchez, O. (2006) 'Tax system reform in Latin America: domestic and international causes', *Review of International Political Economy* 13 (5): 772–801.

Sardanis, A. (2007) *A Venture in Africa: the challenges of African business.* London: I. B. Tauris.

Sarr, B. (2016) 'Assessing revenue authority performance in developing countries: a synthetic control approach', *International Journal of Public Administration* 39 (2): 146–56.

Sharman, J. C. (2006) *Havens in a Storm: the struggle for global tax regulation.* Ithaca NY: Cornell University Press.

Sharman, J. C. (2010) 'Shopping for anonymous shell companies: an audit study of anonymity and crime in the international financial system', *Journal of Economic Perspectives* 24 (4): 127–40.

Shaxson, N. (2011) *Treasure Islands: tax havens and the men who stole the world.* London: Bodley Head.

Sikka, P. and Hampton, M. P. (2005) 'The role of accountancy firms in tax avoidance: some evidence and issues', *Accounting Forum* 29 (3): 325–43.

Spooner, S. (2015) 'Exposed: the Africans named in HSBC Swiss Leaks', *Mail & Guardian,* 13 February. Available at: https://mg.co.za/article/2015-02-13-exposed-the-africans-named-in-the-hsbc-swiss-leaks (accessed 22 January 2018).

Stewart, M. (2002) 'Global trajectories of tax reform: mapping tax reform in developing and transition countries'. Public Law Research Paper 29. Melbourne: University of Melbourne. Available at: https://papers.ssrn.com/abstract=319200 (accessed 8 April 2017).

Story, L. and Saul, S. (2015) 'Stream of foreign wealth flows to elite New York real estate', *The New York Times,* 7 February. Available at: https://www.nytimes.com/2015/02/08/nyregion/stream-of-foreign-wealth-flows-to-time-warner-condos.html (accessed 24 November 2017).

Tait, A. (1990) 'IMF advice on fiscal policy' in G. Krause-Junk (ed.), *Public Finance and Steady Economic Growth.* The Hague: International Institute of Public Finance.

Taliercio, R. J. (2004) 'Designing performance: the semi-autonomous revenue authority model in Africa and Latin America'. Policy Research Working Paper 3423. Washington DC: World Bank. Available at: http://documents.worldbank.org/curated/en/480271468773692962/Designing-performance-the-semi-autonomous-revenue-authority-model-in-Africa-and-Latin-America (accessed 10 April 2017).

Tanzi, V. (2000) 'Taxation and economic structure' in G. Perry, J. Whalley and G. McMahon (eds), *Fiscal Reform and Structural Change in Developing Countries. Volume 2.* Basingstoke: Macmillan.

Tanzi, V. and Zee, H. H. (2000) 'Tax policy for emerging markets: developing countries'. IMF Working Paper 00/35. Washington DC: International Monetary Fund (IMF).

Tax Justice Alliance Uganda (2017) 'Civil society position on tax holidays in Uganda'. Press Release, 27 May. Available at: http://www.seatiniuganda.org/publications/press-statements/149-civil-society-position-on-tax-holidays-in-uganda/file.html (accessed 22 January 2018).

Tax Justice Network (2015) *Financial Secrecy Index 2015: methodology.* Chesham, UK: Tax Justice Network. Available at: http://www.financialsecrecyindex.com/PDF/FSI-Methodology.pdf (accessed 14 December 2017).

Tax Justice Network (2018) *Financial Secrecy Index: 2018 results.* Chesham, UK: Tax Justice Network. Available at: https://www.financialsecrecyindex.com/PDF/FSI-Rankings-2018.pdf (accessed 1 April 2018).

Terpker, S. P. (2008) 'Accounting challenges for semi-autonomous revenue agencies in developing countries'. IMF Working Paper 08/116. Washington DC: International Monetary Fund (IMF). Available at: https://www.imf.org/en/Publications/WP/Issues/2016/12/31/Accounting-Challenges-for-Semi-Autonomous-Revenue-Agencies-in-Developing-Countries-21501 (accessed 10 April 2017).

The Economist (2014) 'Crying foul in Guinea', *The Economist,* 4 December. Available at: http://www.economist.com/news/business/21635522-africas-largest-iron-ore-mining-project-has-been-bedevilled-dust-ups-and-delays-crying-foul (accessed 27 March 2017).

The Economist (2015) 'No representation without taxation', *The Economist,* 5 February. Available at: https://www.economist.com/news/finance-and-economics/21642199-behavioural-argument-higher-taxes-no-representation-without-taxation (accessed 17 November 2017).

Therkildsen, O. (2004) 'Autonomous tax administration in sub-Saharan Africa: the case of the Uganda Revenue Authority', *Forum for Development Studies* 31 (1): 59–88.

Therkildsen, O. (2012) 'Democratisation in Tanzania: no taxation without exemptions'. Paper presented at the American Political Science Association, New Orleans.

Thirsk, W. R. (1993) 'Recent experience with tax reform in developing countries' in R. D. M. Faini (ed.), *Fiscal Issues in Adjustment in Developing Countries.* New York NY: St Martin's Press.

Tilly, C. (1992) *Coercion, Capital and European States, A.D.990–1990.* Oxford: Blackwell.

Titeca, K. (2009) 'The "Masai" and Miraa: public authority, vigilance and criminality in a Ugandan border town', *Journal of Modern African Studies* 47 (2): 291–317.

Titeca, K. and Kimanuka, C. (2012) *Walking in the Dark: informal cross-border trade in the great lakes region.* London: International Alert. Available at: http://hdl.handle.net/1854/LU-4161492 (accessed 10 April 2017).

TJN-A (2015) 'Kenya must review double tax agreement with Mauritius'. Tax Justice Network-Africa (TJN-A) Press Release, 2 November. Available at: http://www.taxjusticeafrica.net/?p=2025&lang=en (accessed 22 January 2018).

TJN-A and ActionAid International (2015) *The West African Giveaway: use and abuse of corporate tax incentives in ECOWAS.* Nairobi and Johannesburg: Tax Justice Network-Africa (TJN-A) and ActionAid International. Available at: http://curtisresearch.org/publications/the-west-african-giveaway-use-and-abuse-of-corporate-tax-incentives-in-ecowas/ (accessed 22 January 2018).

TJN-A and ActionAid International (2016) *Still Racing Toward the Bottom? Corporate tax incentives in East Africa.* Nairobi and Johannesburg: Tax Justice Network-Africa (TJN-A) and ActionAid International. Available at: http://www.actionaid.org/sites/files/actionaid/corporate_tax_incentives_in_east_africa_to_print.pdf (accessed 22 January 2018).

Torgler, B. (2005) 'Tax morale and direct democracy', *European Journal of Political Economy* 21 (2): 525–31.

Transparency International (2013) 'Global corruption barometer: national results'. Available at: https://www.transparency.org/gcb2013/countries (accessed 14 April 2017).

Transparency International (2015) *Just for Show? Reviewing G20 promises on beneficial ownership.* Berlin: Transparency International. Available at: https://www.transparency.org/whatwedo/publication/just_for_show_g20_promises (accessed 20 January 2018).

Transparency International UK (2015) *Corruption on your Doorstep: how corrupt capital is used to buy property in the UK.* London: Transparency International UK. Available at: http://www.transparency.org.uk/publications/corruption-on-your-doorstep/#.WjFtVFVl-pp (accessed 14 December 2017).

Transparency International UK (2017) *Faulty Towers: understanding the impact of overseas corruption on the London property market.* London: Transparency International UK. Available at: http://www.transparency.org.uk/faulty-towers/#.WjF1rVVl-po (accessed 14 December 2017).

Tsui, K. K. (2011) 'More oil, less democracy: evidence from worldwide crude oil discoveries', *Economic Journal* 121 (551): 89–115.

TUAC Secretariat (2015) 'Arm's length principle doesn't work!' Extracts of base erosion and profit shifting (BEPS) consultations at the Organisation for Economic Co-operation and Development (OECD). Available at: https://www.youtube.com/watch?v=hjuhPtmTx64&feature=youtu.be (accessed 20 March 2017).

Twijnstra, R., Hilhorst, D. and Titeca, K. (2014) 'Trade networks and the practical norms of taxation at a border crossing between South Sudan and Northern Uganda', *Journal of Eastern African Studies* 8 (3): 382–99.

UNCTAD (2015) *World Investment Report 2015: reforming international investment governance*. Geneva: United Nations Conference on Trade and Development (UNCTAD). Available at: http://unctad.org/en/pages/PublicationWebflyer. aspx?publicationid=1245 (accessed 20 March 2017).

UNCTAD (2016) *Trade Misinvoicing in Primary Commodities in Developing Countries: the cases of Chile, Côte d'Ivoire, Nigeria, South Africa and Zambia*. Geneva: United Nations Conference on Trade and Development (UNCTAD). Available at: http://unctad.org/en/PublicationsLibrary/suc2016d2_en.pdf (accessed 14 December 2017).

UNECA (2011) *Minerals and Africa's Development: the International Study Group report on Africa's mineral regimes*. Addis Ababa: United Nations Economic Commission for Africa (UNECA). Available at: http://www. foresightfordevelopment.org/sobipro/55/1288-minerals-and-africas-development-the-international-study-group-report-on-africas-mineral-regimes (accessed 25 March 2017).

UNECA (2015) *Illicit Financial Flows: report of the High Level Panel on Illicit Financial Flows from Africa*. Addis Ababa: United Nations Economic Commission for Africa (UNECA). Available at: http://www.uneca.org/publications/illicit-financial-flows (accessed 4 May 2017).

US Department of Justice (2005) 'KPMG to pay $456 million for criminal violations in relation to largest-ever tax shelter fraud case'. Press Release 5-433, 29 August. Available at: https://www.justice.gov/archive/opa/pr/2005/August/05_ag_433.html (accessed 24 November 2017).

van den Boogaard, V. and Prichard, W. (2016) 'What have we learned about informal taxation in sub-Saharan Africa?' ICTD Summary Brief 2. Brighton: International Centre for Tax and Development (ICTD), Institute of Development Studies.

van den Boogaard, V., W. Prichard and S. Jibao (2018) 'Norms, networks, power, and control: understanding informal payments and brokerage in cross-border trade in Sierra Leone'. ICTD Working Paper 74. Brighton: International Centre for Tax and Development (ICTD), Institute of Development Studies.

van Loggerenberg, J. and Lackay, A. (2016) *Rogue: the inside story of SARS's elite crime-busting unit*. Johannesburg: Jonathan Ball Publishers.

Verhoest, K., Peters, B. G., Bouckaert, G. and Verschuere, B. (2004) 'The study of organisational autonomy: a conceptual review', *Public Administration and Development* 24 (2): 101–18.

Vicente, P. C. (2010) 'Does oil corrupt? Evidence from a natural experiment in West Africa', *Journal of Development Economics* 92 (1): 28–38.

von Soest, C. (2007a) 'Measuring the capability to raise revenue: process and output dimensions and their application to the Zambia Revenue Authority', *Public Administration and Development* 27 (4): 353–65.

von Soest, C. (2007b) 'How does neopatrimonialism affect the African state's revenues? The case of tax collection in Zambia', *Journal of Modern African Studies* 45 (4): 621–45.

Wang, J. (2013) 'The economic impact of special economic zones: evidence from Chinese municipalities', *Journal of Development Economics* 101 (C): 133–47.

Waris, A. (2017) 'How Kenya has implemented and adjusted to the changes in international transfer pricing regulations: 1920–2016'. ICTD Working Paper 69. Brighton: International Centre for Tax and Development (ICTD), Institute of Development Studies.

Wiens, D., Poast, P. and Clark, W. R. (2014) 'The political resource curse: an empirical re-evaluation', *Political Research Quarterly* 67 (4): 783–94.

World Bank (2012) *Creating Fiscal Space through Revenue Mobilization*. Washington DC: World Bank. Available at: http://documents.worldbank.org/curated/en/683271468300543858/Creating-fiscal-space-through-revenue-mobilization (accessed 6 March 2017).

World Bank (2015a) 'Net official development assistance and official aid received' in *World Development Indicators*. Washington DC: World Bank. Available at: https://data.worldbank.org/indicator/DT.ODA.ALLD.CD (accessed 22 January 2018).

World Bank (2015b) 'Total natural resources rents (% of GDP)' in *World Development Indicators*. Washington DC: World Bank. Available at: https://data.worldbank.org/indicator/NY.GDP.TOTL.RT.ZS (accessed 24 November 2017).

World Bank (2016a) *Commodity Markets Outlook. Resource development in an era of cheap commodities*. World Bank Quarterly Report, April. Washington DC: World Bank.

World Bank (2016b) *Commodity Markets Outlook. From energy prices to food prices: moving in tandem?* World Bank Quarterly Report, July. Washington DC: World Bank.

World Bank (2016c) *International Debt Statistics 2016*. Washington DC: World Bank. Available at: https://data.worldbank.org/products/ids (accessed 24 November 2017).

World Bank (2016d) *Paying Taxes 2016*. Washington DC: World Bank. Available at: http://documents.worldbank.org/curated/en/559251467992040456/Paying-taxes-2016 (accessed 6 March 2017).

World Bank (2016e) 'Population growth (annual %)' in *World Development Indicators*. Washington DC: World Bank. Available at: https://data.worldbank.org/indicator/SP.POP.GROW (accessed 7 December 2017).

WTO (2013) *World Trade Report 2013*. Geneva: World Trade Organization (WTO). Available at: https://www.wto.org/english/res_e/booksp_e/world_trade_report13_e.pdf (accessed 24 November 2017).

Yohou, H. D. and Goujon, M. (2017) 'Reassessing tax effort in developing countries: a proposal of a Vulnerability-Adjusted Tax Effort Index (VATEI)'. Ferdi Working Paper 186. Clermont-Ferrand: Fondation pour les Études et Recherches sur le Développement International (FERDI). Available at: http://www.ferdi.fr/sites/www.ferdi.fr/files/publication/fichiers/p186-ferdi_hyohou-mgoujon.pdf (accessed 3 April 2017).

Young, C. (1994) *The African Colonial State in Comparative Perspective*. New Haven CT and London: Yale University Press.

Zake, J. O. (2011) 'Customs administration reform and modernization in Anglophone Africa : early 1990s to mid-2010'. IMF Working Paper 11/184. Washington DC: International Monetary Fund (IMF). Available at: https://www.imf.org/external/pubs/cat/longres.aspx?sk=25141.0 (accessed 14 April 2017).

Zambia Tax Platform (2016) *Pre-tax and Non Tax Proposals for the 2016 National Budget*. Lusaka: Zambia Tax Platform Secretariat. Available at: http://www.actionaid.org/sites/files/actionaid/press_releases/zambia_tax_platform.pdf (accessed 22 January 2018).

Zeng, Z. (2015) 'Global experiences with special economic zones: focus on China and Africa'. Policy Research Working Paper 7240. Washington DC: World Bank. Available at: http://documents.worldbank.org/curated/en/810281468186872492/Global-experiences-with-special-economic-zones-focus-on-China-and-Africa (accessed 14 April 2017).

Zinnbauer, D. (2017) 'Urban land: a new type of resource course' in A. Williams and P. le Billon (eds), *Corruption, Natural Resources and Development: from resource curse to political ecology*. Cheltenham: Edward Elgar Publishing.

Zucman, G. (2014) 'Taxing across borders: tracking personal wealth and corporate profits', *Journal of Economic Perspectives* 28 (4): 121–48.

GLOSSARY OF TERMS

AEOI	Automatic Exchange of Information
ANCIR	African Network of Centres for Investigative Reporting
ASYCUDA	Automated System for Customs Data
ATAF	African Tax Administration Forum
BEPS	Base Erosion and Profit Shifting
BSGR	Beny Steinmetz Group Resources
CEO	Chief Executive Officer
CEQ	Commitment to Equity
CIT	Corporate Income Tax
CNMC	China Nonferrous Mining Corporation
CREDAF	Centre de Rencontres et d'Études des Dirigeants des Administrations Fiscales
DBCFT	Destination-Based Cash Flow Taxation
EITI	Extractive Industries Transparency Initiative
EPZ	Export Processing Zone
EU	European Union
FATF	Financial Action Task Force
FSI	Financial Secrecy Index
FTSE	Financial Times Stock Exchange
G8	Group of Eight
G20	Group of Twenty
GDP	Gross Domestic Product
GIS	Geographic Information System
GIZ	Deutsche Gesellschaft für Internationale Zusammenarbeit
GST	Goods and Services Tax (also known as VAT)
HNWI	High Net Worth Individual[1]
ICIJ	International Consortium of Investigative Journalists
ICTD	International Centre for Tax and Development
IFSC	International Financial Service Centre
ILO	International Labour Organization
IMF	International Monetary Fund
KRA	Kenya Revenue Authority
MCAA	Multilateral Competent Authority Agreement
MNC	Multinational Corporation

NFCA	Non-Ferrous China Africa
NGO	Non-Governmental Organisation
NRA	National Revenue Authority (Sierra Leone)
ODA	Official Development Assistance
OECD	Organisation for Economic Co-operation and Development
OFC	Offshore Financial Centre
PAYE	Pay As You Earn
PIT	Personal Income Tax
SARA	Semi-Autonomous Revenue Authority
SARS	South African Revenue Service
SDG	Sustainable Development Goal
StAR	Stolen Asset Recovery Initiative
TADAT	Tax Administration Diagnostic Assessment Tool
TIEA	Tax Information Exchange Agreement
TIN	Tax Identification Number
TJN-A	Tax Justice Network-Africa
TNMM	Transactional Net Margin Method
TUAC	Trade Union Advisory Committee (OECD)
UN	United Nations
UNCTAD	United Nations Conference on Trade and Development
UNECA	United Nations Economic Commission for Africa
URA	Uganda Revenue Authority
VAT	Value-Added Tax
WBG	World Bank Group
WTO	World Trade Organization

NOTES

Chapter 1

I   A recent Afrobarometer survey, covering 34 countries, found that more than one-third (35%) of the respondents said that 'most' or 'all' tax officials were corrupt, and another 39% thought that at least some of them were (Aiko and Logan 2014). According to the *Bribe Payers Index 2008*, the customs administration is perceived by business executives to be one of the most corrupt sectors of government in many African countries (Riaño and Hodess 2008). This is supported by an Afrobarometer survey, covering 18 sub-Saharan African countries, which found that the most discredited institutions were the police and tax administration, including customs (Lavallée et al. 2008). Case studies from individual countries and regions across the continent provide a grim picture of the situation (Fjeldstad 2003; 2006). In a study of customs in the East African Community, Edward Kafeero (2008) argues that traders are so used to corruption that they consider it normal. One trader interviewed by Kafeero put it simply: 'You bribe Customs and prosper or you stick to the ethical principles and perish.'

Chapter 2

I   For information on colonial taxation, see Due (1963), Frankema (2010), Gardner (2012), Mkandawire (2010) and Young (1994).

2   In a number of countries, including Tanzania and Uganda, pre-existing agricultural marketing co-operatives, especially those dealing in coffee, were taken over by central government and used as instruments for extracting a surplus from coffee producers.

3   If we define aid dependence as net ODA as a percentage of gross national income, the 20 most aid-dependent countries in Africa in 2015 were Liberia (62%), the Central African Republic (31%), Somalia (23%), Sierra Leone (23%), South Sudan (22%), Malawi (17%), São Tomé and Príncipe (15%), Rwanda (13%), Mozambique (12%), Niger (12%), Burundi (12%), The Gambia (12%), Comoros (12%), Cabo Verde (10%), Mali (9%), Burkina Faso (9%), Guinea-Bissau (9%), the Democratic Republic of Congo (8%), Mauritania (7%) and Senegal (7%) (World Bank 2015a).

4   Note that the figures for total aid to Africa and for aid as a % of GDP for the average Africa country appear very different. This is because many bigger countries, including Nigeria, Sudan and Congo, received little aid per head of

the population. Large volumes of aid were generally concentrated on relatively smaller countries, where they tended to overshadow governments' own tax collections.

5   In Nigeria and in a few other countries, such as Angola, Equatorial Guinea, Sudan and South Sudan, government revenues come almost entirely from oil and gas.

6   There are many questions about the accuracy of both the revenue and the GDP figures. However, there is no reason to think that the collection figures for sub-Saharan Africa are consistently biased upwards. They likely omit more subnational revenues than do the figures for Latin America and South Asia.

7   The average tax effort – revenue collections as a proportion of potential or likely collections – for the 14 sub-Saharan African countries in the sample, excluding South Africa, was 75%. By contrast, the average for six Latin American countries was 59%, and for four South Asian countries it was 51% (IMF 2011: 59–60).

8   Surveys show a steady increase in the proportion of people who agree with the statement that tax authorities always have the right to make people pay taxes. This information derives from the regular Afrobarometer surveys. In the third round of the survey, conducted in 2005–06, for the first time respondents were asked what became a standard set of questions about their attitudes to taxation. There have since been three further Afrobarometer survey rounds, the latest in 2014–15. The tax questions were not asked in every country in every survey round. Over the four rounds, they were asked 69 times in 24 countries. If we use only the data for the seven countries where the tax questions were asked in each of the four survey rounds, we find that the average proportion of respondents who agreed with the statement 'The tax authority always has the right to make people pay taxes' increased steadily from 60% in 2005–06 to 69% in 2014–15. The results are almost identical if we instead average all the available results. See also Aiko and Logan (2014: 7) and Isbell (2017).

Chapter 3

1   'Dependencies' refers to smaller countries that were colonies of the larger Western powers, and Great Britain in particular. Many of the well-known 'tax havens' are British overseas territories, including Bermuda, the British Virgin Islands and the Cayman Islands. More than half of offshore companies implicated in the leak from the Panama-based Mossack Fonseca were registered in British overseas territories.

2   The 'big four' are the four largest international firms working in this area. Ordered by size they are: PricewaterhouseCoopers (PwC), Deloitte, Ernst & Young and KPMG. In 2012 they had a combined turnover of $112 billion, 2,800 offices and over 700,000 employees worldwide. All four companies have businesses in over 150 countries. These firms have been repeatedly

fined by OECD countries for facilitating tax evasion and avoidance but have nonetheless remained both highly active and major advocates for the status quo. A few examples: in 2005, KPMG was fined $456 million for engaging in fraud that generated at least $11 billion in phony tax losses for wealthy individuals, costing the US Treasury over $2.5 billion in evaded taxes (US Department of Justice 2005). Eight years later, Ernst & Young was fined $123 million for promoting and defending abusive tax shelters to rich individuals, helping them dodge $2 billion in taxes to the US between 1999 and 2004 (Novack 2013). A leak of documents in 2014 revealed that PwC was marketing arrangements for multinational companies that artificially diverted profits to Luxembourg through intra-company loans. In its report, the UK's Public Accounts Committee called PwC's activities 'nothing short of the promotion of tax avoidance on an industrial scale' (Public Accounts Committee 2015).

3   Among the most notable are the 'Panama Papers' leak in 2016 and the 'Paradise Papers' leak in 2017.

4   Illustratively, a recent investigative report by the *New York Times* found that over half of luxury apartment sales in 2014 in New York were via shell companies designed to obscure the beneficial owners (Story and Saul 2015).

5   For example, a report by Transparency International UK (2015) found that, in London, 89% of the 40,725 property titles held by foreign companies were held by companies incorporated in secrecy jurisdictions. Further, of the £180 million worth of property under criminal investigation as suspected proceeds of corruption since 2004, 75% used offshore secrecy to hide the owners' identities. Another report, titled *Faulty Towers*, found that in 14 landmark London property developments worth £1.6 billion, almost 40% of future homes were sold to investors from countries at high risk of corruption or those hiding behind shell companies (Transparency International UK 2017). In the UK as a whole, 86,000 properties are owned by companies incorporated in secrecy jurisdictions, 87% of which keep information about the real owners secret (Leon and Hirst 2017). See also Story and Saul (2015).

6   Tellingly, third-party information from banks and others is often not easily available to African tax authorities even within national borders, owing to laws that control the flow of information. This speaks to the scope for unilateral measures by African governments to improve enforcement, which is discussed later.

7   For example, total assets frozen in OECD countries until the end of 2012 amounted to $2.6 billion, of which only $400 million had been returned to the countries of origin (Gray et al. 2014).

8   For more detailed explanations, see Picciotto (2017) and Christians (2007).

9   See Palan et al. (2010), Fuest et al. (2011), Sikka and Hampton (2005), Christensen et al. (2007), ActionAid (2012), Lewis (2013), IMF (2014), Prats et al. (2014), ActionAid (2015) and UNCTAD (2015).

10 Transfer mispricing is especially likely to take place in transactions between related parties in MNCs, but it also can and does occur between independent companies where there is sufficient trust.

11 In a study on the 'spillover' effects of tax havens, IMF researchers estimated global tax losses at $600 billion annually (Crivelli et al. 2015). UNCTAD's 2015 *World Investment Report* estimated that developing countries lose $100 billion annually only from conduit foreign direct investment through tax havens. The OECD (2015a) estimated tax losses to be $100 billion to $240 billion per year. Cobham and Jansky (2017) estimate global tax losses at $500 billion per year.

12 For example, a widely cited UNCTAD (2016) study claims that as much as 67% of export revenues were misappropriated by mining and oil companies in five countries through transfer mispricing between 2000 and 2014. For South Africa, this would amount to $102 billion. However, subsequent critiques provide compelling evidence that these numbers are likely to be dramatically inflated, due to weaknesses in the methodology (Eunomix Research 2017).

13 The OECD Development Assistance Committee reports total aid to sub-Saharan Africa of $54 billion in 2014 (OECD 2016).

Chapter 4

1 In 2013, the International Consortium of Investigative Journalists (ICIJ) received millions of leaked files from two financial service providers, a private bank in Jersey and the Bahamas corporate registry, which revealed how tax havens around the world are used to hide wealth. These became known as the 'Offshore Leaks'. In 2015, a leak from the Swiss branch of HSBC Bank ('Swiss Leaks') revealed how the bank profited from doing business with tax evaders from around the world. In 2016, a leak of over 11.5 million financial and legal records from Panamanian law firm Mossack Fonseca (the 'Panama Papers') uncovered over 214,000 offshore entities connected to people in over 200 countries and territories, including many celebrities, sports stars and criminals, as well as 140 public officials and politicians. In 2017, 13.4 million leaked files from the offshore law firm Appleby and the company registries of 19 secrecy jurisdictions exposed the offshore activities of some of the world's most powerful people and companies (ICIJ 2017a; 2017b). Dubbed the 'Paradise Papers', they revealed the offshore interests of over 120 politicians and world leaders. These leaks all received extensive media attention around the world.

2 Despite the G20 adopting a set of principles on beneficial ownership at the 2014 summit and identifying financial transparency as a 'high priority' issue, a subsequent assessment report by Transparency International (2015) found progress to be limited. Nevertheless, there has been positive progress, with the Ukraine and Norway implementing public registers in 2015, the UK pledging to

create a register of overseas companies that own UK property and participate in public procurement in 2016, new EU legislation (Fourth Anti-Money Laundering Directive) that will require EU companies to make their owners public, and a group of other countries making beneficial ownership commitments (Kraus 2018). However, major barriers remain, as the system as a whole can be held back by a handful of slow reformers, and a variety of countries – including the United States and various UK overseas territories and crown dependencies – have made only slow progress, while the real estate sector in particular continues to have weak, if any, regulation in place in many countries.

3   Here, tax authorities may split the profits of an MNC in order to reflect the distribution of value added across countries by using case-specific 'allocation factors' that reflect the specific nature of the business. For example, India and China argue that MNCs that locate portions of their supply chain in those countries achieve an improved financial outcome relative to alternative locations because of specific features such as access to low-cost skilled labour and large consumer markets, superior infrastructure, incentives and cost savings. As comparables do not account for these unique market features, China and India have begun using 'location-specific advantages' to increase the calculated taxable profit made by subsidiaries based in their countries (Chakravarty et al. 2015).

4   Such a formula could, in principle, be universal, or it could be sector-specific.

5   A prominent case has been that of Zain in Uganda. In 2010, Zain International BV (Netherlands) sold the shares of Zain Africa BV (Netherlands) for $10.7 billion to a Dutch subsidiary of the Indian multinational Bharti Airtel International BV. As a pan-African mobile telephone business, Zain Africa BV included the Kampala-registered mobile phone operator Celtel Uganda Ltd. The Uganda Revenue Authority (URA) asked Zain International BV to pay $85 million in capital gains tax for selling its operations in Uganda, but Zain disputed the claim, arguing that the URA did not have jurisdiction as the sale took place between companies registered in the Netherlands. Uganda's appeals court ruled that the URA did have jurisdiction, but Zain argues that the Uganda–Netherlands tax treaty prevents Uganda from taxing the transaction, and the case remains unresolved. In a similar case, involving a dispute between Vodafone and the government of India, the supreme court ruled that the Indian Tax Authority did not have jurisdiction to tax the relevant offshore sale, pointing towards the broader difficulties encountered by many developing countries (Platform for Collaboration on Tax 2017).

6   The most important regional institutions are the African Tax Administration Forum (ATAF) and the Centre de Rencontres et d'Études des Dirigeants des Administrations Fiscales (CREDAF), but efforts by both to develop an influential global voice are relatively recent. Other initiatives include the United Nations Economic Commission for Africa's High Level Panel on Illicit Financial Flows, and the African Parliamentary Network on Illicit Financial Flows.

7 A variety of civil society organisations have pushed for these negotiations to be shifted away from the OECD, in favour of the UN Tax Committee. However, to date, China in particular has appeared to favour continued reliance on the technical expertise of the OECD, while vesting political leadership in the G20 and expanding the breadth and depth of consultation.

8 This is true of the case-specific application of profit-split methods allowed for under OECD rules where it is impossible to credibly apply the arm's length principle to separate out local profits. It is also true of the ability to assume a minimum profit rate on simple firms that bear little risk, such as distributors, and therefore should not reasonably be expected to report losses.

9 Such taxes are quite common, at least on paper, in Francophone African countries. However, there has not been any research of which we are aware into their overall effectiveness in Africa.

10 One recent report by Hearson (2015), for example, presents evidence that Africa's tax treaties have, on average, systematically limited their ability to tax international firms and individuals, while generating direct tax losses of 1% of more of tax revenue – and potentially much larger indirect losses. A more recent report from ActionAid (2016b) provides evidence that treaties between lower-income countries and OECD countries take away more rights to tax than treaties with fellow non-OECD countries, and that they are getting worse over time.

11 India and Mongolia have perhaps been the most high-profile initial examples.

12 Rwanda, for example, renegotiated its treaty with Mauritius in 2013, as Mauritius has been a major conduit for investments into Eastern and Southern Africa based in significant part on tax treaties that have facilitated tax avoidance and evasion.

Chapter 5

1 For more information on the issues in this chapter, see Aarsnes and Lundstøl (2013), Africa Progress Panel (2013), Daniel et al. (2010), UNECA (2011), IMF (2012), Laporte and Quatrebarbes (2015), Lundgren et al. (2013) and Lundstøl at al. (2015).

2 See the figures on profit rates on Vedanta's investment in Zambia cited by its chairman, Anil Agarwal (Das 2014). For more details on this deal, see Sardanis (2007).

3 In 2014, the African continent accounted for only 7% of total global energy production from oil, gas and coal, and for 8% of the total production, by weight, of bauxite, copper, lead, nickel, tin and zinc (World Bank 2016a: 17).

4 Between 2010 and 2014, fuel and minerals and metals products accounted for 62% of sub-Saharan Africa's total exports (Chuhan-Pole 2015).

5 Unlike, for example, in the Middle East or Latin America, state-owned companies play a small role in the extractive sector in sub-Saharan Africa. The most obvious exception is the state-owned Sonangol group in Angola, which

is responsible in varying degrees for exploration, production and exporting. However, Sonangol has become notorious both for the close degree of control exercised by a very small political elite tied to the president of Angola and for highly secretive oil-marketing arrangements, based on links with at least one Chinese businessman, that seem designed to transfer profits into private hands.

6   Data from the Extractive Industries Transparency Initiative (EITI 2016b) indicates that, between 2010 and 2012 (various single years, according to data availability), the annual total production from mining activities in the 17 African countries with the most comprehensive reporting was worth about $176 billion (i.e. $176 thousand million), while the reported total revenue collection by governments from the companies responsible was $5.5 billion – or 3% of the total value of production. Oil and gas extraction activities in ten countries – excluding the second-largest oil producer, Angola, which is not a member of EITI and so does not report – generated annual production worth $153 billion, and government revenues of $84 billion – 55% of the total. This difference in this very crudely calculated 'tax rate' between the two components of the extractive sector is only indicative. Some might stem from differences in the ratio of production costs to output values. More concretely, low revenues from mining probably in part reflect high levels of new investment in the sector in the first decade of this century. Some of this investment has not yet generated production or taxable profits. Even so, the difference between a crude 'tax rate' of 3% and one of 55% is dramatic.

7   The Natural Resources Governance Institute currently classifies 58 countries into four groups according to the quality of the governance of their natural resource sectors. This includes 17 sub-Saharan Africa countries. None of them are in the top group, and all but four are in the two bottom groups (National Resource Governance Institute 2015).

8   For more details, see *The Economist* (2014) and Keefe (2013).

9   This is a simplification. Investigations have revealed that secretive oil-marketing deals orchestrated by members of Angola's small political elite are used to transfer some of these enormous rents into private hands (Mailey 2015).

10 Over the period 2005–13, natural resource rents, which were almost entirely from oil, gas and minerals, accounted on average for 19% of the total GDP of the region (World Bank 2015b).

11 This phenomenon has long been termed the 'resource curse'. There is a large literature on it, including Collier (2010), Vicente (2010), Tsui (2011), Barma et al. (2012) and Ross (2012).

12 We are dealing only with large-scale mining here. Small-scale or artisanal mining is likely more important in Africa in terms of the employment it generates. The sector, however, contributes very little to public revenue.

13 In addition, relative to the energy sector, mining activities are more widely distributed among the countries of sub-Saharan Africa.

14   For example, an analysis of the 'FTSE 100' – the 100 companies with the largest market capitalisation on the London Stock Exchange – revealed that mining and oil and gas were the two sectors that ranked highest on a secrecy score. That score takes into account both the location of subsidiaries (using the Financial Secrecy Index) and the level of control of the parent company. The 13 mining, oil and gas companies in the FTSE 100 collectively had 3,454 subsidiaries, of which 2,148 (62%) were located in what are classified as non-transparent jurisdictions by the Financial Secrecy Index. Of these 2,148 subsidiaries, 1,471 were not reporting any data to the outside world. This gave the mining and oil and gas sectors the distinction of having the largest proportion (46% and 40% respectively) of subsidiaries in secrecy jurisdictions that reported no data at all (Prats et al. 2014).

15   After initial agreements are signed, relations between governments and companies are regulated by informal interactions that are inaccessible to outsiders. Tax administrations are typically outsiders. One of the authors recalls a conversation in which the head of tax affairs of a transnational mining company, talking of the efforts of a national tax agency to apply the tax rules literally to the company's operations, complained that 'the tax people did not grasp that the company and the government had a good working relationship, and sorted things out in their own way'.

16   By far the most widely quoted exception is Botswana. Diamond mining in Botswana has long been conducted on a joint venture basis between the government and the world's premier diamond company, DeBeers. The government of Botswana now owns a share of DeBeers. Mining contributes more than 30% of the country's GDP and, until recently, 50% of its tax revenues. There is a substantial literature that attempts to explain Botswana's exceptionalism: why it managed to avoid the 'resource curse' and generally use mining revenues productively. The most convincing explanation for the relatively high quality of governance is based on the interaction of a series of historical factors going back more than a century, including the unusual nature and context of colonial rule in Botswana (Robinson et al. 2003). There are no easy lessons here for other African countries.

17   Note that not every campaigner's criticism of the ways in which mining is taxed in Africa is valid. For example, governments are sometimes 'exposed' for exempting new mining activities from VAT. This might, however, make perfect sense. Mine operators in Africa typically import a large share of their production inputs (notably capital equipment) and export almost all of their product. They would ultimately be required to pay little VAT, because the value of their exports would be offset against the VAT they pay on imports. Many African revenue authorities find it difficult to give VAT refunds that are legally due. Exemption from VAT, especially during the early years of a project, can provide investors with a more predictable tax regime at little cost.

18 This example relates to the broader issue of 'ring-fencing'. Governments would like to ensure that the finances of each separate extractives project are reported separately. Companies prefer to amalgamate projects in their financial and tax reporting to the host government, because this gives them more scope to minimise tax obligations. This is almost a domestic equivalent of the 'transfer mispricing' discussed in Chapter 3.

19 Sufficient, that is, to reduce the chances of: (1) extractives projects being forced by the fiscal regime into loss-making when global product prices are low; and (2) obvious or widely perceived under-taxation when product prices are high.

20 The statistics relate to the period 2003–12 (see World Bank 2016a: 14).

Chapter 6

1 The detailed information on Somaliland was obtained by one of the authors in the course of an advisory assignment in the country in 2016. The statistics are not publicly available in published form.

2 For more detailed information on these senior staff movements, see Moore (2014: 105–6). By 2010, the alumni of the Revenue Authority included two ministers of finance.

3 In fact, the level of 'tax effort' in Rwanda – the ratio of actual revenue collection to what one would expect of a country with that level of income and economic structure – is rather low (Dom 2017: 66).

4 It is not currently possible to do this rigorously, but it soon will be. Starting in 2015, national tax administrations are being evaluated and scored according to a standard method: TADAT (Tax Administration Diagnostic Assessment Tool). Most African tax administrations have not yet received a TADAT assessment but they are becoming more common. Most of the assessments that have been completed remain confidential but they are likely to be leaked or released into the public domain.

5 Manuel became finance minister in 1996. From 1999, he worked closely with the new commissioner of SARS, Pravin Gordhan.

6 There has been less reform of revenue systems in Francophone African countries (Fossat and Bua 2013).

7 The shift to cooperative compliance reflects the wider availability of digital technologies and changing patterns of economic activity and transactions, including: the digitalisation of economic transactions; more complex contracting, subcontracting and value chains; and the growing expense of employing tax staff to directly check tax returns.

8 There is a large literature on this topic; see in particular Ahlerup et al. (2015), Fjeldstad and Moore (2008a), Mann (2004), Prichard and Leonard (2010), Sarr (2016), Taliercio (2004), Terpker (2008), Therkildsen (2004) and von Soest (2007b).

9   A continuing if largely covert conflict is still being waged between Anglophone and Francophone networks of tax specialists and consultants over the creation of SARAs. The Anglophones have been very much in favour while the Francophones continue to resist, and so far have given ground only in Burundi and Togo.

10 There are more ideologically driven arguments, based on the assumption that SARAs genuinely will have considerable autonomy from ministers and presidents, that do not apply in sub-Saharan Africa (Fjeldstad and Moore 2008a).

11 Probably over half of the commissioners-general who are currently CEOs of revenue authorities in sub-Saharan Africa have extensive prior experience in the private sector.

12 In some cases the establishment of SARAs led to large-scale dismissals of existing tax collectors, aimed at removing inefficient and corrupt officials. In other cases, most existing staff were transferred to the new organisation.

13 When applied to an organisation such as a revenue authority that ultimately has to be answerable to government, the concept of 'autonomy' eludes easy definition. One very useful piece of theory suggests that we can measure autonomy on six dimensions: managerial, policy, structural, financial, legal and interventional (i.e. the extent of reporting requirements against set goals) (Verhoest et al. 2004).

14 The standard measure of the efficiency of VAT systems is 'C-efficiency': the percentage of potential VAT revenue that is actually collected. In 2010, the estimated average C-efficiency of VAT clustered around 55% for all major regions of the world except sub-Saharan Africa, where it was 37% (Keen 2013: 9).

15 The most consistent current efforts to assess the impact of fiscal activities on income distribution at national level are being made by CEQ Institute (2017). They have results for a few countries in sub-Saharan Africa, but in every case the databases are weak.

16 Delays may also be caused by the way in which VAT refunds are funded. In Tanzania, for instance, one constraint on paying VAT refunds is that VAT revenue is remitted to the treasury on a gross basis, and in turn the Tanzania Revenue Authority is required to request budget allocations from the treasury to pay VAT refunds. This budget arrangement does not reflect the nature of VAT, which is a net revenue-based tax (IMF 2016b). Some African countries have taken the extreme step of enacting legislation to deny all outstanding VAT repayment claims after a certain period of time (Harrison and Krelove 2005).

17 Cross-country comparative studies indicate that, although countries with VAT raise somewhat more revenue than those without, the effect is particularly weak in sub-Saharan Africa (Keen 2012). By contrast, Ebeke et al. (2016) find that the adoption of VAT in sub-Saharan Africa has had a significant and positive impact on non-resource tax revenues.

18 This section is based on considerable recent research, including Cantens and Rabelland (2017), Bilangna and Djeuwo (2013), Cantens (2012a; 2012b), Cantens et al. (2013; 2014), Cuvelier and Mumbunda (2013), Twijnstra et al. (2014) and Zake (2011).

19 The extent of operational integration varies. Customs tends to retain some operational independence for several reasons, including: its distinctive and generally growing responsibilities for border security; the strength of historical and professional links to the World Customs Organisation in Brussels; and the availability of standard information management software designed specifically for customs operations – ASYCUDA (Automated System for Customs Data).

20 Official statistics do not tell us how much VAT is collected by customs. In 2009–13, taxes on international trade accounted for an average of 24% of total tax collection in the 37 African countries for which data is available – and 19% of total revenue collection (38 countries) (ICTD/UNU-WIDER 2017).

21 The average for sub-Saharan African countries is likely the same, but we do not have reliable figures for a sufficiently large number of countries to justify using a particular figure. In some African countries, PIT is also a tax on incomes earned from small-scale enterprises.

22 The data that underpins this claim is scarce and scattered. The most recent version of the OECD's Revenue Statistics in Africa (OECD 2017) contains adequate data for five African countries: Ghana (p. 176), Kenya (p. 178), Rwanda (p. 187), Swaziland (p. 193) and Uganda (p. 199). For those five countries, in 2015, withholding taxes collected by employers on the income of employees through PAYE on average accounted for 97% of total income tax collection from individuals.

23 Information obtained from the Uganda Revenue Authority.

24 There are different types of zones. Export processing zones (EPZs), for instance, are enclaves where foreign companies engaged in the manufacturing of products for export enjoy preferential (tax) treatment compared with the rest of the economy. Special economic zones offer locational flexibility and have a wider application than EPZs by granting such treatment to firms producing for the domestic market as well.

25 The figures are in IMF et al. (2015: 9). This publication is an excellent summary of what we know about tax exemptions.

26 A detailed analysis of tax expenditures in Ghana revealed that people and organisations in a category labelled 'Government, Privileged Persons, Organisations' were major beneficiaries of exemptions from customs duties (OECD 2013).

27 In Mauritius, incentives related to the corporate income tax system and VAT made up the bulk of the post-reform tax expenditure figure, with excise and customs duties accounting for smaller proportions.

28 The proportion of respondents who believed that 'most' or 'all' tax officials

were corrupt ranged from 9% in Mauritius to 59% in Cameroon (Aiko and Logan 2014).

Chapter 7

1   Evidence from elsewhere in the world also indicates that informal taxation is regressive (Olken and Singhal 2011).

2   This parallels Logan's (2009: 119) finding that, for 12 of the 15 countries on which she had Afrobarometer survey data, traditional authorities were more trusted than formal local governments. The exceptions were South Africa, Tanzania and Uganda.

3   For a good review of the literature on taxing the informal sector, see Joshi et al. (2014).

4   For a summary of the evidence, see Mascagni and Mengistu (2017).

5   Business licences were abolished in Tanzania in 2004. They previously accounted for between 20% and 30% of the total 'own' revenue in municipalities. In 2011, they were reintroduced.

6   Agricultural land is not taxed in most of Africa. In the absence of good agricultural land ownership records that are kept up to date, it would not make sense for most governments to consider beginning to tax agricultural land. However, there are some exceptions. In Ethiopia, all agriculturalists have to pay a recurrent land tax, while Namibia introduced a land tax on commercial farmers in 2004 to fund a land reform programme. Land taxation is also being extended to (large) rural properties in South Africa (Franzsen 2007).

7   We focus here on recurrent property taxes in urban areas, because they are a potential source of significant additional revenue for subnational governments. Note, however, that national governments have similar scope to raise additional revenues, efficiently and fairly, through transfer taxes on changes in ownership of real estate.

8   There are substantial variations among African countries. For example, for the period 2006–08, property tax accounted for about 14% of the total revenues of local assemblies in Ghana; about 6% for local councils in Sierra Leone; and, in Liberia, where local councils are not allowed to collect revenue, property tax accounts for about 1% of total revenues of the central government (Jibao 2009). As we noted above, in most Francophone countries property taxes are in the hands of central government.

9   In recent years there have been some interesting examples of internationally supported systems enjoying some success, including Norwegian-developed systems being used in North Kivu, Democratic Republic of Congo, a South African-designed system employed in Kampala, Uganda, and an ambitious World Bank-supported system in Tanzania. However, the sustainability of international management over time remains open to question. Costs are a major consideration.

10 The figures for the South African and Botswana tax administrations are very close (African Tax Administration Forum 2017: 143–5).

11 This refers to ongoing research by Anna Mbise and Marius Siebert.

12 The most obvious exception is the German technical assistance agency GIZ, which does work extensively on subnational revenue issues.

13 Almost without exception, governments across the world assign more expenditure functions to local authorities than can be financed from their own revenue sources. This is also the case across Africa. However, the level of intergovernmental transfers varies widely between countries and also between rural and urban councils within individual countries (Chitembo 2009). In Botswana, for instance, rural councils receive 92% of their total revenues from central government, compared with 62% for urban areas. In Uganda, local government is heavily dependent on transfers from central government (88% of total revenues in 2007), while local governments in South Africa, on average, generate the bulk of their revenues from 'own' sources (89% in 2007). Transfers and grants constitute the biggest share of total receipts to local councils in Anglophone West Africa (Jibao 2009). For instance, in 2007, local councils in Nigeria received on average almost 78% of their revenue from transfers; in Sierra Leone they received 74% of their revenue from transfers; in Ghana 69%; and in the Gambia 65%. In Liberia, local councils rely 100% on transfers from central government since revenue collection is centralised.

Chapter 8

1 This chapter draws heavily on Prichard (2016b).

2 This alternative formulation has been used widely, including in Herb (2005), Prichard (2015), and a recent article in *The Economist* (2015).

3 The earliest such cases documented in research come from Kenya, where a National Taxpayers' Association aimed to actively link discussion of tax payments to more effective public expenditure monitoring. This built on some neighbourhood communities in Nairobi that had refused to pay taxes until public services were improved. More recently, this type of approach appears to have spread, and has figured, for example, in the 'Tax Power' campaign carried out by various ActionAid country programmes.

4 This possibility was central to early academic models of tax bargaining, which predicted that governments may seek to make targeted concessions to small groups of taxpayers instead of pursuing general improvements in public services and accountability (Levi 1988).

Chapter 9

1 The Kenya Revenue Authority awards a prize for 'Best Tax App Idea' at its Annual Tax Summit, the 2016 edition of which was subtitled 'Kenyan Solutions to Kenyan Challenges'.

Glossary of terms

1   HNWI denotes an individual or a family with high net worth, generally quoted in terms of liquid assets over a certain figure. Traditionally, the term used was 'millionaire', but in recent years this alternative term has become the descriptor of choice.

INDEX

Also available in the African Arguments series

Women and the War on Boko Haram: Wives, Weapons, Witnesses
BY HILARY MATFESS

'An original, innovative, and much-needed addition to the growing literatures on both women and conflict in Africa and the Boko Haram insurgency.'

Brandon Kendhammer, Ohio University

'The author's intensive fieldwork reveals previously unseen layers of complexity. Matfess is right to conclude the fate of Nigeria is tied to the fate of its women, and her book is an important contribution to that discussion.'

Valerie Hudson, Texas A&M University

Congo's Violent Peace: Conflict and Struggle Since the Great African War
BY KRIS BERWOUTS

'Essential reading for all those who want to understand the current situation. *Congo's Violent Peace* has all the makings of a classic.'

Séverine Autesserre, author of *The Trouble with the Congo and Peaceland*

'Few people have a better grasp of the key players than Kris Berwouts. From diplomat parties to refugee camps, from warlords to the presidential entourage, this book is essential reading for anyone truly interested in the DRC.'

David Van Reybrouck, author of *Congo: The Epic History of a People*

Africa: Why Economists Get It Wrong
BY MORTEN JERVEN

'A highly readable and absolutely devastating critique of an increasingly extensive and influential body of work by economists seeking to explain "what's wrong with Africa".'

James Ferguson, Stanford University

'Morten Jerven provides a valuable reminder of the need not just to cite statistics but to question them.'

Financial Times